HERITAGE

Historic sites, memorials, national parks, museums … we live in an age in which heritage is ever-present. But what does it mean to live amongst the spectral traces of the past, the heterogeneous piling up of historic materials in the present? How did heritage grow from the concern of a handful of enthusiasts and specialists in one part of the world to something that is considered to be universally cherished? And what concepts and approaches are necessary to understanding this global obsession?

Over the decades since the adoption of the World Heritage Convention, various crises of definition have significantly influenced the ways in which heritage is classified, perceived and managed in contemporary global societies. Taking an interdisciplinary approach to the many tangible and intangible 'things' now defined as heritage, this book attempts simultaneously to account for this global phenomenon and the industry that has grown up around it, as well as to develop a 'toolkit of concepts' with which it might be studied. In doing so, it provides a critical account of the emergence of heritage studies as an interdisciplinary field of academic study. This is presented as part of a broader examination of the function of heritage in late-modern societies, with a particular focus on the changes that have resulted from the globalisation of heritage during the late twentieth and early twenty-first centuries.

Developing new theoretical approaches and innovative models for more dialogically democratic heritage decision-making processes, *Heritage: Critical Approaches* unravels the relationship between heritage and the experience of late-modernity, whilst reorienting heritage so that it might be more productively connected with other pressing social, economic, political and environmental issues of our time.

Rodney Harrison is a Lecturer in Museum and Heritage Studies at the Institute of Archaeology, University College London. He has a broad range of experience teaching, researching and working across the fields of cultural and natural heritage management in the UK, Australia and North America. Prior to his current position, Rodney worked for the Open University, where he was responsible for teaching, research and public broadcasting in global heritage studies.

HERITAGE

Critical Approaches

Rodney Harrison

Routledge
Taylor & Francis Group

LONDON AND NEW YORK

First published 2013
by Routledge
2 Park Square, Milton Park, Abingdon, Oxon OX14 4RN

Simultaneously published in the USA and Canada
by Routledge
711 Third Avenue, New York, NY 10017

Routledge is an imprint of the Taylor & Francis Group, an informa business

British Library Cataloguing in Publication Data
A catalogue record for this book is available from the British Library

Library of Congress Cataloging in Publication Data
Harrison, Rodney, 1974–
    Heritage : critical approaches / Rodney Harrison.
       p. cm.
    Includes bibliographical references and index.
    1. Cultural property. 2. Historic preservation. 3. Culture policy. I. Title.
    CC135.H37 2012
    363.6'9–dc23
                    2012001075

ISBN: 978-0-415-59195-9 (hbk)
ISBN: 978-0-415-59197-3 (pbk)
ISBN: 978-0-203-10885-7 (ebk)

Typeset in Bembo
by Taylor and Francis Books

CONTENTS

FIGURES

TABLES

PREFACE AND ACKNOWLEDGEMENTS

While the idea for this book first started to take form during the period in which I worked for the Open University after 2007, many of the questions that motivated it have been with me for much longer. I was trained as an archaeologist in Australia, and since the mid-1990s I have been involved as a 'producer' of heritage in a number of different ways, as an educator, bureaucrat, researcher and private consultant, and even longer as a 'consumer' of museums and heritage sites. Like many other Australian archaeologists, as a new graduate I began to work as an advisor on a wide variety of short-term consultancies, each of which required me to assess the impacts of various different developments on archaeological and other cultural heritage 'resources'. Over time, it became apparent not only that heritage was changing in significant ways, but that I was living in a world in which heritage was becoming more abundant, as well as increasingly socially, economically and ontologically prominent. Nonetheless, there seemed to me to be little academic interest in heritage, which, despite its increasing significance, tended to be treated as a technical issue by those other 'experts' who, like myself, were engaged to provide advice on how to 'do' it. At the same time, I was becoming increasingly uncomfortable with the gap that seemed to be developing between heritage professionals and laypersons. In my professional heritage assessments, focused on technical and scientific concerns, it seemed difficult to include the viewpoints of the stakeholders and community members who lived every day with the heritage on which I was engaged to provide professional advice. It became obvious to me that many of the laypersons and other community members with whom I worked often had quite different ways of understanding and relating to heritage to myself and my colleagues, and much of their understanding of the values of heritage seemed to be left out of the professional advice we were being asked to provide as consultants.

Over the period 2000–04, I worked in the Cultural Heritage Division in what was then known as the New South Wales National Parks and Wildlife Service in Sydney, first as a historical archaeologist and subsequently as Aboriginal Regional Heritage Studies Coordinator in a multidisciplinary research team concerned with developing innovative approaches to the management of heritage. During this period, I worked closely not only with a range of other 'cultural' heritage advisors, but also with Aboriginal people, park rangers and 'natural' heritage professionals. This experience was significant in giving me pause to think about the relationship between natural and cultural heritage, issues that I explore in more detail in Chapter 9 of this book. I subsequently took up a research fellowship in what was then the Centre for Cross-Cultural Research at the Australian National University in Canberra, which included a comparative analysis of the ways in which Indigenous people, resource managers, government and archaeologists worked together in Australia and in North America. Again, the comparative element of this research helped me to develop a wider view of heritage as a global phenomenon.

In 2007, I was engaged as the first Lecturer in Heritage Studies at the Open University in the UK. With the help of colleagues, I subsequently began the task of developing an interdisciplinary undergraduate module that explored heritage and its place in contemporary societies as a global phenomena, which would be suitable for distance undergraduate teaching throughout the English-speaking world. The module, *Understanding Global Heritage*, was presented to students for the first time in October 2009, following the co-publication of a series of three course-books by the Open University and Manchester University Press, and a series of films and other materials that were produced for our students and associate lecturers to use as part of the course.

Part of the process of developing the module required a consideration of what heritage studies 'was' and, perhaps more importantly, what it could be. While much had been written about heritage from particular disciplinary perspectives, there were few critical cross-disciplinary studies of heritage that took into account the major changes I had observed occurring in relation to the globalisation of heritage over the late 1990s and early 2000s. During this period, I was fortunate enough to be able to visit and observe the operation of a number of World Heritage sites, which confirmed my view that these places, and accounts of their implementation of (or resistance to) the World Heritage Convention, held much promise for exploring the ways in which local issues were having a global impact on the changing definitions of heritage. Thus the idea began to emerge of a book that would draw together and summarise the work of other scholars who were developing critical, cross-disciplinary approaches to heritage, as well as consider the changes which had occurred in relation to the globalisation of heritage over the previous few decades. It was important that such a book would not only summarise existing work, but provide an agenda for a new interdisciplinary field of critical heritage studies in the future. At the time I started thinking about writing a single-authored book on this topic, I was also invited to join the editorial board of the *International Journal of Heritage Studies*, which has done much to bring together scholars working across many different fields to explore heritage in a comparative way. This conjunction of events provided the impetus for beginning to write *Heritage: Critical Approaches*.

In addition to its comparative perspective and its focus on the *abundance* of heritage and various changes that have occurred as a result of the globalisation of heritage over the late twentieth and early twenty-first centuries, where this book differs markedly from other current interdisciplinary critical studies of heritage is in its focus on three linked themes of *materiality, connectivity* and *dialogue*. These themes, discussed in more detail within the book, developed out of my particular experiences working with Indigenous Australians who have consistently challenged the modern Cartesian dualisms of nature/culture and matter/mind, and the ways in which they inform various global, national, regional and local processes of cultural heritage management. I suggest that notions of connectivity, and a model that sees heritage as a product of the dialogue between people and things, have the potential to address the contemporary *crisis* of the abundance of heritage, which I argue arises from a late-modern sense of *uncertainty* and redundancy (itself in many ways related to the current global financial crisis and other by-products of late capitalism). These new themes and definitions of heritage also have much to contribute to opening up new avenues of research for critical interdisciplinary heritage studies, which I argue (in general terms) has tended to under-theorise the affective qualities of heritage, and to focus instead on issues arising from the politics of representation. My aim in this book is to link these two ways of approaching heritage to develop a critical material semiotic approach to heritage and its role in contemporary global societies.

In the book I have tried to address heritage in an explicitly interdisciplinary fashion, treating it as a broad social (and simultaneously *material*) phenomenon, rather than restricting my analysis to one particular 'type' of heritage. Such interdisciplinarity poses a serious challenge of bridging multiple literatures and critical traditions appropriately, and some readers may find that I have emphasised particular kinds of heritage and particular aspects of the heritage literature with which I am more familiar, to the detriment of others. Similarly, I have tried to draw on international examples wherever possible, although of course I have tended to explore the regions with which I am familiar in most detail, in particular, the UK, North America and Australia. It is also important to note here that my discussion limits itself specifically to anglophone literatures, and hence largely Western examples. Having said this, I argue for the need to look at heritage as an issue of broad social, economic, political and environmental concern in contemporary global societies, and I hope those who do not see their own field or region emphasised strongly in the book will nonetheless read on and recognise the broad themes and their application to their own particular areas of interest. In the spirit of greater cross-disciplinary engagement, there is also a pressing need to pay more attention to non-anglophone (and, indeed, non-Western) heritage literatures, histories and traditions, and I hope those who read this book who are able to comment on those alternative traditions might be challenged to do this.

When I came to write the book, I drew selectively on the work I had done for the Open University module *Understanding Global Heritage*, in almost all cases significantly reworking and redrafting the original material. While very little of what has made it into this book bears direct resemblance to the original sections of the chapters on which I drew, having been completely reworked and reorganised, it is important to acknowledge the original places of publication of those on which I draw here. The chapters in question were originally published as 'What is heritage?', 'Critical approaches to heritage' (co-authored with Audrey Linkman), 'Heritage, colonialism and postcolonialism' (co-authored with Lotte Hughes) and 'The politics of heritage' in *Understanding the Politics of Heritage* (Manchester University Press, 2010), edited by Rodney Harrison; 'Natural heritage' (co-authored with Donal O'Donnell) and 'Heritage as social action' in *Understanding Heritage in Practice* (Manchester University Press, 2010), edited by Susie West; and 'Multicultural and minority heritage', 'Intangible heritage' (co-authored with Deborah Bird Rose) and 'Heritage and the recent and contemporary past' (co-authored with Rebecca Ferguson and Daniel Weinbren) in *Understanding Heritage and Memory* (Manchester University Press, 2010), edited by Tim Benton.

While I was writing this book, I benefited greatly from various conversations that emerged as part of the Advanced Seminar 'Reassembling the Collection', which I co-organised with Sarah Byrne, Anne Clarke and Robin Torrence, sponsored by the School of Advanced Research in Santa Fe, New Mexico. Although that Advanced Seminar focused particularly on the issue of museums and Indigenous agency, it nonetheless had a significant influence on the ways in which I came to think and write about collections more generally, and the World Heritage List in particular. In Chapters 2, 6 and 9 of this book I draw on parts of the Introduction and my own chapter, which are both currently in preparation for publication in quite different forms in SAR Press's Advanced Seminar book series. I thank all of the participants in that Advanced Seminar for their insights and comments on the chapters on which I have partially drawn here.

Most of the chapters in this book have been presented in one form or another at various conferences and seminars. In particular, I thank members of the Open University's Interfaculty Heritage Studies Research Group for their comments on various preliminary versions of chapters in this book. I owe a great debt to my colleagues Susie West and Tim Benton, with whom I worked through many of my early thoughts in developing the Open University Course *Understanding Global Heritage*, which I have subsequently reworked here. In addition, early versions of parts of Chapters 3 and 4 were presented as part of the 'Inquiry: Historic Preservation' public lecture series at the Graduate School of Architecture and Planning (GSAPP) at Columbia University in 2010; parts of Chapter 6 were presented at the US Theoretical Archaeology Group Conference 'The Location of Theory' at Brown University and the 'Making European Heritage' Seminar at the University of Manchester in 2010; and parts of Chapter 9 were presented at 'The things that matter most: Conversations in localism, landscape and the meanings of place' research seminar at the University of York in 2011. I thank all those who attended these seminars, contributed to discussions or followed up with questions. I thank GSAPP in particular for making it possible for me to speak at Columbia University in 2010, and the British Academy for supporting my travel to Brown University in the same year.

I would particularly like to thank Tim Benton, Kevin Hetherington, Uzma Rizvi, Laurajane Smith and Susie West, who generously gave their time to read and provide detailed comments on an early draft of this book. These comments and suggestions helped me substantially in reworking the draft manuscript for publication, and I hope you see the time you generously gave to read and comment on it reflected in the final text.

I have benefited from an ongoing dialogue with a number of friends and colleagues who have challenged me to think about heritage in new and innovative ways. First amongst these I must thank the many local stakeholders and community members with whom I have worked and conversed over the past fifteen years, who have taught me so much about the values which heritage holds for them. Several individuals are mentioned by name within the text, but there are many others whose profound insights have touched me in many ways, and I want to thank and acknowledge all of these people for encouraging me to question the division of 'natural' and 'cultural' heritage, and the roles of 'laypersons' and 'experts' in heritage management. Similarly, my work with Aboriginal sites officers, park rangers, 'natural' heritage staff, and other members of the Cultural Heritage Division at the former NSW National Parks and Wildlife Service had a profound influence on the ideas developed in this book, and I want to acknowledge and thank all those individuals who took the time to share their thoughts with me. Open University colleagues, associate lecturers and students on the *Understanding Global Heritage* course have generously shared their comments and insights on global heritage, and I thank all of them for doing so. In addition to those people already mentioned, I would like to thank Tony Bennett, Denis Byrne, Martin Gibbs, Graham Harvey, Cornelius Holtorf, Lotte Hughes, Jorge Otero-Pailos, Siân Jones, Ian Lilley, Sharon Macdonald and John Schofield, who have all at various points provided encouragement, inspiration and intellectual nourishment, which has been important in developing the ideas in this book. I look forward to many more conversations about heritage with all of you in the future. The final stages of the production of the book were completed as I moved across to take up a new position as Lecturer in Museum and Heritage Studies at the Institute of Archaeology, University College London, and I thank staff, students and colleagues at the UCL Centre for Museums, Heritage and Material Culture Studies for their warm welcome.

Finally, and most importantly, I would like to thank my family and friends for their ongoing support and encouragement. Vicky, as ever, has provided constant guidance and strength, and has supported me in every way possible. Matt saved the day with last minute technical assistance with figures. I dedicate this book to my mother Eunice, who taught me to balance looking to the past in the present with moving on to the future.

1

INTRODUCTION

Heritage everywhere

It is Monday lunchtime in Chelsea Market, New York City, and the office workers, locals and tourists buy their sandwiches, browse for produce, and promenade through the ruined shell of the former National Biscuit Company complex, strolling amongst the rusted fans, exposed air vents and partially demolished brickwork (Figure 1.1). An example of an 'adaptive re-use' heritage project, like many others we have become used to in contemporary cosmopolitan cities, this physical experience of being, working and dwelling amongst the old and the new, of living with the polished patina of the past, has become familiar to most of us in the late-modern world. As its website notes, 'a visit to the market offers ghostly evocations of the site's history' (Chelsea Market 2011). Such 'ghostly evocations' are no longer spontaneous incidents, but frequently staged experiences that are an increasingly common part of our everyday urban and suburban landscapes. Walking down any major street in just about any city in the world will reveal dozens of monuments, memorials, listed buildings, ecological conservation zones, sites of memory and the heterogeneous piling up of the traces of the past in the present. To persist with our example of the Chelsea Market, a short walk across town to Broadway finds us on one of the busiest urban thoroughfares in Manhattan. A walk down this street north to south reveals dozens of listed buildings, a number of memorials and commemorative plaques, parks, gardens and several museums within a single block on either side of this road, which dissects the city. This is not atypical, and any other major world city would reveal similar numbers of heritage sites, monuments to the past amongst thriving metropolises. Heritage, and the formally staged experience of encountering the physical traces of the past in the present, has become an all-pervasive aspect of contemporary life, a series of components that act as building blocks for the design of contemporary urban and suburban spaces. The first theme of this book is what we might term the *abundance* of heritage in our late-modern world, and its social, economic and political function in contemporary global societies.

FIGURE 1.1 Chelsea Market, New York City, November 2011. (Photograph by the author.)

At the time of writing, not far from this busy thoroughfare is a protest camp of some several hundred people assembled under the banner 'Occupy Wall Street' (OWS). This group of people are gathered in protest against the deregulated late capitalist system which brought about a series of global financial crises in the early part of the new millennium. At first, these two spaces—Chelsea Market with its commercial heritage-chic, and the OWS protest camp with its battered tents—appear to be completely unrelated. But I suggest that these are linked by a sense of crisis and uncertainty, which has grown in significance in contemporary postindustrial societies throughout the late-modern period. The Occupy movement stands as a brave and ambitious protest against the systematic inequalities which have emerged from the globalised financial services industry that contributed directly to the late 2000s global financial crisis, and the inherent uncertainties that have been generated by the resulting high rates of unemployment and inflation, falling house prices, foreclosures and 'credit crunch'. This same sense of growing uncertainty has had a significant, escalating effect over the past few decades of the twentieth century and into the twenty-first, in encouraging us to stockpile the redundant, the disused and the outmoded as potential raw materials for the production of memories that we feel we are unable to risk losing, even when we are powerless to articulate what their possible value might be. Following Richard Terdiman (1993), it is possible to characterise this as late-modernity's 'memory crisis'. This sense of *crisis* is a product of a number of factors—the sense of speed and rate of late-modern technological, social and environmental change; the pervading sense of uncertainty that accompanies a series of social, economic, humanitarian, political and environmental emergencies; the haunting of the present by the past; the growth of nostalgia; and the rise of the experience economy amongst them. This speaks to the second major theme of the book, which is the relationship between heritage and modernity, and in particular, the role of *uncertainty* in accounting for heritage as a global cultural phenomenon.

We live in an age in which heritage is ubiquitous. But what does it mean to live amongst the spectral traces of the past, the heterogeneous piling up of historic materials in the present? How did heritage grow from the concern of a handful of enthusiasts and specialists in one part of the world to something which is considered to be universally cherished? Why did heritage become such an omnipresent cultural phenomenon? And what concepts and approaches are necessary to understanding this global trend? Although components of these material traces of the past have been conserved for many years, I argue that we live in a time that is distinctive in the ways in which definitions of heritage have expanded to such an extent that almost anything can be perceived to be 'heritage', and the mechanisms for the categorisation, cataloguing and management of the past have become so sophisticated in their design that we have become largely blinded to this rapid and all-pervasive piling up of the past in our quotidian worlds. This process has, to date, largely been neglected by academics and under-theorised by practitioners. This book attempts simultaneously to account for this global phenomenon and the industry that has grown up around it, as well as to develop a 'toolkit of concepts' (cf. Rabinow 2003) with which to study it.

The central aim of this book is to provide a critical account of the emergence of 'heritage studies' as an interdisciplinary field of academic study, as part of a broader consideration of heritage as a social, economic and political phenomenon of late-modern societies, with a particular focus on various changes that have occurred as a result of the globalisation of heritage during the late twentieth and early twenty-first centuries. I argue that over this period there have been a number of fundamental 'crises' for heritage, the resolution of which has had (and continues to have) a significant impact on the ways in which heritage is defined, perceived and managed in contemporary global societies. These changes relate in part to the dominance of notions of heritage that have been promulgated since the 1970s through the work of the World Heritage Committee (Di Giovine 2009), but also relate to a series of widespread social and economic shifts in late-modern societies involving processes of globalisation, deindustrialisation, and the rise of the contemporary experience economy. So in addition to providing an overview of heritage studies, the book also attempts to provide a critical account of these new developments in heritage and to suggest new frameworks within which they might be explored. In doing so, it aims to begin to map out a new agenda for the interdisciplinary study of heritage, and suggests new approaches with broad implications for the practices of heritage identification, conservation and management in the twenty-first century. In particular, I emphasise a series of interlinked concepts—*materiality*, *connectivity* and *dialogue*—which I suggest are central to understanding the role of heritage in contemporary societies and in reorienting heritage so that it might be more closely connected with other contemporary social, political, economic and environmental concerns.

In a postmillennial period that has been rocked by various economic, humanitarian, environmental and political dilemmas, the reader might be forgiven for wondering why the study of heritage is important. Haven't we more pressing things to think about than 'the past'? By investigating heritage as a social, political and economic phenomenon within a particular historical context, I hope not only to explore the broad changes that have occurred in our relationship with heritage over the course of the decades since the introduction of the World Heritage Convention in the early 1970s, but also to suggest that heritage is primarily *not* about the *past*, but instead about our relationship with the *present* and the *future*. As such, heritage poses urgent questions that arise as a result of our consideration of contemporary geopolitical issues. Heritage is not a passive process of simply preserving things from the past that remain, but an active process of assembling a series of objects, places and practices that we choose to hold up as a mirror to the present, associated with a particular set of values that we wish to take with us into the future. Thinking of heritage as a creative engagement with the past in the present focuses our attention on our ability to take an active and informed role in the production of our own 'tomorrow'. Understanding our era's obsession with preservation will allow not only heritage researchers and practitioners, but also informed laypersons, to exercise greater agency in the decisions that governments, NGOs, communities and other individuals make about actively forming our past in the present. So while this book aims to provide an overview and critical analysis of the direction of heritage studies as a newly emerging academic discipline, it also seeks to provide a new critical framework for heritage studies for the twenty-first century. It does this through suggesting a new 'dialogical' model in which heritage is seen as emerging from the relationship between people, objects, places and practices, and that does not distinguish between or prioritise what is 'natural' and what is 'cultural', but is instead concerned with the various ways in which humans and non-humans are linked by chains of *connectivity* and work together to keep the past alive in the present for the future. I will argue that this dialogical model of heritage has radical implications not only for the study of heritage, but also for breaking down the bureaucratic divide between laypersons and experts, suggesting new models for heritage decision-making processes in the future.

What is heritage?

Heritage today is a broad and slippery term. It might be used to describe anything from the solid—such as buildings, monuments and memorials, to the ethereal—songs, festivals and languages. It often appears as a positive term, and in this guise might be found in use in selling everything from houses ('period features', 'historic neighbourhood', 'Grade II listed') to food (for example through the European Union's legal system of Protected Geographical Status) and bars of soap ('classic glycerine and triple-milled heritage blend'). Finally, the term encompasses a range of things from large to small, grandiose to humble, 'natural' to constructed. It can be used to describe everything from whole landscapes to tiny fragments of bone, stone and charcoal in archaeological sites; grand palaces to ordinary dwelling places; wilderness areas to modern city landscapes. The concept of heritage not only encompasses a nation's relationship to history and history-making, but also refers increasingly to the ways in which a broad range of other constituencies are involved in the production of the past in the present. Increasingly, too, heritage has come to describe globalised and globalising processes of broad international concern. Thus heritage can be seen to operate at a range of different spatial, temporal and institutional scales.

By way of example of this breadth, consider the list of 'types' of cultural heritage that UNESCO produced in 2002 during the United Nations Year for Cultural Heritage (UNESCO nd). UNESCO included the following items on its list:

- cultural heritage sites (including archaeological sites, ruins, historic buildings)
- historic cities (urban landscapes and their constituent parts as well as ruined cities)
- cultural landscapes (including parks, gardens and other modified landscapes such as pastoral lands and farms)
- natural sacred sites (places that people revere or hold important but that have no evidence of human modification, for example sacred mountains)
- underwater cultural heritage (for example shipwrecks)
- museums (including cultural museums, art galleries and house museums)
- movable cultural heritage (objects as diverse as paintings, tractors, stone tools and cameras—this category covers any form of object that is movable and that is outside an archaeological context)
- handicrafts
- documentary and digital heritage (the archives and objects deposited in libraries, including digital archives)
- cinematographic heritage (movies and the ideas they convey)
- oral traditions (stories, histories and traditions that are not written but passed from generation to generation)

- languages
- festive events (festivals and carnivals and the traditions they embody)
- rites and beliefs (rituals, traditions and religious beliefs)
- music and song
- the performing arts (theatre, drama, dance and music)
- traditional medicine
- literature
- culinary traditions
- traditional sports and games.

The list covers an enormously broad range of categories. However, this list includes only those things that might be considered for listing by UNESCO as *cultural* heritage, and thus does not even begin to consider various categories of *natural* heritage, nor those aspects of heritage that are, for whatever reason, not recognised as listable. Nonetheless, this does give a sense of the vast number of objects, places and practices to which the term might be considered to apply 'officially' at the turn of the twenty-first century. It also introduces a concept that is central to heritage—categorisation and listing.[1] 'Heritage', at least insofar as those agencies charged with managing it are concerned, cannot exist independently of a process of categorising, ordering, listing and subsequently conserving and/or archiving it. The implications of this are discussed further in Chapter 2.

I am certainly not the first to observe how broad is the range of things to which the term 'heritage' might be applied. However, even in the years since the publication of David Lowenthal's famous critique, *The Past is a Foreign Country* (1985: xv), in which he argued that 'the landscape of the 1980s seems saturated with "creeping heritage"', we have seen a dramatic and exponential growth in the number and range of objects, places and practices that are defined, conserved and exhibited as 'heritage'. Indeed, I would argue that what is distinctive about heritage today is not so much the characteristic or quality of that which is considered to merit the use of the term, so much as its abundance, the sheer amount of stuff in the world that it can be used to describe, and the ways in which those categories of 'things' (a term I use to include both tangible and intangible heritage) that are defined as heritage have multiplied exponentially. I discuss this growth in heritage in more detail in later chapters of this book, but I think it is worth bearing in mind here that, although the notion of 'heritage' as things and traditions from the past has been with us for a long time, there are a number of ways in which heritage is defined, managed and under-stood that are distinctive to our late-modern period. Similarly, there are other notions regarding heritage that are much older, and belong to the development of ideas about what it means to be 'modern' which were formed in the period following the Enlightenment. These older ideas about heritage and the nature of the past and present often persist alongside those ideas that have developed more recently. So heritage as a concept is constantly evolving, and the way in which the term is understood is always ambiguous and never certain. This provides one of the main incentives for taking a critical approach to heritage in contemporary society, so that we can begin to understand what role the concept plays in any given context in which it is invoked, and the unique cluster of knowledge/power effects that it brings to bear on any given situation.

Indeed, the context in which heritage is deployed as a concept is crucial. In addition to appearing as something that is desirable, and that has a commercial, political or social value, heritage is often invoked in the context of debates and protests about things and practices that are considered to be threatened or at risk. That risk might simply be the implicit threat of time itself—forgetting, decaying, eroding or becoming worn with age. More often, the threat is one of demolition or destruction—the flattening of a building, the bulldozing of a tree, the destruction of a tract of landscape by mining, perhaps, or even more seriously, the extinction of a plant or animal species, or the genocide of a group of people during times of war. The element of potential or real threat to heritage—of destruction, loss or decay—links heritage historically and politically with the conservation movement. Even where a building or object is under no immediate threat of destruction, its listing on a heritage register is an action that assumes a potential threat at some time in the future, from which it is being protected by legislation or listing.

I don't want to define heritage further here, as I want to give this issue the detailed consideration it deserves in the next chapter. It is sufficient for now to say that heritage is generally invoked as a positive quality, that it assumes some relationship with the past, and that it relates to ways of categorising and classifying 'things' and traditions in the world. Moreover, it often implies a sense of threat, or at least some vulnerability, and various other qualities that set it apart from the everyday. Most importantly, heritage today is distinctive as a concept in the broad number of different categories of things it might be found to describe. The 'industry' that has grown up around the identification, preservation, management and exhibition of these many and varied forms of heritage has assumed an important place within the operation of contemporary global societies. For this reason, heritage needs to assume a central place in any consideration of what it means to be a global citizen in the early twenty-first century. It is, after all, not only that our taxes pay for the work of governments in conserving heritage, but perhaps more importantly, that our futures are imagined and made possible through the pasts which are produced through heritage in our present.

What is heritage studies?

The very rapid expansion of heritage objects, places and practices throughout the world in the past forty years has created new industries, professions and a wide range of intellectual speculation. Uzzell (2009: 326) colourfully describes heritage studies as 'the lovechild of a multitude of relationships between academics in many disciplines, and then nurtured by practitioners and institutions'. For this reason, heritage has often been perceived to be compromised by its contingent relationship to other areas, tourism and the leisure industries in particular. Historians have tended to see the heritage industries as popularisers of history at best, and as the producers of 'bad' history at worst (e.g. Lowenthal 1985, 1998). Architectural historians and archaeologists have voiced disquiet about the simplification of questions of authenticity and meaning in the interests of popular education and political expediency in relation to heritage. Sociologists and those writing from a cultural studies perspective have pointed to a reverence for selected material aspects of the past as an integral characteristic of late-modern society. Geographers have approached heritage through the lens of urban studies and planning, and its relationship to processes such as regeneration and gentrification. Ecologists, biologists and natural geographers have been concerned with concepts of biodiversity and ecological sustainability. Heritage studies as a discipline does not therefore emerge naturally from any single current academic field. It is an area rich with interest, covering research into what we choose to conserve and why, the politics of the past, the processes of heritage management, and the relationship between commemorative acts and public and private memory, but at present it is without a 'home' in any particular academic discipline. I argue that this is both a disadvantage in the sense in which heritage has tended not to be treated 'seriously' by academics until recently, but also potentially a source of creative dynamism for a newly emerging field of interdisciplinary academic investigation with links to policy making in the 'real' world.

Perhaps it is important to ask a more fundamental question here: why might we be interested in delineating a 'field' of interdisciplinary heritage studies at all? In the past, heritage has tended to be explored from particular, highly specialised, clearly defined subject positions that have discouraged us from considering heritage as an overarching contemporary global phenomenon. Archaeologists have been interested in the conservation of archaeological sites and objects; historians in the promotion of accurate public history; anthropologists in the relationship between heritage and tradition; geographers in natural and cultural landscapes; biologists and ecologists in the conservation of plant and animal species. Furthermore, the way in which heritage has been driven largely by compliance with municipal, state and national legislation, and has become caught up in processes of the production of local, regional and national identity and cultural economies, means that we have tended not to look across national borders to explore areas of common concern. The challenge of Indigenous and other minority and non-Western peoples in applying alternative models to the definition and methods of management of both cultural and natural heritage (perhaps even in suggesting the absence of distinction between these two categories) has provided another important and, in its own way, highly specialised input into this diverse assemblage of ideas. Yet there are very good reasons why we might want to think about heritage in a holistic and comparative way. In this book, I argue that the form of our contemporary global responses to heritage—whether the desire to conserve a historic landscape, an animal species, an endangered language or a small scatter of prehistoric stone artefacts—are ultimately driven by a common series of concerns that relate to the experience of globalisation and the conditions of late-modernity. Further, since the 1970s, the work of international NGOs, in particular the UNESCO World Heritage Committee and its advisory bodies, has promulgated a particular approach and a series of underlying values towards heritage, which are now part of a common, universal language of heritage management. For this reason, from Hong Kong to Nanking, York to Nantucket, and Arnhem Land to Switzerland, heritage is increasingly officially defined and governed by a common set of philosophies that have their origins in a particular, modern, Euro-American way of thinking about the relationship between the past and present, a desire to order and categorise and a late-modern obsession with vulnerability, uncertainty and risk. The friction that has developed between this way of thinking about heritage and other local, regional or national approaches has provided an important series of challenges that has in turn begun to lead to the creative transformation of this 'universal' system of heritage management itself. The fact that heritage is such an all-pervasive, global phenomenon, which has had a fundamental influence on how we have made and remade our built and natural environments, coupled with its powerful cultural influence in contemporary global societies, suggests that developing an oversight and a sense of its common concerns is both urgent and long overdue.

In Chapters 3 and 4 of this book, I identify three broad phases in the history of heritage, the first two occurring principally in Euro-American contexts prior to around 1970, and the third in response to the emergence of globalised heritage discourses and changes in the social and economic context of heritage in the later part of the twentieth century. I argue that the academic debates about heritage that materialised during the 1980s and 1990s have had an important influence on the practice of heritage in the late twentieth and early twenty-first centuries, and the form that heritage has taken during the past few decades. While one of the main academic criticisms of heritage has focused on the dominance of tangible objects and buildings in heritage at the expense of intangible cultural values, I argue that official practices of heritage and academic heritage studies have actually increasingly distanced themselves from material 'things' and have become dominated by the discourse of heritage. I refer to this as heritage studies' 'discursive turn'. While the discursive turn has been important in drawing attention to the knowledge/power effects of heritage and its processes of identification, exhibition and management, it has also tended to deprivilege the significant affective qualities of material things and the influences the material traces of the past have on people in the contemporary world. And while certain critiques draw on alternative models of heritage from Indigenous and non-Western contexts, I argue that they fail to appreciate the significant ways in which these same traditions conceptualise heritage as an emergent property of the *dialogical* relationship between human beings and a range of other human and non-human actors and their environments. In the light of this, I think it is important to reconsider the affective qualities and the material aspects of heritage. Developing a dialogical model of heritage, which implies an ontology of connectivity and more democratic processes of heritage decision-making, I argue that this alternative way of studying and understanding heritage has important implications for the ways in which we might deal with the overwhelming presence of the past in contemporary society, and allow us to connect heritage with broader issues such as sustainability and environmental change. This dialogical model implies an ethical stance in relation to others, and a belief in the importance of acknowledging and respecting alternative perspectives and worldviews as a condition of dialogue, and provides a way to connect heritage with other pressing social, economic, political and environmental issues of our time. I discuss these issues in further detail later in the book.

Acknowledging heritage as a process with deep historical roots, I argue that new approaches to heritage emerged in the mid twentieth century in response to the 'cult of memory' that developed in North America, the UK and Western Europe following the Second World War, and accelerated in response to a series of changes that occurred in postindustrial societies after 1970. Elsewhere, this set of changes has been summarised to highlight the way in which it has influenced our late-modern engagement with the past (Harrison and Schofield 2010). These changes can be seen to include:

- processes of deindustrialisation
- the growth of new communicative technologies and electronic media
- the globalisation of technology and its association with altered patterns of production and consumption
- the widespread experience of mass migration and the associated rise of transnationalism (in terms of capital, technology, labour and corporations)
- new modes of capitalism involving more flexible forms of capital accumulation and distribution
- changes in the experience of time and space associated with a perception of accelerated change and 'speed'

(Harrison and Schofield 2010: 128).

My intention is to locate the globalisation of heritage within the historical, social and political context of the second half of the twentieth century and the early part of the twenty-first. While academic heritage studies have provided a series of critiques of heritage that have influenced its development over the past four decades, I suggest that their impact has been limited by a narrow focus on certain themes, in particular the politics of representation and discursive processes of meaning-making. While these studies have provided important insights, I suggest that we need to develop a broader critical agenda for heritage studies as a newly emerging academic discipline, one that is more attuned to the affective qualities of heritage, the ways in which it is caught up in local and global processes, and the distribution of power within the various administrative and governmental networks surrounding it. I conclude with some observations regarding the future of heritage, and the need for a broader integration of heritage and heritage studies with a consideration of other pressing issues of political, social, economic and environmental concern.

It is important to identify some limits to the present volume. Fundamentally, it deals with the modern Western traditions of heritage that gave rise to the 1972 World Heritage Convention, and their application to non-Western contexts. It does not, for example, engage with the alternative histories of heritage conservation that developed in Asia, for example (see Byrne 2007; Daly and Winter 2011). It also limits itself to the anglophone literature on heritage. There is a large practical and theoretical literature on heritage and conservation techniques published in French, Italian and Spanish, for example, that is not covered in this book. There remains an important task of documenting the non-Western discussions around heritage, making them available to a broader audience and subjecting them to the same critical analysis that this book advocates for anglophone traditions, which I hope scholars who are trained and knowledgeable in these fields will feel challenged to explore in response to this volume.

Structure of the book

This book is divided into four broad sections. This introduction and the second chapter introduce a series of central concepts that inform the rest of the book. Chapter 2 looks at the relationship of heritage to modernity as a philosophical and political concept, arguing that heritage is informed by the particular relationships between modernity and time, a sense of uncertainty, vulnerability or 'risk', and processes of ordering, classifying and categorising (or 'listing') that were developed in the modern historical sciences. Further, it introduces a series of ways of conceptualising and studying the relationships between people and 'things', drawing on actor–network theory, assemblage theory and symmetrical archaeology, which help frame the discussion of the diversification of heritage in the late twentieth and early twenty-first centuries in Chapters 6–10. These chapters provide the foundation for the themes of materiality, connectivity and dialogue that I develop in subsequent sections of the book.

Chapters 3 and 4 provide a brief historical account of the rise of heritage in Western societies in the late eighteenth and early nineteenth centuries, and its global spread during the second part of the twentieth century, exploring how various modern notions influenced the development of the 'idea' of heritage over this period. Chapter 3 focuses on the emergence of the concept of the public sphere and the modern concepts of risk and distance from the past, which informed the first official attempts to conserve heritage objects and places during the late eighteenth and nineteenth centuries. It then explores the increasing state control and regulation of heritage throughout the late nineteenth and early twentieth centuries, which arose as a result of the idea of the past as threatened and precarious resource. Finally, it examines various global developments that occurred following the Second World War in relation to the history of the Aswan High Dam and various international safeguarding campaigns, which were instrumental to the development of the World Heritage Convention. Chapter 4 considers the globalisation of heritage and the post-1970 'heritage boom'. It explores the way in which notions of collection and curation from the late nineteenth century museum were deployed in the context of global economic change and deindustrialisation, providing models for the musealisation of places, cities and landscapes in the 1970s and 1980s. Further, it explores the changes in late-modern societies that help explain the widespread growth of public interest in the past that occurred during this period, which have led to the pervasive 'saturation' of heritage we experience in the contemporary world.

Chapter 5 provides an outline of the rise of the critical interdisciplinary field of academic heritage studies, and an overview of the major areas of debate that have come to define the field as it is emerging today. It explores its roots in early discussion of the relationship between heritage and nationalism, and subsequent debates about the relationship between heritage and economic decline in the UK. In the United States, heritage studies emerged from discussions of the public understanding of the past in the academic field of history, and developed alongside professional studies of the 'interpretation' of heritage sites and tourism studies. Another major contribution to heritage studies has been questions relating to the politics of representation, which developed separately in cultural studies and postcolonial studies and in the context of the 'new museology', and were subsequently brought together in the work of sociologists and cultural anthropologists in relation to debates about the ownership of cultural property. Finally, the chapter explores more recent discussions of heritage as a 'discourse' in relation to Foucauldian models of governmentality and critical discourse analysis. It is argued that these debates have set the broad parameters of heritage studies as they are presently understood.

Chapters 6–9 shift to focus in detail on one or two of a series of linked conceptual 'crises' that have arisen as a consequence of the diversification and global spread of heritage over the late twentieth and early twenty-first centuries: new concerns that have emerged in relation to various social, economic and political shifts that have occurred in relation to heritage as a result of processes of globalisation and late-modern change. Chapter 6 focuses on the new categories of cultural landscapes and intangible heritage, which were developed by the World Heritage Committee in the 1980s and 1990s, and their impact on definitions of heritage globally. Chapter 7 looks in more detail at processes of globalisation and transnationalism and the issues they have produced in relation to heritage, particularly in multicultural societies. The chapter also considers issues regarding the universal rights to cultural diversity as expressed by UNESCO and their relationship with heritage more broadly. Chapter 8 explores the problem of memorialisation of the past in relation to political and social change, and the issues that arise in relation to heritage in the case of changes of political regime, looking at iconoclasm and its relationship with collective forgetting, and the emergence of 'absent heritage' and virtual heritage as further exemplars of the heterogeneous piling of the past in the present, which is characteristic of contemporary heritage conservation. Finally, it considers recent arguments that suggest late-modern societies are becoming overwhelmed by the past, conserving 'too much' heritage, and arguments about the 'need' for societies to forget, alongside a developing literature on deaccessioning heritage. Completing this section, Chapter 9 considers the challenge of Indigenous and non-Western models of heritage for global heritage practices and for the idea of a 'universal' World Heritage, and proposes an alternative dialogical model of heritage based on the connectivity of people, landscapes and things. This dialogical model suggests new ways of connecting heritage with broader social, political, economic and environmental concerns.

Chapter 10 concludes by looking briefly towards the future of heritage, outlining a broad agenda for critical heritage studies in the new millennium. It reiterates the book's central themes of abundance, uncertainty, materiality, connectivity and dialogue to explore potential new areas of study and ways in which the new models of heritage suggested here might be employed in developing future research directions. In particular, it reinforces the ways in which a dialogical notion of heritage might help us all to engage more actively with the production of the past in the present, and provide the basis for more democratic models of heritage decision-making in the future.

2

SOME DEFINITIONS

Heritage, modernity, materiality

Introduction

This chapter introduces some broad definitions and concepts that underpin the arguments that follow. In the first part I consider a number of definitions of heritage and explore some important fundamental differences between the ways in which heritage has been perceived in the United Kingdom and Western Europe on the one hand, and in North America on the other. Following this, I discuss the relationship of heritage to modernity as a philosophical concept, arguing that heritage is informed by the relationship between modernity and time, the idea of 'risk' or threat, and the role of ordering, classifying and categorising in modernity, as background to the historical accounts of the rise of heritage in Chapters 3 and 4. One of the key concerns of this book is a series of crises that have arisen over the course of the past few decades as a consequence of the diversification and global spread of heritage over the late twentieth and early twenty-first centuries. In exploring these crises, I focus particularly on the relationship of various actors—practitioners, state officials, local stakeholders, academics—to the material aspects of heritage and the particular circumstances of the debates in which various local issues have influenced global and national heritage practices. In the final part of this chapter, I introduce a number of approaches concerned with helping elucidate the relationships between actors and the various environments in which they operate, including actor–network theory and assemblage theory. Part of my argument in this book is that a major outcome of the debates about heritage that have been central to the rise of critical heritage studies as an academic discipline over the past three decades has been a process of 'dematerialising' heritage by introducing an ever-increasing emphasis on the intangible aspects of heritage and tradition as part of an exponential growth in the objects, places and practices that are considered to be defined as heritage. As a result, I also introduce a number of concepts that derive from a growing literature on new approaches to material culture in the social sciences, which are integral to a dialogical model of heritage that I explore later in the book. This chapter contains theoretical and conceptual material that underpins much of the rest of the volume.

Some definitions of heritage

It is important at this point to introduce some definitions which will help guide the discussion that follows. Heritage has often been perceived to be a 'conveniently ambiguous' concept (Lowenthal 1998; Davison [2000] 2008), and has been put to many different social and political ends (Samuel 1994). However, it could also be argued that its ambiguity lies at the root of many of the problems that have arisen within global heritage management (e.g. Breglia 2006), and various arguments over the critical academic analysis of heritage. As I have already noted, the word 'heritage' has been used to describe everything from buildings to cooking styles, songs to personal belongings, ethnicity to religion. With such a broad range of meanings in circulation within contemporary global societies, it is not surprising that the term has become problematic.

It is perhaps helpful in the first instance to point out that heritage is not a 'thing' or a historical or political movement, but refers to a set of attitudes to, and relationships with, the past (Walsh 1992; Harvey 2001, 2008; Smith 2006). These relationships are characterised by a reverence and attachment to select objects, places and practices that are thought to connect with or exemplify the past in some way. The form this set of relationships takes varies both geographically and chronologically (e.g. Byrne 1991; Bradley 2002), but people must 'work' to produce these relationships (Byrne 2008), which are co-produced (Dicks 2000) and formed as a result of the relationships between people and other human and non-human actors. Perhaps most importantly, heritage is formed *in the present* (Tunbridge and Ashworth 1996: 20; Lowenthal 2004: 19–23; Graham and Howard 2008: 1) and reflects inherited and current concerns about the past. The form of this connection with the past is also variable, and might manifest as a set of relationships with an object, building or place, but may also manifest as a particular set of intangible practices that appear to be separate from material things. Nonetheless, as I go on to argue, such practices are thoroughly embedded in a set of physical relationships with objects, places and other people, and in this sense, to speak of intangible heritage as somehow separate from the 'material' world is inaccurate. I've already introduced the phrase 'objects, places and practices' as a gloss to describe the range of different ways in which heritage might be recognised in contemporary societies. So it is important to realise that heritage is not one thing, but can take many different forms.

Throughout this book, I use the term *official heritage* to refer to a set of professional practices that are authorised by the state and motivated by some form of legislation or written charter. This represents what most of us would recognise as a contemporary 'operational' definition of heritage as the series of mechanisms by which objects, buildings and landscapes are set apart from the 'everyday' and conserved for their aesthetic, historic, scientific, social or recreational values. This broadly Euro-American set of practices emerged in some places as early as the mid-nineteenth century, but accelerated rapidly in North America, the UK, Western Europe and many of their former colonies following the Second World War. The history of the rise of official heritage is discussed in detail in Chapter 3. In contrast, I use the term *unofficial heritage* to refer to a broad range of practices that are represented using the language of heritage, but are not recognised by official forms of legislation. Unofficial heritage may manifest in the rather conventional form of buildings or objects that have significance to individuals or communities, but are not recognised by the state as heritage through legislative protection, or may manifest in less tangible ways as sets of social practices that surround more tangible forms of both official and unofficial heritage, but are equally not protected by legislation (for a more detailed exposition of the differences between official and unofficial heritage, see Harrison 2010a: 8–9).

An example of the relationship between official and unofficial heritage can be drawn from the World Heritage site of Stonehenge in south-east England. The official heritage of Stonehenge could be understood as residing in its legislative protection, as a Scheduled Ancient Monument and as part of the Stonehenge, Avebury and Associated Sites World Heritage Site, which was inscribed in 1986. However, its unofficial heritage might be seen as residing in the set of practices surrounding its use by a range of different neo-pagan and druidic groups, who have been gathering to witness the Summer and Winter Solstices at the site since the early twentieth century, gatherings that in recent years have seen thousands of visitors from around the world assemble at the site. While the solstice practices of neo-pagans are tolerated and managed by English Heritage, which now allows special access to the stone circle for these purposes, Stonehenge's significance is thought to lie primarily in its archaeological values, not in its contemporary uses. However, to consider this as simply a distinction between the 'past' and 'present' values of the site would be inaccurate. In the same ways in which contemporary neo-pagans make and remake the meaning and significance of this object from the past in the present, its archaeological significance also represents a form of ascribed value assigned to it by generations of practitioners who have remade the meaning of Stonehenge to address contemporary archaeological debates. So we can see that objects, places and practices may sometimes have both official and unofficial heritage status, and that status has nothing to do with the particular qualities of the 'thing' itself, but are defined by values ascribed by those who hold positions of expertise and authority and whose viewpoints are recognised and acted upon by the state (Smith 2004, 2006).

In other cases, unofficial heritage values may surround an object, place or practice that remains completely unrecognised by the state. For example, in the case of places and buildings which fall into categories that allow them to be defined as official heritage, these might be recognised by a community or interest group as important, but fail to achieve official recognition of heritage status. A well known example is the unsuccessful campaign in 1963 to stop the demolition of the Old Pennsylvania ('Penn') Station building in New York City, which is widely perceived to have contributed directly to the founding of the New York City Landmarks Preservation Commission under a new historic preservation act passed in 1965 as the Landmarks Law (Moore 1999; Gray 2001; but see Wood 2007; Mason 2009: x). This

FIGURE 2.1 Hundreds of druids and pagans celebrate the winter solstice at Stonehenge on 22 December 2009 in Wiltshire, England. Hundreds of people gathered at the famous stone circle to celebrate the sunrise closest to the winter solstice, the shortest day of the year. (Photograph by Matt Cardy/Getty Images.)

was perhaps a rather 'conventional' example, in which the protest group represented a number of professional interests, particularly architectural historians and planners, and catalysed around a building, a category that has long received protection as official heritage. In other cases, unofficial heritage could be less conventionally represented by a series of values and practices that exist at a local or community level, but are not included within the state's perception of its patrimony or national story. Examples include local festivals that are not recognised as of interest to the state, or the heritage of migrant groups or the working classes. They might also include places that are not officially 'listed' but are nonetheless actively preserved by local or regional interest groups.

In some cases, what had previously been 'unofficial' becomes 'official' heritage as the state's relationship to that heritage changes, or as particular objects, places and/or practices are recognised as heritage by the state. One example is the promotion of the former maximum security political prison on Robben Island as a museum and heritage site by the post-apartheid government of South Africa. Another example is President Nicolas Sarkozy's suggestion in 2008 that the correct methods for preparing classic items of French cuisine might be considered for protection as part of the UNESCO World Heritage List. This move, although facilitated by changes in the way heritage is defined by UNESCO, nonetheless represented a shift from older models of official

FIGURE 2.2 Protesters marching with placards outside Penn Station to save the building from demolition, New York City, 1963. (Photograph by Walter Daran/Hulton Archive/Getty Images.)

heritage in France, which were focused on the monument (Nora 1996, 1997, 1998), to one that also embraces traditional practice. The different forms that unofficial and official heritage might take have blurred significantly since the beginning of the new millennium as a result of the increased recognition of 'intangible' forms of heritage by the state and international heritage authorities (see Chapter 6). What is important to recognise here is that there is no formal change in the nature of the 'thing' itself (although with time, there might be some change relating to the way in which it becomes managed as a piece of official heritage). I want to emphasise that the recognition of something as official heritage or unofficial heritage is simply a matter of definition, and does not necessarily denote some intrinsic quality of an object, place or practice.

Unofficial heritage also often refers to what, without a sense of threat or loss, we might refer to as 'custom' or 'tradition': a set of repetitive, entrenched, sometimes ritualised practices that link the values, beliefs and memories of communities in the present with those of the past. Both of these terms are derived from socio-cultural anthropology, and in the public mind are often associated with small-scale societies and the everyday practices that can be understood to generate 'culture'. I place particular emphasis on the 'everydayness' of such practices here. Traditions and quotidian aspects of culture are very rarely conceived of as 'heritage' in the absence of uncertainty, risk, a perception of threat, or the need to compete for attention with other interests that are perceived to be detrimental to them. One of the important distinctions that existed in heritage practice in the West prior to around 1980 was that official forms of heritage management tended to recognise only the remarkable— the greatest, oldest, biggest and best. In this way, a *canonical* model of heritage was produced that was distinguished markedly from the everyday. The object of such forms of heritage was to draw a clear distinction from the past, in that the buildings and objects that were being preserved were seen as separate from (and, perhaps most importantly, more valuable than) those from the quotidian present. In subsequent chapters I suggest that it was only when official heritage attempted to broaden its remit to deal with not only remarkable objects, buildings and landscapes, but also traditional social practices and their association with more quotidian places, that it found itself in crisis, and conflict arose between models of heritage that emphasised the remarkable and those that emphasised the everyday. I characterise such models as 'continuous', in the sense in which they emphasise the connection between the past and the quotidian present. The approaches to heritage that emerged from this crisis saw official heritage switch from canonical to more *representative* approaches, and encompass aspects of both 'high' and 'popular' culture. Part of this new approach was also driven by emerging neoliberal economic approaches in the West, and by the ways in which heritage was forced to market itself to broader audiences as it was incorporated into an emerging experience economy. I explore these issues in more detail in Chapters 4 and 5.

In using the general terms 'official' or 'unofficial' heritage, I do not want to suggest that there is no variation in the definition of heritage employed by those who operate within each category. There should be multiple conceptions of heritage active within authoritative groups at any one time, which we would also expect to shift in relation to other social, political and economic forces. Similarly, there is clearly a gulf of difference that separates the unofficial heritage values of Stonehenge for contemporary neo-pagans, and those values to which protesters were attempting draw attention in debates around the future of the Old Pennsylvania Station in New York City. My point in drawing this distinction between official and unofficial heritage is simply

FIGURE 2.3 Prison cell in the former High Security Prison on Robben Island in South Africa, where Nelson Mandela was imprisoned from 1964 until 1982. In 1996 Robben Island was gazetted as a South African National Monument and National Museum, and in 1999 it was listed as a World Heritage site. (Photograph by iStockphoto.)

to suggest that certain forms of heritage are authorised by legislation or charter, while others are not. I have introduced these definitions here because I want to suggest that a vast majority of the arguments relating to heritage—in an academic sense, at the level of public policy, and in relation to individual campaigns and protests—can be reduced to a series of issues relating to the recognition (or lack of recognition) of unofficial heritage, or in other words, arguments about the definition of 'heritage' itself. Returning to the example of Penn Station, it was the absence of formal mechanisms to recognise the importance of the building to people's sense of place, and the lack of recognition of the building within existing frameworks for heritage conservation, which led to its demolition. Once these new frameworks were in place, similar buildings were subsequently able to be defined and conserved as 'heritage', as was the case with the New York City Grand Central Terminal, which was successfully preserved under this legislation in the US Supreme Court case Penn Central Transportation Co. *v.* New York City (1978). This raises another important point, which is that the categories of 'official' and 'unofficial' heritage are not fixed, and ideas about what constitutes heritage in one 'arena' significantly influence those in another. In part, the expansion of the categories of what is considered to constitute heritage has occurred as a direct result of ideas about what constitutes heritage in the 'unofficial' realm becoming officially recognised. On the other hand, ideas about what heritage is and does that circulate within 'official' heritage can also significantly influence what people believe constitutes their own 'unofficial' heritage, whether it is recognised by the state or not. So these categories are locked in a dialectical or recursive process in which each influences the definition of the other. A number of the changes in heritage described in Chapters 6–9 of this book relate to the outcomes of this process over the course of the late twentieth and early twenty-first centuries, in particular the formal recognition of intangible heritage by UNESCO, discussed in Chapter 6.

Comparing ways of understanding heritage in North America, the UK and Western Europe

I have made reference to official heritage as a set of broadly Euro-American practices, and in doing so have implied that we should see certain similarities between the practices of heritage in North America, the UK and Western Europe and their present and former colonies. While most authors would acknowledge this connection (e.g. Lowenthal 1985, 1998), the histories and contemporary practices of historic preservation in North America conventionally have been considered separately from those of the UK and Europe. A number of factors have colluded in this separation, not the least being differences in terminology ('preservation' in North America, 'conservation' in the UK and Europe, for example) and the administration of heritage, which tends to be managed at the national level in the UK and Europe, but administered at many different levels (federal, state and local) in the USA (as it is in other countries, such as Australia). Official practices of heritage have been understood to reflect quite different meanings in different countries. As historian David Lowenthal notes:

> Heritage in Britain is said to reflect nostalgia for imperial self-esteem, in America to requite angst for lost community, in France to redress wartime disgrace, in Australia to surplant the curse of European recency with indigenous antiquity. But no explanation specific to one people can account for a cause so contagious. What is involved is a cluster of trends whose premises, promises and problems are truly global.
>
> *(Lowenthal 2004: 23)*

This volume seeks to take up the challenge laid down by Lowenthal to consider heritage in a critical and comparative fashion as a global phenomenon, while recognising the need to consider not only the similarities, but also the differences in how heritage is defined, managed, understood and used in different countries. Some of the problems inherent in trying to take such a comparative perspective have been exacerbated by a lack of attention to the history of the historic preservation movement in the USA. The national story of heritage conservation has been examined in detail by a number of authors in the UK (Briggs 1952; Wright 1985; Hewison 1987; Hunter 1996; Ross 1996; Delafons 1997; Mandler 1997; Carman 2002; Cowell 2008), in countries such as France (Nora 1996, 1997, 1998) and Greece (Herzfeld 2004; Hamilakis 2007), and in a European context more generally (Choay 2001; see Jokilehto 2002; Stubbs 2009 for international comparative histories of architectural conservation). However, in the USA this work has been limited mainly to the multiple volume history by Charles Hosmer (1965, 1981), Kenneth Murtagh's textbook *Keeping Time: The History and Theory of Preservation in America* (2006) and the collection *Giving Preservation a History*, edited by Max Page and Randall Mason (2004; see also Rosensweig and Thelen 1998). As Page and Mason note, the absence of critical accounts of the history of the preservation movement in the USA has led to the development of a series of unquestioned foundation myths and an absence of groundwork for critical analysis of the field. While this book cannot explore the diverse micro-histories of preservationism in North America, which have begun to be explored by scholars such as Randall Mason (2009) and contributors to *Giving Preservation a History* (Page and Mason 2004), it is intended to provide a broad reflection on heritage practices throughout the Western world, particularly over the course of the late twentieth and early twenty-first centuries, and the impact of these practices at a global level. For this reason, I hope readers will forgive any generalisations that might gloss over significant national and regional variations in heritage practices, but will find some resonance in the book's assessment of the *global* impact of the various crises and the associated shifts in practice and definition that it describes.

As others have noted before me, the North American tradition of historic preservation has its roots in European culture, but it has also diverged from this tradition in a number of important ways (see further discussion below and in Chapter 3). Nonetheless, the histories of historic preservation in the UK and North America can be seen to share a number of similarities, and to mirror one another in some matters. This is reflected in their shared historical trajectories and the mythologies that have grown up around them. For example, the UK has its own equivalent of the 1963 destruction of New York Penn Station discussed above, which is also viewed as part of the foundation history of historic heritage conservation in that country, in the furore surrounding the destruction of the Euston Railway Arch in London in 1961 (see Chapter 3). Similarly, both the UK and USA draw on the mythology of a 'founding mother' to explain the origins of their heritage movements. In the USA, this founding mother is Ann Pamela Cunningham, who spearheaded a campaign to save President George Washington's historic home at Mount Vernon in the 1850s. In the UK, it is Octavia Hill, who was responsible for helping to establish the National Trust in the 1890s. Both 'founding mothers' (the gender politics here are clearly interesting and worthy of consideration in their own right) feature prominently in the historiography of the heritage movements in their respective countries.

I don't raise these points of comparison flippantly, but to suggest that there are a number of broad similarities in the history of heritage conservation movements in the UK, North America and Western Europe and their present and former colonies, which make worthwhile their consideration as part of a broader pattern of Euro-American responses to the material remains of the past in the context of urban planning (see Chapter 3). It is also important to emphasise that it was this broad tradition of historic preservation on which UNESCO drew in developing the World Heritage Convention, and from which many issues have subsequently developed in attempts to apply this model globally. However, while I have emphasised some of the broad similarities that exist between forms of official heritage management in North America and the UK, Western Europe and their former colonies, there is one fundamental difference in the historical trajectory of heritage in America and Europe, which it is important to highlight at this stage. This has to do with the colonial foundations of old and new world states.

While North America and Europe (including the UK) shared a history of the growth of heritage legislation in the late nineteenth and twentieth centuries, there are some major differences in the ways in which heritage has manifested itself in North America as a settler society when compared with European non-settler societies (e.g. Smith 2004, 2006). I use the term 'settler society' here to refer to the postcolonial reimagining of places established as colonies or outposts of Western European empires, in which existing Indigenous populations were dislocated by settler-colonists (Eddy and Schrueder 1988; Lilley [2000] 2008). Elsewhere, drawing on the work of Arjun Appadurai (2006, [2001] 2008), I have suggested that heritage in settler societies must assume a 'predatory' role, in which certain forms of recollection manifest in the selection and management of particular cultural heritage places require the elimination or removal of other memories or forms of recollection (Harrison 2008: 178ff). Because of their peculiar colonial histories, heritage management in settler societies must work to metaphorically and/or physically erase the traces of prior Indigenous occupation as a way of emphasising the roots of contemporary nationhood in colonial settlement (see also Trigger [1989] 1996; Byrne 1996; Smith 2004). These processes are obvious not only in a North American context, but also in former and current European colonies such as Australia (Byrne 1996; Harrison 2004; Smith 2004, 2006). Some of these differences manifest themselves in the different approaches to nature conservation in the UK and USA, for example (Harrison and O'Donnell 2010). This is not to say that heritage does not also take predatory forms in non-settler societies (Ashworth et al. 2007), but simply to point out the particular dynamics of settler societies with regard to the heritage of their Indigenous populations. For now, it is important to remember that there are certain differences between heritage conservation strategies that arise from the different historic trajectories of settler and non-settler societies.

Heritage and its relationship with modernity

Having defined what heritage 'is', and the important differences between the categories of 'official' and 'unofficial heritage', I want to suggest that are a number of characteristics of the way in which heritage is defined, understood and managed today, which derive from a way of perceiving the world that is a product of the experience of *modernity*. While we can probably assume all human societies have some form of relationship with objects, places and practices to which they attribute significance in terms of understanding the past and its relationship to the present (Lowenthal 1985; Harvey 2001; Bradley 2002), there are a number of ways of conceptualising and experiencing the world that are peculiar to modern societies. These worldviews have directly informed the contemporary practice and definition of heritage; identifying them can help us understand its character and history over the course of the past two centuries (see also Walsh 1992; Brett 1996). In this section, I explore this relationship between heritage and modernity in more detail.

Most commentators place the origins of the philosophies that underlie Western approaches to heritage management in the context of late Enlightenment thought and the rise of nation-states in the eighteenth and nineteenth centuries. While the origins of museums and other collections of cultural objects, such as the various 'lists' of canonical regional, national and 'World' heritage places, lie much earlier in the work of antiquarians and private collectors, heritage is widely held to be a distinctively *modern* notion. By using this term 'modern', I mean not only that it developed relatively recently, but that it emerged within the context of a series of distinctive philosophies and social and political movements that we would recognise as belonging to a modern sensibility, and that have helped define (and produce) the modern period. While sociologists, political historians and art historians have tended to define modernity differently, it is generally associated with a set of ideas and social and economic conditions that emerged in the course of the Enlightenment, and is linked historically with the rise of nation-states and political forms based on liberal government. Sociologist Anthony Giddens defines modernity in these terms:

> At its simplest, modernity is a shorthand term for modern society, or industrial civilization. Portrayed in more detail, it is associated with (1) a certain set of attitudes towards the world, the idea of the world as open to transformation, by human intervention; (2) a complex of economic institutions, especially industrial production and a market economy; (3) a certain range of political institutions, including the nation-state and mass democracy. Largely as a result of these

characteristics, modernity is vastly more dynamic than any previous type of social order. It is a society – more technically, a complex of institutions – which, unlike any preceding culture, lives in the future, rather than the past.

(Giddens and Pierson 1998: 94)

This cluster of ideas and their underlying social, political and economic movements both facilitated and underpinned the development of a particular set of relationships with the past, which were necessary prerequisites to the development of contemporary notions of heritage, including an increased emphasis on empiricism and reason as the primary source of knowledge and authority (Smith 2004, 2006), and a way of defining the present in opposition to the past (Lucas 2004, 2005, 2010; Harrison 2011) and rooting the 'invented traditions' of new nation-states by creating a history for them (Hobsbawm 1983a, 1983b; Kosselleck 1985).

However, it is important to note that modernity can be understood as not simply a set of ideas and philosophies, but also a quality of *lived experience*; as both a sociological and a phenomenological category (Osborne 1995: 5). As Marshall Berman notes in his famous account of modernity, *All That is Solid Melts into Air*:

> There is a mode of vital experience – experience of space and time, of the self and others, of life's possibilities and perils – that is shared by men and women all over the world today. I will call this body of experience 'modernity'. To be modern is to find ourselves in an environment that promises us adventure, power, joy, growth, transformation of ourselves and the world – and, at the same time, that threatens to destroy everything we have, everything we know, everything we are. Modern environments and experiences cut across all boundaries of geography and ethnicity, of class and nationality, of religion and ideology: in this sense, modernity can be said to unite all mankind. But it is a paradoxical unity, a unity of disunity: it pours us all into a maelstrom of perpetual disintegration and renewal, of struggle and contradiction, of ambiguity and anguish. To be modern is to be part of a universe in which, as Marx said, 'all that is solid melts into air'.
>
> *(Berman 1983: 15)*

The experience of modernity is thus one of novelty, progress, speed and rupture from the traditions of the past. Modernity emphasises itself as new, dynamic and distinctive from that which came before it. I use the term 'modernity' here in an active sense, following Jürgen Habermas's description of modernity as a 'project'. In his account, 'the project of modernity formulated in the Eighteenth century by the philosophers of the Enlightenment consisted of their efforts to develop objective science, universal morality and law, and autonomous art according to their inner logic ... for the rational organisation of everyday social life' (Habermas 1981). While we could argue about whether modernity really is a project, or simply the form taken by a particular historical consciousness as Osborne (1995: 23) suggests, the important point to note is that modernity produces a distinctive sense of its own time. As Bruno Latour notes, reminding us of the many alternative ways of thinking about time (as cyclical, for example):

> The moderns have a peculiar propensity for understanding time that passes as if it were really abolishing the past behind it ... since everything that passes is eliminated forever, the moderns ... sense *time as an irreversible arrow*, as capitalisation, as progress.
>
> *(Latour 1993: 68–9, my emphasis)*

This is what Jean-François Lyotard ([1979] 1984) means when he refers to modernity as a cultural condition characterised by constant change and the pursuit of progress. It is the question of what this 'progress' constitutes that goes to the heart of debates around heritage. Very broadly speaking, Marxist traditions emphasise progress as a process of human emancipation, while liberal and free market traditions emphasise progress as the continuous expansion of capital. Both of these traditions take an ambiguous position on the retention of 'old things' and see the past as something to be managed carefully. This emphasis on progress, historical change and a break with tradition in modernity throws up unacknowledged tensions in terms of our relationship with time and its passage, tensions that are at the heart of contemporary understandings of the term 'heritage'.

Heritage and the time of modernity

If one of the most distinctive aspects of modernity is its emphasis on linear progress and the distinct break it perceives between past and present, it follows that it must 'manage' its relationship with the past carefully. There is now a fairly well established argument, perhaps most strongly articulated by Kevin Walsh (1992), which suggests that it is the very way in which modernity contrasts itself in relation to its past that makes heritage such an important factor in determining how modern societies conceptualise themselves (see also Jameson 1991; Brett 1996; Harvey 2001). As Osborne (1995: 13–14) notes, the 'time' of modernity is not straightforward, as it involves a complex doubling in which it defines itself simultaneously as both 'contemporary' and 'new'. In doing so, it constantly creates the present as 'contemporary past' whilst it anticipates the future as embodied within its present. In other words, modernity creates for itself a past that is perceived to be both immanent (contained within) and imminent (impending) in the present (Harrison 2011). This simultaneity of the past in the present is part of the way in which the experience of modernity is emphasised as one of rapid progress and technological and social change (Berman 1983; Virilio 1986; Tomlinson 2007). These processes can be said to have accelerated in the period since the second half of the twentieth century, in what I refer to as the period of 'late-modernity' (see Chapter 4).

One important outcome of this rather peculiar relationship with time is that, in its obsessive attempts to transcend the present, modernity becomes fixated on the past in several distinctive ways. In the first instance, it is haunted by the idea of decline or decay. If progress is inevitable, so is obsolescence. This means that all things are potentially threatened with decline and decay, and those things that persist from the past are necessarily held to be at risk of disappearance. Secondly, in attempting to define itself in opposition to tradition and the past, modernity becomes concerned with defining and categorising it. While, as I discuss below, categorisation is itself an important aspect of the experience of modernity, modernity's oppositional relationship with the past and with tradition makes the task of defining it doubly urgent. It is possible to argue that these two factors, the sense of the inevitability of the passage of time and the need to define and categorise the past in particular ways, work together to generate a nostalgia for 'old things', and for tradition, as the refuge from those aspects of modernisation that are felt to be most alienating and disruptive (Boym 2001; Wilson 2005). This, in turn, reinforces the sense of risk and threat that becomes associated directly with the past and with the passage of time in modernity. Whether these 'traditions' are in fact relatively shallow or deep does not matter, so much as the desire to anchor the values of the present in relation to cultural forms that are believed to have existed in the past.

One of the ways in which modernity has managed the notion of time and progress is through the institution of the museum. Tony Bennett (1995, 2004) has discussed the ways in which the museum and its associated historical sciences (anthropology, archaeology, palaeontology) developed during the nineteenth and twentieth centuries as techniques for both the management and the exhibition of 'progress' using distinctive visual forms associated with evolutionary schema, while at the same time generating new ideas about what it means to be human associated with new forms of cultural governance. Central to these historical sciences were a series of Enlightenment dualisms that separated past and present, body and mind, and nature and culture. But while the museum helped in ordering modernity by re-enforcing these dualisms and putting the past 'in its place', it also simultaneously generated new forms of value for the remnants of the past in emphasising the distance between past and present. If the past is remote, it must also necessarily be rare and valuable. And if heritage is that which remains from the constant march of progress, it is also threatened by the very conditions that produce it. Once again, the ambiguity of modernity's relationship with the past produces what appear to be opposing sentiments in the desire to be unshackled from the past, whilst simultaneously fetishising and conserving fragments of it. This ambiguity is expressed and partially reconciled through the modern concept of 'risk'.

Modernity, heritage and risk

I have already mentioned that heritage is now generally defined against a background of (actual or metaphorical) protest over the potential loss, cessation or erasure of something that is perceived to be of value, within a broader discourse of conservation or preservation. This is because heritage has often been defined in the context of some sort of *threat* to objects, places or practices that are perceived to hold a form of collective value (Lowenthal 1985; Dicks 2000; Smith 2006; Davison [2000] 2008), and in opposition to other things that are perceived to be less important or significant. This threat might manifest as the demolition of historic buildings, the loss of cultural objects, the erosion of social values, or the impact of urban development on natural landscapes. An important point to note is that the physical destruction is perceived to injure not only the object, place or practice in question, but also the group of people who hold that as part of their heritage. So this threat becomes a dual menace that threatens not only the external environment, but also a community of human actors. This structures both the language of heritage and the ways in which it is invoked and deployed within modern societies. This idea of threat to heritage is based on a fundamental notion of risk and uncertainty that, like the notion of time discussed above, is central to the experience of modernity.

Mary Douglas's work on risk is helpful in drawing out some of these issues of the relationship between heritage and modernity. Douglas sees the management of risk as bound up in cultural responses to the threat of transgression. In *Purity and Danger* (1966), she identifies taboo as a universal social mechanism for the maintenance of purity and order, drawing on notions of danger and threat that are structured by a biological model of society in which matter that transgresses the boundaries of the body is perceived to be problematic. She defines dirt as 'matter out of place', and the perception of uncleanliness as synonymous with those things that are ambiguous and do not neatly fit into social categories. Building on this work on risk and threat, which was largely developed with reference to non-modern societies, she turned to explore the idea of risk as part of modernity, and a product of a perception of *vulnerability* as a result of globalisation.

> The idea of risk could have been custom-made. Its universalizing terminology, its abstractness, its power of condensation, its scientificity, its connection with objective analysis, make it perfect. Above all, its forensic uses fit the tool of the task of building a culture that supports a modern industrial society.
>
> *(Douglas 1992: 15; cited in Lupton 1999: 48)*

These ideas were central to Ulrich Beck's development of the idea of a modern 'risk society' (1992; see also Giddens 1990, 1991), in which danger is perceived as an inherent quality of the experience of modernity and the result of its preoccupation with the future. Beck defines risk as 'a systematic way of dealing with hazards and insecurities induced and introduced by modernisation itself. Risks … are consequences which relate to the threatening force of modernisation and to its globalization of doubt' (1992: 21).

Anthony Giddens suggests that one way in which modern societies manage risk and uncertainty is through placing increased trust in 'experts' and abstract 'expert systems' over local forms of knowledge (1991: 29–32). An important insight into risk and its relationship with heritage and the conditions of modernity comes from Michel Foucault's work on governmentality. Foucault wrote of governmentality as a broad strategy that has dominated Western societies since the eighteenth century, concerned with the management of individuals and populations in relation to a wide range of variables that are used in the production of the individual or collective subject (Foucault 2007, 2011). In doing so, particularly in his later works, Foucault identified a field of power relations which he referred to as bio-technical-political, a field that exists in both the discursive and non-discursive realm, which is produced and actively managed using a broad ensemble of technologies, techniques and practices. Paul Rabinow suggests the bio-technical-political field might be better rendered in English as a concern with 'welfare' (1989: 8). Welfare is directly related to risk. As Lupton notes, risk functions in Foucault's conception of modern societies as 'a governmental strategy of regulatory power by which populations and individuals are monitored and managed' (1999: 87). Risk is calculated and defined by a range of 'experts' who produce statistics and data that make risk calculable and hence manageable. Integral to this process of managing risk, which we might think of using the terms 'welfare' or 'care', is the process of identifying and classifying it. I explore the links between the increasing bureaucratisation and professionalisation of heritage as modern strategies for the care and management of heritage 'risk' in Chapters 3 and 4.

Modernity, classification and ordering

If classification is a method for ordering, and hence identifying, risk or vulnerability, and the perception of risk is integral to the conditions of modernity itself, it follows that classification can be understood as central to the project of modernity. And if it is modernity's relationship with the past that defines it, then it follows that time must be ordered and organised. As we have already seen, Berman (1983) characterised the experience of modernity as one that is inherently disorderly, and in response to this experience of disorder and alongside the increased emphasis on science and reason, the historical sciences began to organise the past into linear sequences, drawing on an evolutionary schema (Bennett 1995). The process of classification, ordering and cataloguing is an integral part of what it means to be modern. As Bowker (2005) notes (see also Bowker and Star 2000), classificatory systems are not only structures for the organisation of information, but they are, perhaps equally importantly, 'memory practices', that is, structures for the production and maintenance of knowledge systems that shape the way in which we perceive the past and present. In *Organizing Modernity* (1994), John Law speaks of 'modes of ordering' as expressions of the project of modernity that are strategies for patterning the networks of the social. He shows how these modes of ordering not only characterise, but also define and hence *generate*, the qualities of different materials—objects, texts, agents, organisations, as well as their patterns of distribution and modes of representation. Following this line of reasoning, the way in which we perceive and experience the subject of a classificatory system can also be understood to be a product of the classificatory system itself. Returning to *Purity and Danger* (1966), Douglas notes that anomalies within classificatory systems are treated with distrust because they represent potential sources of social disorder and threat. One way of dealing with such anomalies is to purify them by rendering them to the realm of myth. Another is to build more elaborate systems of classification that can take account of them. So classificatory systems should not be considered as fixed, and the process of classification should be considered a dialectical one between the system and its subjects (as noted above of the relationship between official and unofficial heritage).

Processes of collecting, cataloguing and classifying also connect with the project of modernity in another important way. Bruno Latour has shown how the history of the modern sciences is, in part, a history of the mobilisation of objects and forms of data that can be reassembled in the laboratory, which comes to act as a centre of collection and calculation.

> How large has the earth become in their chart rooms? No bigger than an *atlas* the plates of which may be flattened, combined, reshuffled, superimposed, redrawn at will. What is the consequence of this change? The cartographer *dominates* the world that dominated Lapérouse … A centre (Europe) has been constituted that begins to make the rest of the world turn around itself. One other way of bringing about the same Copernican revolution is to gather *collections*. The shapes of the lands have to be coded and drawn in order to become mobile, but this is not the case for rocks, birds, plants, artefacts, works of art … . Thus the history of science is in large part the history of the mobilisation of anything that can be made to move and shipped back home for this universal census.
>
> *(Latour 1987: 224–5, original emphases)*

Latour's model describes the construction of scientific knowledge by way of the production and accumulation of 'immutable and combinable mobiles'—objects, specimens, charts, maps, tables, field notebooks and other recorded observations—which are collected from the peripheries (or 'field') and returned to a centre (such as a laboratory) where they may be combined and interpreted in different ways. This allows laboratories, and by extension, museums and other collections of heritage, to 'act at a distance' (Latour 1987: 229) on the fields of collection through the same networks of collection and distribution by which the mobiles are returned, as well as new networks that are created as a result of the assembling and reassembling of these mobiles at the centre (see Bennett 2005, 2009, 2010, in press a on the application of this model to museum collecting, and Harrison in press b on heritage lists and registers).

Clearly, the issue of classification, ordering and cataloguing has a whole range of implications for heritage in its 'official' guise. Central to the museum are processes of assembling, categorisation, comparison, classification, ordering and reassembling (Stewart 1993; Baudrillard 1994; Elsner and Cardinal 1994; Bennett 1995, 2004; Pearce 1995; Byrne et al. 2011; Harrison in press a, b), processes that relate to modern scientific practices more generally (Latour 1993; Law 1994; Bowker 2005; Hopwood et al. 2010; Schlanger 2010). Similarly, the listing of heritage sites on various registers, and the classificatory schemes that accompany these processes, can be seen to be linked directly to the project of modernity and its management of time and risk. Before moving on from this point, I think it is worth exploring in more detail what some of the *consequences* of classification are, so that they can be explored in relation to heritage in the chapters that follow. Law (1994: 110–11) lists nine general attributes of modern modes of ordering that might help structure our investigations, which I summarise briefly.

- *Materials*: modes of ordering might characterise and hence generate the qualities of things (including 'agents, devices, texts, social relations and architectures') and the patterning of relationships between them.
- *Size*: modes of ordering might determine the relative relationships of size in relation to standard or normative measures.
- *Dualisms*: modes of ordering might introduce the definition of dualistic differences that work against one another (the distinction between body and mind, for example, or the distinction between nature and culture).
- *Agency*: modes of ordering might generate asymmetrical models of power relationships that empower and disempower particular entities in relation to one another.
- *Representation*: modes of ordering might generate characteristic modes of representation, that is, forms of speaking and activity that stand in for those disempowered as a result of the process discussed above.
- *Distribution*: modes of ordering might produce standard expectations of distributions.
- *Problems*: patterns in distribution that are not normative will be perceived to be problematic and require a 'solution'.
- *Boundary relations*: modes of ordering will embody ways of dealing with other modes of ordering when they cut across one another, that is, they will establish boundaries and rules for the maintenance of those boundaries.

An example of this is demonstrated by historian Tim Rowse (2008), who has shown how indigeneity, a category developed to describe a heterogeneous series of peoples in modern colonial contexts spread across the world (see Chapters 6 and 9), is itself a grouping generated by the perception of vulnerability and risk. He notes that the category of 'Indigenous people' was first used in the 1920 Covenant of the League of Nations and subsequently found definition through the work of the United Nation's International Labor Organization (ILO) in the 1930s in relation to the potential of 'native' labour and the idea that responsibility for the welfare of 'native' people should be removed from the nation-state and entrusted to an international body. Indigeneity has subsequently been defined as a result of the delineation of a series of threats and associated forms of vulnerability in relation to the development work of international organisations such as the World Bank. Indigeneity has also formed as a category through the work of international conventions, in particular the ILO's Indigenous and Tribal Populations Convention (1957) and its revision the Convention on Indigenous and Tribal Peoples (1989). Francesca Merlan shows how contemporary definitions of indigeneity emphasise vulnerability, citing Martinez Cobo (1986: 5, para. 379) for the United Nations, who defines Indigenous communities, peoples, and nations as 'those which have a historical continuity with preinvasion and pre-colonial societies that developed on their territories, consider themselves as distinct from other sectors of societies now prevailing in those territories ... and are deter-mined to preserve and transmit to future generations their ancestral territories, and their ethnic identity, as the basis of their continued existence as peoples' (cited in Merlan 2008: 305). The sense of survival and continued existence in this statement is haunted by potential threat and vulnerability in the notion that indigeneity by definition requires active preservation (and hence categorisation and collection, for example in museums and lists of intangible heritage).

Theorising heritage

Heritage and actor–networks

In the Introduction I suggested that one of the key concerns of this book is the identification and examination of a series of crises that have arisen over the course of the past few decades as a consequence of the diversification and global spread of heritage during the late twentieth and early twenty-first centuries. In studying these crises, I want to explore what anthropologist Anna Tsing refers to as 'zones of awkward engagement' (2005), spaces of friction in which the relationship between local actors and global processes are revealed to explore these shifts in heritage and their social and material consequences. In doing so, I emphasise the relationships between people, 'things', institutions, corporations, governments and the environment, as well as the ideological and epistemological structures that animate and give them meaning. An actor–network framework is helpful in drawing out these issues of connection between the local and the global.

Actor–network theory (ANT) was developed by sociologists and scholars working in the field of science and technology studies as a critique of conventional social theory (Latour and Woolgar 1979; Latour 1987, 1993, 1996, 1999, 2005; Callon et al. 1986; Callon 1989; Serres and Latour 1995; Law and Hassard 1999). It has been described as a material semiotic method (Law 2004) that simultaneously maps the relationships between 'things' and 'concepts', using the network as a metaphor for understanding the ways in which these are interconnected. Bruno Latour (2005) outlines a series of strategies for studying contemporary social phenomena, including a focus on the local spaces where the global is in the process of being assembled (and the actors involved in the production of social processes or movements), to look at the ways in which the local itself is generated, and to study the connections between these sites. ANT defines 'the social' in a particular way. The term does not define a field or a quality of a particular thing, but instead refers to

> a movement, a transformation ... an association between entities which are in no way recognizable as being social in the ordinary manner except during the brief moment when they are reshuffled together. To pursue the metaphor of a

supermarket, we would call 'social' not any specific shelf or aisle, but the multiple modifications made throughout the whole place in the organization of all the goods—their packaging, their pricing, their labelling—because those minute shifts reveal to the observer which new combinations are explored and which paths will be taken (what later will be defined as a 'network'). Thus, social, for ANT, is the name of a momentary association which is characterized by the way it gathers together into new shapes.

(Latour 2005: 65)

Latour uses the term 'actor' or 'actant' to stand for anything that modifies any particular state of affairs: the 'agent' or 'actor' is a conduit for change. Thinking this way shifts the emphasis from what objects 'symbolise' to the affective qualities of things, and the ways in which material objects are involved in particular forms of interactions that create social 'features', such as inequalities or shifts in power, through momentary or more persistent networks of social connection. We can trace the creation of these social features by looking to the shifts or movements during which new combinations of associations are made available to collectives by considering the associations they choose to explore. These shifts or movements provide sources for a consideration of the networks of connection that allow local actors to have global influences.

Heritage and agency

Exploring heritage as a production of the past in the present leads to a reassessment of who and what is involved in the process of 'making' heritage, and 'where' the production of heritage might be located within contemporary societies. This directly invokes the question of agency. One of the outcomes of these and other related approaches in the social sciences is that it is becoming customary to consider agency not as an individual act of will, but as something that is distributed across collectives. Importantly, these collectives (or 'assemblages') are considered to be composed of both humans and non-humans, and are seen to include plants, animals, the environment and the material world. While different disciplines and authors draw on different versions of this notion—the 'distributed action and cognition' approach of Hutchins (1995), Gell (1998) and Strathern's 'distributed agency' (1988, 2004) in anthropological studies of art, the distributed agency that arises from the actor–network framework of ANT (Latour 2005) or the assemblage theory of Deleuze and Guattari, which sees social life as composed 'semiotic flows, material flows and social flows simultaneously' ([1988] 2004: 25; see further discussion below)—all share a radically transformed notion of social collectives and the ways in which agency is manifested within them. Fundamental to this new notion of 'the social' is the dissolution of familiar, modernist dualisms such as 'nature' and 'culture', 'human' and 'non-human', 'social' and 'natural' (Latour 1993; Law 1994), which themselves are based on a Cartesian separation of matter and mind. Agency is thus contingent and emergent within social collectives, involving both human and non-human actors, and taking many different forms (see also Joyce and Bennett 2010: 4). The World Heritage List, for example, might constitute one of these forms, involving as it does a collective of people—bureaucrats, local stakeholders, NGOs, tourists; and 'things'—the heritage sites themselves, the varied visitor facilities and interpretive apparatuses, and so on. The World Heritage List constitutes a collection that allows many of these human and non-human agents to act 'at a distance' without ever being present together on the site, through bureaucratic processes, for example, or through the production and dissemination of various representations and texts that influence a site's management.

Michel Callon (2005: 3–5) has provided a summary of these arguments insofar as they relate to the question of agency. He notes that action is a collective property that 'naturally overflows', and that, to be recognised as such, agency has to be framed in particular ways. For this reason, agencies are characterised as 'multiple and diverse', and depending on how they are framed, can be perceived to be collective or individual, adaptive or reflexive, interested or disinterested. These agencies are distributed amongst collectives that include humans, their bodies, the technologies they employ, and the natural world that surrounds them. These collectives are arranged in specific ways, and agency is made or remade through the assembling or reassembling of these collectives. Despite employing a 'flat' notion of the social (Latour 2005) in which all parts of the collective are potentially involved in the distribution and redistribution of agency, asymmetries between agencies may be considerable, and certain arrangements of collectives may be capable of deploying particular forms of agency strategically while others have less capacity for free will. In relation to this point, it is perhaps helpful to think of 'handicaps' to account for 'relations of domination–exclusion between agencies, and to interpret behaviors of resistance or recalcitrance' (Callon 2005: 4–5, see also Callon 2003). For this reason, in the same way that individuals can behave in ways that are not always strategic and that might betray mixed allegiances to different, even opposing interests, so different agencies can be perceived to mix and merge with one another in ways that are not necessarily unidirectional nor always adaptive. Throughout this book, I refer to the term 'relations' in preference to 'social relations' to emphasise these mixed social/material collectives and the ways in which agency is expressed and distributed across them. Focusing on agency will allow us to shift to see both official and unofficial heritage as a process that involves a number of agents and that might be directed towards multiple and conflicting ends. This framework allows a more realistic and sophisticated exploration of the way in which heritage is utilised and produced by the diverse groups and individuals who make appeals to it.

Heritage as an assemblage or agencement

This notion of heritage as a mixed social/material collective brings me to another key concept—the assemblage or *agencement*. I want to suggest that we can think about heritage as an assemblage in two different ways (see also Bennett 2009; Macdonald 2009b). The first is a conventional way in which heritage is thought of as a series of objects, places or practices that are gathered together in a museum or on a list, register or catalogue of some form. I have already suggested that categorisation is integral to the definition and management of heritage and its relationship with modernity, and we see this manifested in the many and varied modes of ordering that have been established to facilitate the collection, categorisation, preservation and management of heritage objects, sites and practices in the modern world. The second notion of the assemblage draws on Manuel de Landa's (1997, 2006a, 2006b) articulation of Deleuze and Guattari's 'assemblage theory' (see also J. Bennett 2010). Deleuze and Guattari ([1988] 2004) used the term 'assemblage' (*agencement*) to refer to a series of heterogeneous groupings in which the grouping itself could be distinguished as a whole from the sum of its parts. Importantly, such groupings are mixed, and social or cultural groupings are not distinguished from natural ones (or *vice versa*). Assemblage theory exists as an alternative to the metaphor of society as a living organism that has dominated social theory throughout the twentieth century. In perceiving social structures as assemblages as opposed to organisms, de Landa (2006a) indicates that the properties of such natural/cultural groupings are not the result of the functions of the components themselves, but instead exist as the product of the exercising of their capacities—they are not an inevitable outcome of the function of their components (i.e. they are not logically necessary), but they are a product of their particular histories and their relationships with other parts of the assemblage (i.e. they are contingently obligatory) (2006a: 11). Unlike organisms, assemblages are not governed by a central 'nervous system' or head. In this way, agency is distributed across and through the assemblage, as well as within it.

Far from simply being a semantic point, de Landa (2006a) shows how replacing the organismic metaphor with that of an assemblage has a series of implications for the way in which we study past and contemporary material–social relations. In the first instance, thinking of assemblages as heterogeneous groupings of humans and non-humans has the effect of flattening the hierarchy of relationships that exists within modern Cartesian thinking, which separates matter and mind, nature and culture, humans and non-humans. This focuses our attention on the ways in which things and people are involved in complex, interconnected webs of relationships across time and space, rather than seeing objects and ideas about them as somehow separate from one another. Secondly, the notion of the assemblage connects with Latour's argument that 'the social' should not be considered a separate domain, but 'the product of a very peculiar movement of re-association and reassembling' (2005: 7). In this way, the notion of the assemblage helps us to concentrate on the formation and reformation of social processes across time and space. Jane Bennett's (2010) discussion of assemblage theory also emphasises the ways in which agency is distributed throughout an assemblage, which functions as a 'federation' of actants, in which all material and non-material things are participants. Latour speaks of a 'parliament of things' (1993: 144–5) to describe such collectives.

Callon (2005) and Hardie and Mackenzie (2007; see discussion in Ruppert 2009) show how the English translation of the French *agencement* as 'assemblage' does not fully realise the sense in which the term also refers to the ways in which agency is configured in relation to specific socio-technical arrangements.

... agencies, like Hobbes' Leviathan, are made up of human bodies but also of prostheses, tools, equipment, technical devices, algorithms, etc. The notion of a cyborg aptly describes these *agencements*. Because agencies are made they can be (re)made, at least to some extent. (Re)configuring an agency means (re)configuring the socio-technical *agencements* constituting it, which requires material, textual and other investments.

(Callon 2005: 4)

Thus agencies cannot be separated from the ways in which they are arranged and the affordances of the socio-technical assemblages in which they are caught up. Thinking of heritage as an assemblage or *agencement* means paying attention not only to individuals and corporations and the discourses they promulgate or resist, but also to the specific arrangements of materials, equipment, texts and technologies, both 'ancient' and 'modern', by which heritage is produced in conversation with them. These specific arrangements of materials might include not only the 'historic' fabric of a heritage site itself, along with the assortment of artefacts and 'scars' that represent its patina of age and authenticity, but also the various technologies of tourism and display by which it is exhibited and made visitable as a heritage site. We might think of the governmental capacities of these various socio-technical components, which together make up the heritage *agencement*, in relation to the concept of an apparatus or *dispositif*, as it was developed by Michel Foucault in his work on governmentality.

Heritage as an apparatus or dispositif

Throughout this book, I emphasise the importance of an attentiveness to 'things' in relation to the study of heritage. This is not only a reflection of my particular disciplinary background, nor simply a reaction against what I characterise as the 'discursive turn' in heritage studies, but relates to specific ways of understanding heritage as a strategic socio-technical and/or bio-political assemblage composed of various people, institutions, apparatuses (*dispositifs*) and the relations between them. Thinking of heritage in this way not only helps us to understand the way it operates at the level of both material and social relations, but also helps us to focus our attention on the particular constellation of power/knowledge effects that it facilitates, that is, the relationship between heritage and governmentality (see also Smith 2006). Paul Rabinow (2003: 49ff) has shown how Michel Foucault defined an apparatus as a device or technology that specifies (and hence helps to create) a subject so that it might control, distribute and/or manage it. Agamben further defines an apparatus as 'anything that has in some way the capacity to capture, orient, determine, intercept, model, control, or secure the gestures, behaviors, opinions, or discourses of living beings' (2009: 14) (and indeed, the system of relations between them). We might think here of the governmental capacities of the various modern and historic material interventions at heritage sites—conservation methods and equipment, crowd-controlling devices, infrastructure associated with movement around a site, the various interpretive appliances that have been introduced alongside the affordances of the material that forms the heritage site itself, and the texts and discourses that give each of them their authority to control behaviour in specific ways. These devices and texts are arranged and assembled in precise and identifiable ways, the study of which allows their capacity to control and regulate behaviour, and the various networks of agency in which they are distributed, to be better understood.

Heritage and approaches to material culture

Over the past decade, there have been a number of major shifts in how material culture is studied in several academic disciplines across the humanities and social sciences, which have been referred to by some authors as a broad 'material turn' (Hicks 2010; Joyce and Bennett 2010; Olsen 2010; see also Tilley et al. 2006). Central to these changes are new ideas that explore the agency of objects and the relationships between objects and human actors. This is a necessary outcome of an actor–network framework in which the social is perceived to be 'flat', and priority is not attributed to any particular actor, whether human or non-human, within the network.

Latour (1999: 198) and Serres (1987: 209) argue that since prehistory, humans and non-humans have been integrally connected by a series of relationships in which their essential characteristics were perceived to be mixed or shared (Olsen 2003, 2007). As Olsen notes, it is conventional to narrate human history as a history of the intimacy of human relations to technology:

> If there is one historical trajectory running all the way down from Olduwai Gorge to Post-Modernia, it must be one of increasing materiality: more and more tasks are delegated to non-human actors, more and more actions mediated by things (Olsen 2003). Only by increasingly mobilizing things could humans come to experience 'episodes' of history such as the advent of farming, urbanization, state formations, industrialization and postindustrialization. The features we associate with historical change, the attributes we connect with development and 'progress', were all made possible by humans increasingly extending themselves in intimate relations with non-humans.

Olsen rejects this familiar approach by insisting that there are two sides to the history:

> The important lesson entailed in a symmetrical approach, however, is that these other entities did not just sit in silence waiting to be embodied with socially constituted meanings. Landscapes and things possessed their own unique qualities and competences which they brought to our cohabitation with them.
> *(Olsen 2007: 586)*

The seriousness with which 'things' are treated within ANT raises the possibility of a consideration of the fundamental ontological indivisibility of objects and humans

(Webmoor and Witmore 2008: 59). In applying these ideas to heritage, human and non-human agents are seen to work together to recreate the past in the present through everyday networks of association. While I consider these ideas in more detail later in the book, it is sufficient to suggest at this point that this way of thinking helps refocus our attention on the affective qualities of things and the important role of materiality and non-human agency in heritage studies.

Symmetrical archaeologies

Drawing on the work of ANT scholars, and a long-established tradition in archaeology of considering the relationship between humans and material things, symmetrical archaeology (Olsen 2003, 2007, 2010; Webmoor and Witmore 2004, 2008; Shanks 2007; Webmoor 2007; Witmore 2007) pushes the relevance of an approach that does not see people and objects as ontologically distinct as a way of overcoming the fundamental modernist impulse to separate 'objects' and 'humans', 'nature' and 'culture', 'subject' and 'object' (Witmore 2007: 546; see further discussion of this ontological separation in relation to archaeology in Thomas 2004, 2009; Lucas 2004; Shanks et al. 2004; Olsen 2010). As its title indicates, symmetrical archaeology is concerned primarily with the thorough entanglement of humans and non-humans in the world:

> a symmetrical archaeology attends, not to how 'individuals' get on in the world, but rather to how a distributed collective, an entanglement of humans and things, negotiates a complex web of interactions with a diversity of other entities (whether materials, things or our fellow creatures).
>
> *(Witmore 2007: 547)*

A fundamental feature of symmetrical archaeology is the idea that the past is actively created in the work of archaeologists.

> This requires us not to presume that the way the past was will win through into our understanding because of the 'force of evidence'. Instead, the past has to be worked at. A successful account of the past is not so much a measure of accordance between the way things were and our archaeological account, as it is a personal and social achievement. This is one of the major propositions of a symmetrical archaeology – that we need to look to the work of archaeologists in coming to understand the past.
>
> *(Shanks 2007: 589–90)*

I have suggested above that heritage should be considered to be the creation of a past *in the present*. If we broaden the quote above to take in not only archaeology, but all of the disciplines which are drawn on to produce heritage—art and architectural history, archaeology, history, engineering, biology and earth sciences—we can see how heritage is a product of not only the human imagination, but the entanglement of humans and objects, pasts and presents.

The process of creating the past in the present is one of mediation (Witmore 2006; Shanks 2007). As archaeologist Michael Shanks notes:

> The creative process of working upon what is left of the past is one of translation and mediation, of metamorphosis, of turning the remains into something else. The archaeological site and its finds become text or image, account or catalogue, recombined into a museum exhibition, revised into the narrative of a synthetic textbook or TV program, reworked into the rhetoric of a lecture course for an archaeological program.
>
> *(Shanks 2007: 592)*

Like archaeology, heritage is a creative process, and one in which individual objects may go through a series of transformations that, whilst altering their efficacy and agency with respect to humans, may not necessarily alter the fabric of the object itself. The desire to preserve the fabric of objects, buildings and places in an unaltered, 'authentic' state is one of the most pervasive aspects of official heritage's character. Archaeology, like the other historical sciences mentioned above, is intimately implicated in this process. Think for a moment of a historic object, such as an old gramophone in a museum. Its relationship with humans is changed fundamentally by its mode of exhibition and its transformation from a functional 'tool' to an object of display, in its shift from living room to museum display case, even though the fabric of the object itself is not changed. So heritage, like archaeology, becomes a form of mediation in the process of creating the past in the contemporary world (see Harrison 2006 for a detailed consideration of the material agency of particular forms of museum object and their symmetrical relationships with archaeologists, museum staff and Indigenous artisans), a specific set of material aesthetic practices which highlight and mediate the endings of things (Otero-Pailos 2006). Controversially, much of the work of preservation could be understood as having an impact on the materiality (and thus transforming) heritage objects themselves, for example, cleaning (Otero-Pailos 2007), processes of chemical and physical conservation, reconstruction of monuments, the active management of biodiversity in conservation areas, etc. Given that this 'work' is defined precisely as the 'absence' of interaction with the physical, as the *arrest* of decay, this is worthy of further exploration.

The implications of symmetrical archaeological approaches for the study of heritage have recently been explored by Timothy Webmoor in relation to the UNESCO World Heritage site of Teotihuacan, Mexico (Webmoor 2007, 2008). He focuses particularly on the relationship between archaeology and public and stakeholder involvement with the site, showing how the site is not simply a material backdrop for the interactions of archaeologists, locals, tourists and 'new age' visitors, but structures and forms a part of these interactions in many different ways.

Tracing the associations formed through an 'Aztec bailador' or dancer reveals the active quality of things, or a swapping of properties between things and humans. The stepped causeways of tezontle, or volcanic rock, surrounding the plaza of the Pyramid of the Sun determine now (as they did in the prehispanic period) where such performances are carried out. As elevated boundaries, these things also provide seating for tourists seeking a spectacle. But the movement of tourists to the dance spectacle is equally guided by the modern system of fences and gates of the Instituto Nacional de Antropología e Historia (INAH) which arrest ambulation at the plaza before the performative spectacle. Instead of nationalist identity politics or valorization of Teotihuacan as constitutive of a mythic and unifying past, things, both past and present, equally enervate the spiritual spectacle ... The 'archaeological engine' drives all these associations at Teotihuacan, mixing humans and things in inter-connected networks that extend well beyond any ideational or meaning privileging notion of 'heritage'.

(Webmoor 2007: 573)

As Webmoor demonstrates, symmetrical approaches to archaeology are full of potential for the study of heritage. The most important ideas I want to emphasise here are the thorough mixing or entanglement of objects and humans in the process of 'creating' heritage, and the ways in which both are equally implicated in a process of producing the past in the present. This more continuous and integrated way of understanding the relationships between past and present, and objects and humans, underpins my discussion of dialogical models of heritage in the final chapters of this book.

Conclusion

In this chapter I have established a series of definitions and concepts that underpin, and are explored in more detail throughout the rest of the volume. I suggested that many of the attitudes towards the past that are implicit in contemporary official approaches to heritage are related in fundamental ways to Western, post-Enlightenment understandings of the world and to the experience of modernity. In particular, heritage reflects a modern, linear notion of time that emphasises progress in its separation of past from present. In turn, this sense of linear time and the speed of its passage produces an underlying sense of *uncertainty* and vulnerability in its insistent focus on the overthrowing of tradition to focus on the future. Modes of ordering, classifying and organising heritage simultaneously represent strategies for managing this sense of risk and uncertainty, whilst creating the ordered, linear sense of time on which these ideas of progress rest. Heritage is thus both a product and producer of Western modernity.

I have also introduced a series of theoretical perspectives to help frame the study of the relationships between the global and the local, objects and people, and the net-works of relationships between them, drawing particularly on ANT and assemblage theory. In doing so, I have tried to emphasise the themes of *materiality* and *connectivity*

FIGURE 2.4 Tourists at the World Heritage site of Teotihuacan, Mexico. (Photograph by Isabelle Le Fournis. © UNESCO/Isabelle Le Fournis.)

to suggest that symmetrical models of archaeology and material culture might help establish some new ways of understanding heritage as *dialogical*. I have also suggested that thinking of heritage as composed of different apparatuses or *dispositifs* helps us to explore the governmental capacities and knowledge/power effects of its specific socio-technical and bio-political arrangements in the contemporary world. I have drawn on these interlinked themes of materiality, connectivity and dialogue to address aspects of the various crises that have emerged from the application of the UNESCO World Heritage model to places and communities with radically different conceptions of heritage. In Chapter 3, I explore the 'prehistory' of World Heritage as it was developed as a concept in Western Europe, the UK and the USA, and the emergence of a sense of common, 'universal' interests in heritage that gave rise to the World Heritage Convention in 1972.

3

PREHISTORIES OF WORLD HERITAGE

The emergence of a concept

Introduction

This chapter describes the background to the development of the World Heritage Convention and its underlying definition of heritage as a distinctive set of official, state-led practices and ways of engaging with the past. I argue that the World Heritage concept emerged from a long history of thinking in particular ways about the relationship between objects and the past, and about the role of the state in using particular objects to tell particular kinds of stories about its origins and to establish a series of norms with which to govern its citizens. The chapter charts the early connection of the Enlightenment concept of the public sphere with a concern for the preservation of the natural and cultural environment that developed in Western Europe, Britain and North America and some of their colonies during the nineteenth century, and the subsequent increasing control of heritage established by their nation-states throughout the twentieth century. These models of heritage, which were developed in a post-Enlightenment, modern, Euro-American context, were critical to the definition of heritage that underpinned the World Heritage Convention, and that the World Heritage Committee subsequently attempted to apply globally. I argue later in this book that it was this very attempt to apply a particular definition of heritage to countries and communities with radically different ideas about heritage that led to a series of conceptual crises that have contributed to the transformation of heritage practice in the later twentieth and early twenty-first centuries, alongside other broad changes in late-modern societies and their relationships with the past.

Integral to the emergence of the World Heritage Convention were a series of specific safeguarding campaigns that had been established in the years preceding the drafting of the Convention text. These campaigns, forged in the uncertain context of particular threats, established the sense of urgency that heralded its arrival, and had a strong overall influence on the form and characteristics of the Convention. In the second part of this chapter, I look in more detail at the first of these campaigns and its influence on the concept of 'World Heritage' and on the World Heritage Convention text in particular. In Chapter 1, I argued that the specific circumstances of various heritage campaigns have led to a series of crises that subsequently influenced the drafting of UNESCO policy. This idea is fundamental to understanding the trans-formation and diversification of heritage that occurred following the introduction of the World Heritage Convention in the later part of the twentieth century. So the object of this chapter is to explore how the formal processes and language of heritage developed in a particular social and historical context, to chart the 'heritage' of the World Heritage idea, before exploring the conflicts that have arisen subsequently in the application of this model of heritage to alternative, largely non-Western con-texts, and the emergence of an academic critique in response to UNESCO's apparent hegemonic position (e.g. Byrne 1991).

At this stage, I want to introduce a loose three-phase framework into this history of heritage. One of the problems with some previous academic work on heritage is that it has often assumed that heritage is all the same thing (Davison [2000] 2008; Harvey 2008), but even within the European, British and North American contexts in which it was developed, heritage has undergone major shifts over the past 150 years. The first phase of heritage is associated with the connection of the Enlightenment concept of the public sphere with a concern for the preservation of the natural and cultural environment, which developed in Euro-American contexts during the nineteenth century. The second phase delineates a period of increased state control of heritage throughout the twentieth century, and the emergence of the World Heritage concept. The third phase relates to the period after the introduction of the World Heritage Convention in 1972 and the emergence of postindustrial economies and new forms of late-modern capitalist societies. This final phase is also associated with a popular heritage 'boom', in which the public developed a greater vernacular interest in the past for a variety of reasons, considered in more detail in Chapter 4.

Heritage and the emergence of the public sphere

'Heritage' is, perhaps rather appropriately, an old word, the meaning of which has shifted through time (Davison [2000] 2008: 31; Littler and Naidoo 2004). Its etymology lies in medieval Old French and Latin terms to describe the property that was inherited by a person's 'heirs'. In the eighteenth and nineteenth centuries in North America and the UK, the word was closely linked with the great estates and properties belonging to the landed classes. At this time, the word had also begun to be used to refer to a religious or spiritual bequest. During the nineteenth and early twentieth centuries, this use of the term broadened and it increasingly came to refer to a cultural or intellectual legacy linked to the creation of a series of 'invented traditions' (Hobsbawm 1983a) associated with the rise of new nation-states, predominantly in Britain, France and Germany (Bennett 1995; Hunter 1996; Smith 2006: 17) and North America (Page and Mason 2004). This was associated with a newly emergent interest in studying the past and its physical traces through archaeology (Kohl and Fawcett 1995; Trigger

[1989] 1996: 248ff) and the preservation of monuments (Choay 2001) and natural landscapes (Oelschlaeger 1991).

Carman and Sørensen (2009: 13–16) point to the importance of the concept of civic duty in separating earlier interests in the past from more modern notions of heritage as a store of 'things' held in trust by (and for) the public. As part of a process that they see beginning in France during the late eighteenth century (with the establishment of the first government agency concerned with the preservation of monuments), and spreading to Western Europe (including the UK) and North America during the nineteenth century, they chart the coming together of a valorisation of the past with a concern for its preservation through material things as a result of the development of a distinct idea of a 'public sphere' (Carman 2002; see also Bennett 1995, 2004; Merriman 2004). The public sphere has been defined by Habermas (1989) as a space in which individuals and groups can gather to formulate ideas that influence public opinion and the rules that govern societies. However, we need to be aware that the notion of who this 'public' was, and their real power to influence opinion, varied considerably over the period in question, and it is perhaps more helpful to think of multiple publics and varied spheres of interest. Whatever the case, it was not until the middle of the nineteenth century that the idea of the conservation of objects, buildings and landscapes became closely connected with that of the preservation of intellectual and cultural traditions. This period saw the increasing professionalisation of heritage practices through the widespread passing of property from private ownership to be held in trust in public institutions (such as public museums and the organisations such as the National Trust) and the development of legislation to regulate both this process and the broader conservation of the material remains of the past in the form of objects, buildings and landscapes.

The earliest inventories and the professionalisation of practice

While the idea of a canon of heritage places might be argued to be as old as the notion of a list of 'seven wonders of the world', the earliest government inventory of historic sites was begun in post-revolutionary France in 1837 by the Commission des Monuments Historique, which was charged with the task of taking stock of the nation's historic buildings (West and Ansell 2010: 33–4). The inventory divided up and attributed value to buildings based on their date of construction, architectural style and associated historical events. This established a pattern which would be followed time and again in the inventories adopted by other nation-states, and eventually by UNESCO in its World Heritage List in the later part of the twentieth century. The list was dominated by medieval buildings, which the Commission and its architects encouraged owners and locals to restore rather than replace, attributing great value to existing building fabric as part of the 'essence' of the building and its *patrimoine*, or heritage. This approach to the protection of ancient and medieval buildings was mirrored in the UK in the work of John Ruskin, and in William Morris's Society for the Protection of Ancient Buildings, established in the late 1870s (Cowell 2008: 67ff). In his *Seven Lamps of Architecture* (1849), Ruskin noted:

It is again no question of feeling whether we shall preserve the buildings of past times or not. We have no right whatever to touch them. They are not ours. They belong partly to those who built them, and partly to all generations of mankind who are to follow us.

(cited in Cowell 2008: 72)

I have already noted that the idea of 'expertise' is linked integrally to the modern conception of risk and its management. The professionalisation of practice that was realised through this system of specialised or 'expert' inspectors and conservation architects was an important part of the newly emerging field of heritage during this period (Carman and Sørensen 2009), establishing a set of relationships that would persist to the present day (Smith 2006). The establishment of the Commission des Monuments Historique in France was followed by legislation in Britain that established a list of 'Ancient Monuments' and an associated group of inspectors employed as civil servants, who were charged with the task of advising on their protection. The Ancient Monument Protection Act of 1882 applied to sites of medieval age and earlier, and sites on the list were deemed important enough to be inspected and monitored regardless of ownership (West and Ansell 2010: 34).[1] Similar pieces of legislation and systems of identification and protection of historic sites were subsequently adopted in Germany and the United States, and later exported to Western European colonial interests in Asia and Africa.

Alongside these developments was a parallel movement relating to nature conservation, which saw the establishment of the first national parks. With the spread of industrial capitalism in the eighteenth and nineteenth centuries, romantic artists and writers developed and idealised the notion of spaces that were outside the influence of technology and commercialisation; 'wild' or 'wilderness' areas. In the late eighteenth and early nineteenth centuries, British artists such as John Constable and J.M.W. Turner, and North American authors such as Ralph Waldo Emerson and Henry David Thoreau, were influential in promoting this idea of a wilderness beyond the realms of industrial civilisation. The idea of wilderness was strongly influenced by Judaeo-Christian notions of the fall from grace in the Garden of Eden and the idea of a lost, natural, golden age of humanity in which humans existed in balance with nature (Olwig 2001; see also Olwig and Lowenthal 2006). The idea of the protection of objects, buildings and landscapes in the context of widespread 'loss' through processes of industrialisation and urban growth became a fundamental underlying concept of both the natural and cultural heritage preservation movements.

Yellowstone National Park, which was gazetted by an Act of Congress on 1 March 1872, became the first 'wild' area reserved for recreational purposes under the management of the United States Federal Government, and is widely recognised as the first nature park specifically gazetted for conservation and recreational purposes. The second was the 'Royal' National Park in Sydney, Australia, which was gazetted in 1879. In the UK, the establishment of the Royal Botanical Gardens at Kew in the mid-nineteenth century can be seen to have developed from a similar concern. The North American author John Muir, whose prolific writings on the relationship between humans and nature brought the concept of wilderness to a wide audience in the late nineteenth century and the years leading up to the First World War, is widely credited as the first modern nature conservationist (Oelschlaeger 1991: 172). His activism, and that of the preservationist society known as the Sierra Club, which he founded in San Francisco in 1892, were significant in the establishment of a number of the first US national parks, including Yosemite National Park (based on the model of Yellowstone National Park). In the UK, the Sierra Club's efforts were pre-empted by debates on the preservation of Commons and other open spaces by groups such as the Commons Protection Society (founded in 1866) and the National Footpaths Preservation Society (founded in 1844), who were both influential in the founding of the National Trust for the Preservation of Historic Buildings and Natural Beauty in 1894, whose mission became the task of holding land and buildings in perpetuity 'for ever, for everyone'.

In addition to the important connection between heritage and nation-building, implied in its invocation of the values of patrimony and property, was a developing nostalgia for both 'nature' and 'the past' associated with processes of industrialisation (Olwig 2001). Octavia Hill, one of the founders of the National Trust, emphasised the benefits of the conservation of green spaces for the working classes, whose access to woodlands and other 'natural' places was eroded by the growth of cities and industry. Fundamental to the developing concept of 'wilderness', which underlay the national park movement, was the idea that natural places were good for the human constitution but also fragile and in need of protection from humans and industrial development. These ideas had a profound influence on the scientific study of sustainable forest management in the nineteenth century in Western Europe, British India and the USA (Nash 1967). Similarly, underlying the early cultural heritage legislation was a response to the widespread changes that were occurring in urban and rural landscapes in response to processes of industrialisation.

So by the end of the nineteenth century, a concept of heritage as a list of places and landscapes that were at risk and that needed to be protected from the influence of modern development, the 'solid being melted into air' by nineteenth century industrial capitalism (see Chapter 2), had become established. This concept was underpinned by a series of modern ideals that saw the past as distant from the present, that sought to emphasise the separation of nature and culture, and that established heritage as a 'class' of 'place' which should be set apart from the everyday. At its heart was the concept of the public sphere, and the idea that certain great monuments, buildings and landscapes needed to be conserved by, and for, the public as part of a broader conversation about what was important from the past in forming a set of values for the appropriate functioning of societies in the present. All of these ideas would prove fundamental to the emergence of the World Heritage concept in the later part of the twentieth century.

The origins of state control

The second phase in the history of heritage saw the emergence of the state's control and manipulation of heritage. Heritage became what James Scott (1998) would define as a regulatory process associated with bureaucratic high modernist planning, one of a series of linked state projects of standardisation and management in which the local came under increasingly centralised administration. As Scott notes, states seek to simplify aspects of social, economic and political life so that they can be assessed in aggregate and controlled more effectively. An important part of this process involves defining, standardising and categorising. Ironically, in the case of heritage, the state often redeployed local names and local customs strategically, transforming them and then rolling them out as 'national' values (e.g. chapters in Hobsbawm and Ranger 1983). While Michael Herzfeld (2005) has noted that Scott underestimates the complicity of bureaucrats and locals and the resultant modifications of heritage schemes in local practice (see also Otero-Pailos 2008 and further discussion in Chapter 6), an analysis of legislative changes over the course of the twentieth century in the United States and England demonstrates the ways in which, as the state increasingly sought to control heritage, it also sought to redefine it so as to increase its influence over an ever-broadening range of objects, buildings and landscapes. In this part of the chapter, I consider the explosion of legislation over the late nineteenth and twentieth centuries that was concerned with the definition and regulation of heritage in the United States and England, as examples of the ways in which the definition of heritage was increasingly prescribed and caught up in different bureaucratic processes over this period.

A brief legislative history of heritage in the US National Park Service, 1870 to 1980s

The history of the US National Park Service provides an insightful example of this process and how it operated in relation to federal legislation in the United States. The roots of the first official US federal heritage legislation lie in a series of unrelated private lobbying efforts to conserve aspects of natural and cultural heritage, which were subsequently drawn together under a single government department with responsibility for the management of heritage on federal lands. It is conventional to begin a history of the National Park Service with a consideration of the gazettal of Yellowstone National Park by an Act of Congress in 1872, at which time it became the first 'wild' area reserved for recreational purposes under the management of the US Federal Government. However, perhaps equally important from a legislative point of view was early work by the Bureau of Ethnology, established in 1869 under the directorship of Major John Wesley Powell, to preserve Native American sites on federal lands. Following the gazettal of a number of national parks in the intervening years, The Antiquities Act (1906), which was approved by Congress on 8 June 1906, played a key role in drawing together the various concerns for the conservation of natural and cultural heritage that had been expressed by these earlier developments. The Act gave the president authority

> to declare by public proclamation historic landmarks, historic and prehistoric structures, and other objects of scientific interest that are situated upon the lands owned or controlled by the Government of the United States to be national monuments.

Monuments of military significance would be managed by the Secretary of War, while those in national forests were managed by the Department of Agriculture. Others remained under the jurisdiction of the Department of the Interior. This fragmented system is said to have been instrumental in President Woodrow Wilson's decision in 1916 to create the National Park Service as a separate bureau of the Department of the Interior (Kieley, 1940). The National Park Service Organic Act (1916) specified the role of the National Park Service, to

> promote and regulate the use of the federal areas known as national parks, monuments, and reservations … which purpose is to conserve the scenery and the natural and historic objects and the wild life therein and to provide for the enjoyment of the same in such manner and by such means as will leave them unimpaired for the enjoyment of future generations.

The intervening years saw the expansion of the National Park Service's mission to include the management of parks in the eastern states, as well as the transfer of national monuments held by the US Forest Service; the National Capital Parks in Washington, DC; and battlefields, forts, and monuments from the War Department

FIGURE 3.1 Mammoth Hot Springs Terraces, in what would become Yellowstone National Park, in 1871. (Photograph by William Henry Jackson. Courtesy of Department of Interior, National Park Service Historic Photograph Collection, Harpers Ferry Center.)

FIGURE 3.2 Members of the Historic American Buildings Survey (HABS) team measuring the Kentucky School for the Blind building in 1934. The US National Park Service established HABS as a make-work programme for architects, draftsmen and photographers during the Great Depression. It was formalised as a programme under the 1935 Preservation of Historic Sites Act, and provided an important stimulus for the development of the North American historic preservation movement. (Historic American Buildings Survey, HABS KY-20-19. Library of Congress Call No. HABS KY,56-LOUVI,2-7.)

in 1933. The Preservation of Historic Sites Act (1935) had further important implications, initiating a 'national policy to preserve for public use historic sites, buildings and objects of national significance for the inspiration and benefit of the people of the United States' (National Park Service 2011a), and a national survey to identify historic sites for inclusion within the national park system.

Subsequent developments in the 1960s saw the increasing control of the National Park Service over an ever-expanding portfolio of objects, places and landscapes. This was achieved through a broadening of the definition of heritage, as well as the increasing levels of state control that were realised by way of legislation. The Wilderness Act (1964) allowed the National Park Service to gazette areas that would be conserved primarily for their conservation values, not necessarily based on their values for recreation. This saw the realisation of a conception of wilderness as opposed to the interference, or even the presence, of humans. The National Historic Preservation Act (1966) established the National Register of Historic Places, and required that all parks be entered into this register. It also established the Advisory Council on Historic Preservation, a new federal agency that would review and advise the National Park Service and other federal agencies regarding potential impacts on places on the National Register, in conjunction with state historic preservation officers. Further legislation, including the Wild and Scenic Rivers Act (1968), National Trails System Act (1968), National Environmental Policy Act (1969), General Authorities Act (1970), Endangered Species Act (1973) and Alaska National Interest Lands Conservation Act (1980) increased the Service's powers to control large areas of landscape that were gazetted as natural or cultural heritage. And in the late 1970s, the Archaeological Resources Protection Act (1979) replaced the Antiquities Act to establish penalties for the destruction or theft of archaeological 'resources' on federal lands.

What emerges from this brief review of the legislative history of the US National Park Service from the 1870s to the 1980s is both the increasing number of legislative controls relating to heritage, and the increasing number of objects, places and landscapes to which the term 'heritage' came to be applied, which emerged over the course of the twentieth century. At the same time, similar developments were occurring in relation to heritage and planning legislation at the state and city level in the United States. After the passing of the Historic Preservation Act (1966), Secretary of the Interior Stewart L. Udall undertook to decentralise certain aspects of legislative responsibility for heritage to State Liaison Officers (who would later become known as State Historic Preservation Officers [SHPOs]). SHPOs would take responsibility for surveying and maintaining a register of historic heritage places within their states and developing a plan for their maintenance and preservation (Murtagh 2006: 57). Federal funds were made available for 50 per cent match funding with the states for restoration and rehabilitation of heritage places nominated to the National Register. As a result of the work of SHPOs, between 1966 and 2003 the number of places on the National Register rose from 868 to over 1.3 million individual places as part of 77,000 nominations (Murtagh 2006: 57–8). Another important development was the passing of the 1976 Tax Reform Act, which was succeeded by the 1981 Economic Recovery Tax Act, and the 1986 Tax Reform Act, which incentivised the adaptive re-use of historic building stock by offering tax credits on works to certified historic properties (Murtagh 2006: 58–60). All these developments had a significant influence on the number and nature of places identified as 'heritage', and federal and state governments' control of them.

A brief legislative history of heritage in England, 1870 to 1980s

In England, a similar trajectory is apparent in the increasing levels of state control and the increasingly broad definitions of heritage in the period up to the 1980s (Cowell 2008).

FIGURE 3.3 South-east elevation of Old Slater Mill, Pawtucket, Rhode Island, c. 1968. Slater Mill was the first property listed on the National Register of Historic Places in November 1966. Its statement of significance notes that it was the first successful cotton factory, and the first water-powered spinning mill using the Arkwright system, in North America. (Courtesy of Library of Congress, Prints & Photographs Division, HAER, Reproduction number HAER RI,4-PAWT,3-8.)

I have already mentioned how in England, the Ancient Monuments Protection Act (1882) initiated a system in which (as in France) an Inspector of Ancient Monuments reported to the Commissioner of Works on the condition, and methods for the preservation of, a list of scheduled monuments dated to 1700 and earlier, which stimulated the slow process of developing a schedule that included all the standing stones and ancient monuments throughout the country. It also made provisions for the state to purchase monuments or to take them into its guardianship, while damage to monuments and sites became a punishable offence. Lieutenant-General Augustus Henry Lane Fox Pitt Rivers, the first Inspector of Ancient Monuments, was responsible for the acquisition and listing of forty-three monuments under the Act between 1883 and 1890. The Act was revised in 1900 and 1913, when an Ancient Monuments Board was created to advise Commissioners of Works on the compulsory purchase of significant properties whose protection was a matter of national concern. While the Housing and Town Planning Act (1909) included a provision that schemes should consider the preservation of objects of historical interest, it was not until the Town and Country Planning Act (1932) that provisions were introduced that could be used specifically for the protection of historic buildings in the guise of Building Preservation Orders (Cowell 2008: 107). However, as Cowell points out, these provisions were limited in their usefulness by the need to compensate financially the owners of buildings on whom Building Preservation Orders had been served.

Following the widespread destruction of historic buildings that had begun to occur during the Second World War, major changes in legislation and planning for heritage places were introduced. A series of government departments were created or reinvigorated during the 1940s. The National Buildings Record was established in 1941, and charged with the task of recording historic buildings under threat from bombing raids. The work of this department received renewed vigour in the wake of the infamous Baedeker raids, a series of retaliatory bombing raids on English cities undertaken by the German air force. These raids were initiated in response to the bombing of the cities of Lübeck and Rostock in March 1942. In his book *Among the Dead Cities*, A.C. Grayling (2006: 51) writes that Baron Gustav Braun von Sturm, a German propagandist, is reported to have said on 24 April 1942: 'We shall go out and bomb every building in Britain marked with three stars in the Baedeker Guide [the German tourist guide to Britain].' The raids have been interpreted as an attempt to lower British morale by attacking notable scenic cities, which otherwise had no strategic or military importance.

A number of planning acts were passed during the 1940s, which culminated in the Town and Country Planning Act (1947). This established the parameters of the contemporary listing system in England, in which a system of listing buildings equivalent to the scheduling of ancient monuments was introduced, an Advisory Committee would oversee the survey of the country's historic buildings, and listed buildings would be classified according to various grades of ascending significance (Grades I, II and III). The Historic Buildings and Ancient Monuments Act (1953) established the Historic Buildings Council for England, and gave the state powers to issue grants to owners of listed properties to assist with their upkeep (Creigh-Tyte and Gallimore 1998). During the 1960s, in response to widespread rebuilding programmes and the application of modernist town planning principles, new requirements for special planning consent for alterations to historic buildings were introduced as part of the Town and Country Planning Act (1968). The introduction of this legislation is

FIGURE 3.4 First English Inspector of Ancient Monuments, Lieutenant-General Augustus Henry Lane Fox Pitt Rivers. (Photograph by W. and D. Downey, c. 1890. © Pitt Rivers Museum, University of Oxford.)

FIGURE 3.5 Photograph of bomb-damaged library in Holland House, Kensington, London, *c.* 1940–1945. The widespread damage to historic buildings in England during the Second World War was important in motivating the establishment of the National Buildings Record. (Photograph by Fox Photos Limited. Courtesy of English Heritage National Monuments Record.)

said to have occurred at least partially in response to the public outcry over the destruction of two Grade II listed structures, the Coal Exchange and Euston Railway Station Arch, in London in 1962. Its introduction had a major influence on the levels of state intervention in relation to historic buildings. A similar broadening of control by the state was exercised in relation to archaeological sites by the introduction of the Ancient Monuments and Archaeological Areas Act (1979), which introduced a formal system of Scheduled Monument Consent for any work to a designated monument.

These increasing levels of state control of heritage in England were realised in the National Heritage Act (1983), which created the Historic Buildings and Monuments Commission for England (or 'English Heritage'), disbanding the Ancient Monuments Board and the Historic Buildings Council, and incorporating their functions into a single department.[2] This was significant in bringing the management of archaeological sites and historic buildings under a single umbrella department, consolidating the state's advisory role and legislative control of heritage. The role of English Heritage, set out in the National Heritage Act, was to secure the preservation of ancient monuments and historic buildings; to promote the preservation and enhancement of conservation areas; and to promote the public's enjoyment of, and advance their knowledge of,

FIGURE 3.6 Demolishing the Doric portico at Euston Station, London, 1961. The campaign against the destruction of the Euston Station Arch became something of a *cause celebre* and many protesters argued that the arch should not have been destroyed but dismantled and re-erected on another site. The loss of the portico was a major influence in changing attitudes to the preservation of Britain's architectural heritage. (Photograph by Science and Society Picture Library/Getty Images.)

ancient monuments and historic buildings and their preservation. It inherited the responsibility for the management of over 400 monuments and historic buildings from the Department of the Environment, and became the centralised instrument of heritage planning in England at this time (National Archives 2011).

A century of bureaucratisation: heritage in the United States and England (1870–1980) compared

Although there are distinct differences, which will become more obvious in subsequent chapters when we consider the academic literature that subsequently grew up in each country around heritage, I have tried to emphasise some broad similarities between the histories of heritage legislation in the United States and England. However, such legislative histories gloss over significant variations that occurred in each country, and in the United States in each of the states themselves. Such histories are not appropriate to the job of charting the social and cultural shifts that helped shape contemporary attitudes towards heritage in each country (Page and Mason 2004: 7). Nonetheless, these two case examples clearly demonstrate a process that occurred over the course of the twentieth century, in which the state exercised increasing levels of control over heritage, whilst simultaneously broadening the number of objects, buildings and landscapes over which that definition could be argued to extend. This process accelerated considerably from the late 1960s onwards, after which we can see increasing numbers of legislative measures and an expansion of the role of the state in both defining and controlling heritage through official planning controls. The later part of the process overlapped with the period in which heritage began to come under the purview of some of the post-war international organisations such as the United Nations. The influence of these global organisations is discussed below.

It is also important at this point to consider the ways in which the bureaucratisation of heritage was associated directly with another process of increasing professionalisation of heritage; the two produced a set of professional practices associated with heritage *compliance* (Smith 2004, 2006; Jameson 2008). This took heritage out of the hands of amateurs and enthusiastic members of the public, and put its control into the hands of 'experts'—architects, archaeologists, engineers and museum professionals. This had two important effects. 'Heritage' became less about what people did as part of their everyday lives, and came to be seen as a separate class of extinct objects or places associated with vanished or vanishing cultural practices. Heritage was, by designation, in the past, and defined in opposition to the present. Secondly, heritage was emphasised as a professional activity, one that was outside the understanding of ordinary people. Heritage was a specialised field to be undertaken by professionals, specialists, 'experts', and became increasingly caught up in bureaucratic planning processes. This effectively severed heritage from the local and redeployed it as a national, state-controlled, professionalised practice.

The origins of World Heritage: postwar internationalism, the Aswan High Dam and UNESCO's safeguarding campaigns

Following the Second World War, the issue of heritage received a great deal of attention as part of postwar reconstruction efforts. As the old empires began to gather together their resources and attempt to rebuild, there was a global outcry over the massive destruction of cultural heritage sites that had occurred during the war. Heritage became a part of the purview of some of the new international NGOs, such as the United Nations (UN), which had been established in the immediate aftermath of the war to replace the League of Nations with the stated aim of maintaining peace and promoting international cooperation in addressing economic, social and humanitarian issues. It emerged within the broader context of the idea of an international system of cooperation and regulation from the 1944 Bretton Woods United Nations Monetary and Financial Conference, which established a series of organisations in addition to the UN, including the International Monetary Fund (IMF) to regulate international financial security and aid postwar reconstruction and political stability. These various international organisations have played a key role in globalisation processes, and heritage was very much caught up in these developments (see Chapter 7). In the immediate aftermath of the war, concerns about the impact of armed conflict on cultural heritage led to the development of the Convention for the Protection of Cultural Property in the Event of Armed Conflict (or 'The Hague Convention') adopted at The Hague (Netherlands) on 14 May 1954. The Hague Convention specified that signatories must refrain from damaging cultural properties in their own or other countries' territories during times of armed conflict, and made any act directed by way of reprisals against cultural property a violation of the Convention.

The Hague Convention is significant in that it recognised an explicit connection between cultural heritage and national identity, and the use of heritage in nation-building. It also put the destruction of 'cultural property' in some ways on a par with the killing of civilians, as something that was outlawed in the context of armed conflict. But most significantly, it began to put into practice the idea that cultural heritage might somehow have significance that set it apart and made its management an issue of *international* concern. It seems significant that the symbol chosen for The United Nations Educational, Scientific and Cultural Organization (UNESCO)'s flag in 1945 was the Parthenon, a place whose cultural heritage would later become a major issue of 'global' concern for that agency through the (at the time of writing, as yet unresolved) political battle between the Greek and British Governments for the return of the Parthenon marbles from the British Museum.

The idea of international collaboration on the safeguarding of cultural heritage was first discussed at the Athens Conference on the restoration of historic buildings in 1931, which was organised by the International Museums Office and led to the drafting of the Athens Charter; however, its recommendations were not realised until well after the end of the Second World War. This new sense of global responsibility for cultural monuments found its most important expression after 1954, when the Egyptian Government announced its plans to construct the Aswan High Dam, which would require the flooding of a valley containing ancient Egyptian monuments including the Abu Simbel temples. The Aswan High Dam was a strategic project aimed at regulating the flooding of the Nile river valley and allowing the storage of water for agriculture (it was also later used for the generation of hydroelectric power). It was part of a series of works involving a pre-existing dam (the Aswan Low Dam) some 4 kilometres downriver, which had been built in 1902 and raised several times over the intervening period.

The Aswan High Dam project was announced at a time of complex political and military upheaval for Egypt. In 1952, the 'Free Officers Movement' overthrew the Egyptian monarch King Farouk I, abolishing its constitutional monarchy and establishing a republic. The new government signed an agreement for the removal of British troops in 1954 and began lobbying the World Bank for funding to construct the Aswan High Dam in 1955, shortly after which a tentative funding agreement was reached. However, the USA and UK almost immediately withdrew their financial support as a result of Egypt's alignment with the People's Republic of China in the conflict with (US- and UK-supported) Taiwan. In 1956, Egypt announced the nationalisation of the Suez Canal Company to fund the dam's construction. This led to further tension with the UK, which had strategic military and economic interests in the canal, and which formed an alliance with France and Israel against Egypt, beginning military operations and occupation of parts of Gaza, Sinai and the Canal itself in August. Pressure from the USA, USSR and UN forced the removal of troops in November. All British and French banks and companies were subsequently nationalised, and in 1958 Egypt united with Syria, forming the United Arab Republic. They would subsequently become involved in the civil war in Yemen in 1962, prior to the 1967 Arab–Israeli War, in which they lost control of the Sinai Peninsula and the Gaza strip, and which had long-lasting political and social implications for the whole region, not the least being Egypt's subsequent shift in allegiance from the USSR to the USA under the presidency of Muhammad Anwar El Sadat.

UNESCO's involvement with Egyptian cultural heritage sites began well before the announcement of the first safeguarding campaign at the end of 1959 (Hassan 2007). In 1954, UNESCO had supported the establishment of the Documentation and Study Centre for the History of Art and Civilization of Ancient Egypt in Cairo. In 1955, they sent supplies to begin the process of recording archaeological sites in Nubia. Hassan (2007) reports that in April 1959 Tharwat Okasha, Egyptian Minister for Culture, met with Rene Maheu, assistant Director General of UNESCO, requesting their assistance in safeguarding the Nubian monuments threatened by the Aswan High Dam development. The Sudanese Government's account (NCAM 2010) suggests that an independent approach was made by the Sudanese Minister of Education, Ziada Arbab, in October the same year. In November 1959, the 55th session of the Executive Board of UNESCO adopted the principle of an appeal for international cooperation to assist the Egyptian and Sudanese Governments and authorised preparatory work safeguarding Abu Simbel Temple and archaeological investigations of the sites in Sudanese Nubia to be undertaken as a matter of urgency (UNESCO 2010a, 2010b).

An appeal was subsequently launched by UNESCO Director General Vittorino Veronese, on 8 March 8 1960, to undertake 'a task without parallel in history' (cited in Hassan 2007: 80), a global campaign to save the antiquities of Egypt and Sudan (Säve-Söderberg 1987). The worldwide safeguarding campaign, which would run for twenty years (the construction of the dam itself was completed by 1970), involved a large-scale archaeological excavation and recording programme and a number of major works, including the relocation and reconstruction of the Abu Simbel and Philae temples and other monuments from the valley. Over half of the estimated US$80 million cost of the project was raised from forty-seven donor countries. A series of influential and wealthy individuals formed an 'Honorary Committee of Patrons' to lobby governments on UNESCO's behalf, while an exhibition of Tutankhamen's treasures toured the UK, Europe and North America between 1972 and 1979 to help enlist private support. The bulk of the financial support came from the USA, France, Italy and the Federal Republic of Germany, while private contributions in excess of

US$7 million were received. A tourist tax levied on visitors to Egypt raised almost US$2 million (Hassan 2007: 84).

As part of the safeguarding campaign, twenty-three temples were documented and relocated. In the case of the Egyptian temples, some of these were rebuilt close to their original locations in Nubia, while in Sudan those temples that could be relocated were transported to the National Museum in Khartoum. The temples were reassembled in six groups:

- the temples of Philae island on the island of Agilkia near the former Aswan dam
- the temples of Beit el Wali and Kalabsha and the Kiosk of Qertassi near the High Dam
- the temples of Dakka, Maharraqa and Wadi es Sebua near the former site of Wadi es Sebua
- the temples of Amada and Derr and Pennut's Tomb at Aniba near the former site of Amada
- the temples of Abu Simbel *in situ* but 60 m above their original site
- the temples of Aksha, Buhen, Semna East and Semna West in the museum garden in Khartoum.

(UNESCO 2010b)

The relocation of the spectacular monumental temples of Ramses II at Abu Simbel, completed in 1968, was considered to be one of the great technical achievements of the campaign. Images of these temples occur frequently in UNESCO documentation relating to the successes of their various safeguarding campaigns.

The safeguarding campaign in Egypt and Sudan has become a fundamental part of the origin story of UNESCO, and yet the political context of campaign is consistently ignored in UNESCO's retelling of the events. It appears as a story of international 'cooperation', the first in a series of subsequent campaigns in Venice, Italy (1966–present) following flooding of the lagoon; at Moenjodaro in Pakistan (1974–97), which was threatened with flooding from the Indus River and encroaching salinity; and some twenty other sites throughout the world. Yet it is important to acknowledge the fundamentally political origins of the campaign. This was not simply a benign attempt to help out a fellow nation in need. International expeditions launched by member states demanded that half of the archaeological finds would be taken back to museums in their own countries. This led to the relocation of whole temples to New York, Leiden, Madrid, Turin and West Berlin (Säve-Söderberg 1987: 137–8; Hassan 2007: 80). Furthermore, promises to participating member states were made to give them priority in applying for subsequent permits to excavate outside the reservoir areas. A series of complex political relationships that had developed out of the colonial histories of Egypt and its neighbours drove the patronage of member states and the subsequent carve-up of salvaged archaeological remains. The campaign was an important nation-building exercise, in which the power and influence of various member states was expressed in the level of support offered and, by extension, the number of Egyptian antiquities that flowed back 'home' to act as a material witness to their influence on the world stage.

FIGURE 3.7 Relocation of the temples of Ramses II at Abu Simbel in progress, 1965. (© UNESCO.)

FIGURE 3.8 The temple's sculptures are reassembled at the new site, 1965. (© UNESCO.)

It is not possible to overstate the significance of this international campaign in promoting the idea that heritage was a universal concern, and that individual states could no longer expect to operate independently in the management of heritage deemed to be of international significance. This signalled an important shift from the perception of heritage as something for the management of individual nations, to a more global sense of heritage as something that was collectively owned. In this case, it was something to be drawn up and divided amongst the wealthy and powerful nations who not only gained the benefit of appearing in the role of philanthropist, but also were legitimately able to collect and mobilise relics for display in national museums.

Equally important to the recasting of these old colonial relationships and desires, and the new expression of nationalism through international collaboration, were issues surrounding cultural tourism. Although the area had long attracted visitors, its status as a site of intensive international collaboration over heritage stimulated a boom in tourism, which Egyptian authorities sought to exploit through the imposition of a tourist tax to help fund the safeguarding campaign. The idea that these temples belonged to the common heritage of humanity fuelled this tourist boom. Another important aspect of the safeguarding campaign and its use as part of UNESCO's origin narrative is its ignorance of the displacement of an estimated 100,000 living Nubians, who occupied the area inundated by the dam's construction, over the spectacular stone monumental remains which it saved (Hassan 2007: 83). The emphasis on heritage as monumental and distant from the circumstances of the present would have a powerful influence on the World Heritage Convention text.

The 1972 World Heritage Convention

While the first UNESCO safeguarding campaign was under way, the Second Congress of Architects and Specialists of Historic Buildings met in Venice in 1964 and adopted a number of resolutions. The first created the International Charter on the Conservation and Restoration of Monuments and Sites (the 'Venice Charter'). The Venice Charter took the form of a treaty giving an international framework for the preservation and restoration of historic monuments and buildings. A subsequent resolution, put forward by UNESCO, created the International Council of Monuments and Sites (ICOMOS) to oversee the implementation of the charter. ICOMOS was founded in 1965, and in this same year a White House conference called for a 'World Heritage Trust' to preserve the world's natural and scenic areas and historic sites 'for the present and the future of the entire world citizenry'. The flooding of Venice in November 1966, and the subsequent development of a second international safeguarding campaign, appeared to underline the need for global collaboration on heritage issues, and images of a flooded Venice appeared to give urgency to these developments in the light of a growing sense of the *vulnerability* of global heritage. The International Union for Conservation of Nature (IUCN), formed in 1948 as the International Union for the Protection of Nature (IUPN), echoed the proposals that had emerged from the 1964 Venice Congress proposals, which were presented in 1972 to the United Nations

FIGURE 3.9 A woman wades through the floodwaters in Rialto Square in Venice during the floods of November 1966. The floods stimulated a second international safeguarding campaign and were instrumental in rallying support for the development of a World Heritage Convention. (Photograph by A.F.I. Venise. © UNESCO/A.F.I. Venise.)

conference on Human Environment in Stockholm. The conference developed a draft Convention Concerning the Protection of the World Cultural and Natural Heritage (World Heritage Convention), which was adopted by the General Conference of UNESCO on 16 November 1972 (Bandarin 2007).

The Convention created a World Heritage Committee, which would be advised by ICOMOS, IUCN and the International Centre for the Study of the Preservation and Restoration of Cultural Property (ICCROM). The World Heritage Committee would administer the nomination of places to a World Heritage List, which would contain 'a list of properties forming part of the cultural heritage and natural heritage … which it considers as having outstanding universal value in terms of such criteria as it shall have established'. It placed the question of the identification and management of heritage squarely within the context of the circumstances of late-modern life by appealing to the idea of threat, and suggesting that the threat of the loss of heritage was an issue for the concern of all humanity:

> cultural heritage and the natural heritage are increasingly threatened with destruction not only by the traditional causes of decay, but also by changing social and economic conditions which aggravate the situation with even more formidable phenomena of damage or destruction ... deterioration or disappearance of any item of the cultural or natural heritage constitutes a harmful impoverishment of the heritage of all the nations of the world.

The Convention text is rich with detail, and a great deal of space has been dedicated to unpacking its implications (Walsh 1992; Fowler 2004; Harrison and Hitchcock 2005; Kirshenblatt-Gimblett 2006; Leask and Fayall 2006; Smith 2006; Bandarin 2007; Francioni 2008). There are several points that bear amplification. The first is to note the way in which the Convention text reflected a series of modern Cartesian dualisms. Natural and cultural heritage were to be considered separately, and assessed using separate criteria, emphasising the separation of nature and culture that emerges from a philosophy in which body and mind are separate (an issue I take up in more detail in Chapter 9). We have already seen how various aspects of Enlightenment thought had driven the creation of the heritage concept during the late eighteenth, nineteenth and twentieth centuries in Europe and America, and the Convention text was strongly influenced by this constellation of concepts that had developed around heritage over the course of the previous two centuries.

The second point to note is the way the Convention text defined cultural heritage as something that is either a monument, building or site.

> For the purposes of this convention, the following shall be considered as 'cultural heritage':
>
> - **monuments**: architectural works, works of monumental sculpture and painting, elements or structures of an archaeological nature, inscriptions, cave dwellings and combinations of features, which are of outstanding universal value from the point of view of history, art or science
> - **groups of buildings**: groups of separate or connected buildings which, because of their architecture, their homogeneity or their place in the landscape, are of outstanding universal value from the point of view of history, art or science
> - **sites**: works of man or the combined works of nature and man, and areas including archaeological sites which are of outstanding universal value from the historical, aesthetic, ethnological or anthropological point of view.

In doing so, the Convention text strongly reflected the professional interests of ancient historians, architects and archaeologists, respectively, and made an assumption that heritage is a special class of object that is defined and studied by 'experts'. Furthermore, this classificatory system implicitly defined heritage as something that is extinct or has ceased to function, and hence is separate and remote from contemporary everyday life.

However, the most novel and defining aspect of the Convention text was its concept of 'universal heritage value':

> parts of the cultural or natural heritage are of outstanding interest and therefore need to be preserved as part of the World Heritage of mankind as a whole ... in view of the magnitude and gravity of the new dangers threatening them, it is incumbent on the international community as a whole to participate in the protection of the cultural and natural heritage of outstanding universal value, by the granting of collective assistance which, although not taking the place of action by the State concerned, will serve as an efficient complement thereto ... it is essential for this purpose to adopt new provisions in the form of a convention establishing an effective system of collective protection of the cultural and natural heritage of outstanding universal value, organized on a permanent basis and in accordance with modern scientific methods.

This idea has a clear lineage from the safeguarding campaigns in Egypt/Sudan and Venice, and this single clause has had profound and far-reaching consequences in terms of both contemporary understandings of 'heritage', and the means for its preservation, management and exhibition. In employing this notion, the Convention text represents itself as a totalising discourse representing a global hierarchy of value (cf. Herzfeld 2004). Byrne (1991) suggests that the idea of the universal significance of heritage values is made up of two parts. The first is that all humans necessarily share an interest in the physical aspects of the past as 'heritage', and that they do so in the same way. The second is that people in one country would necessarily be interested and concerned for the conservation of certain types of physical remains of heritage in another country—that certain aspects of heritage transcend physical and political boundaries. For this reason, Byrne and others have criticised the Convention as hegemonic, and as forcing what are essentially Western notions of heritage onto countries that might not otherwise hold such interests in heritage. The final important point to note is that the process of nominating World Heritage sites was determined by state parties, and that there was an expectation that states would necessarily have such places within their boundaries and would be willing to allow them to be catalogued and recorded for the purposes of collective international interest and cooperation.

There was no sense of the number of World Heritage sites that might exist, or how long they might take to identify. Nonetheless, the list grew rapidly. The first inscriptions to the list were made in 1978, and by 1980, eighty-two World Heritage sites had been inscribed in thirty-seven countries, and fifty-five countries had ratified the Convention. These first inscriptions included many familiar sites that had already been subject to intensive state management and utilised in the construction of national identities, such as Yellowstone National Park in the USA, and Chartres Cathedral in France (Figure 3.10). New sites were added regularly to the list, which grew to number 335 by 1990, and had more than doubled again in the following

FIGURE 3.10 Chartres Cathedral in France was one of the early sites to be nominated to the World Heritage List in 1979. (Photograph by Misato Le Mignon, 1997. © UNESCO/Misato Le Mignon.)

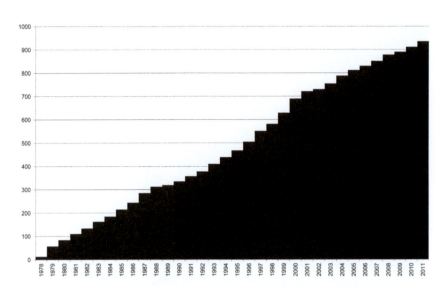

FIGURE 3.11 Cumulative number of World Heritage sites by year, 1978–2011. (Source: UNESCO 2011c.)

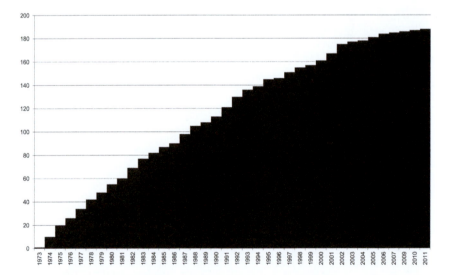

FIGURE 3.12 Cumulative number of States Parties to have ratified the World Heritage Convention, 1973–2011. (Source: UNESCO 2011d.)

decade to 690 by 2000 (Figure 3.11). Similarly, the number of States Parties to ratify the Convention continued to grow (Figure 3.12). By its thirtieth anniversary in 2002, the World Heritage List numbered 730 sites, and 175 States Parties had ratified the Convention. World Heritage had truly become a 'global' success story.

So by the 1970s, 'heritage' had been firmly established as a concept not only within the Euro-American contexts in which it had been developed over the late eighteenth, nineteenth and early twentieth centuries, but also at the international level. The years following the introduction of the World Heritage Convention would see not only an incredibly rapid expansion of the list itself, but also an explosion of popular interest in heritage in general, and the idea of World Heritage more particularly (Di Giovine 2009), which was increasingly utilised as a way of advertising sites for tourism, a phenomenon I consider in more detail in Chapter 4. The process of attempting to apply the Convention globally would have far-reaching impacts not only in terms of our current understandings of heritage, but more broadly in helping shape the contemporary world and our experience of it.

Conclusion

My intention in this chapter was to emphasise the intensification of activity around heritage which occurred in the 1960s and 1970s, which found its apogee in the 1972 World Heritage Convention. The process of the professionalisation of heritage, which had begun in the nineteenth century, had reached its zenith through the work of large advisory groups composed of experts in the fields of architecture, archaeology, history, ecology, biology, and so on. Similarly, heritage had become intensively regulated, and as we saw in the example of the histories of federal heritage legislation in the United States and England, the definition of heritage had grown to embrace an ever-expanding list of objects, places and landscapes. The period following the introduction of the World Heritage Convention would see a series of fundamental changes in heritage, many of which would be generated by the process of trying to apply this quite limited set of ideas on a global stage, as discussed in Chapters 6–9.

The World Heritage Convention appeared at a time that would become a turning point for heritage, when popular interest in the past had begun to accelerate, when the world tourist economy was in the process of restructuring, and when a series of technological changes in communicative technology would have a profound impact on globalisation processes that would radically alter the way in which people engaged with the world. What had begun as a series of ideas about the need to protect certain places from the detrimental effects of modernity had become a global phenomenon. In Chapter 4, I explore how these ideas about heritage shifted from the various bureaucratic contexts in which they had been defined and regulated over the course of the late nineteenth and twentieth centuries to become an issue of widespread popular concern at the end of the twentieth and the beginning of the twenty-first.

4

LATE-MODERNITY AND THE HERITAGE BOOM

Introduction

Chapter 3 provides a brief history of the idea of 'heritage', which found expression in the 1972 World Heritage Convention. This particular constellation of ideas about the relationship between the traces of the past and people in the present developed in North America, Britain and Western Europe (and several of their contemporary and former colonies) as a result of the emergence of the idea of the public sphere, and in the context of widespread industrialisation and accompanying social change associated with the experience of modernity, in which the past was perceived as a vulnerable and threatened resource. The development of the earliest 'lists' of heritage set in motion a trend for heritage to become increasingly bureaucratised and removed from the realm of everyday life. Chapter 3 also charts the way in which heritage became ever more broadly defined and strictly controlled as a result of state intervention and management throughout the course of the twentieth century. These ideas about heritage were deployed strategically by UNESCO within the particular political contexts of a series of early international safeguarding campaigns, and established the idea that there were some buildings, places and landscapes that were so important that their management was a concern not only for nations, but for the international community. The World Heritage Convention was developed as a document to codify and operationalise these concepts.

One major question that remains to be answered is why these ideas about heritage and its management, which had to a large extent been developed in isolation from broader public interests, subsequently gathered pace and were embraced so wholeheartedly by the public that it has become possible for us to speak of a late twentieth century heritage 'boom' (Hewison 1987; Walsh 1992; Lowenthal 1998; Dicks 2003). The period after 1972 saw fundamental shifts in the heritage landscape, and the development of a peculiar constellation of ideas and interests that we would recognise as belonging to a particular 'late-modern' notion of heritage. In this chapter, I want to look in more detail at various changes that occurred during the decades after 1970 in the public interest in the past in general, and in heritage more particularly, which led to heritage becoming an issue of broad public concern. I argue that various changes in the public's relationship with the past and its material traces, including processes of rapid technological change, deindustrialisation, the restructuring of the tourist gaze, reconfigurations in civic governance, and the widespread commercialisation of the past as 'experience', led to an expansion of public interest in the past as heritage. I also argue that the idea of the museum as a space for the relic, archaic or obsolete object, and its framework for the categorisation, collection, curation and exhibition of objects from the past, had a very important influence on the rise of heritage as a global phenomenon in the later part of the twentieth century in the context of large-scale processes of deindustrialisation and social and economic change. Central to this chapter is an exploration of the relationship between World Heritage and late-modern globalisation. As Barbara Kirshenblatt-Gimblett (2006) points out, while World Heritage is offered as a remedy for the homogenisation of culture which globalisation is thought to produce, it is itself a product of globalisation and a series of economic and political transformations in which cultural tourism has come to dominate aspects of the world economy. It is with this process of 'heritagisation' (a term that Kevin Walsh (1992) uses to refer to the process by which objects and places are transformed from functional 'things' into objects of display and exhibition) that the current chapter is concerned.

The late twentieth century and the heritage boom

It is clear, looking from an early twenty first century perspective, that heritage has become an all-pervasive industry in contemporary global societies. Heritage has become ubiquitous in our late-modern cities and urban and rural landscapes, and visiting and 'experiencing' the past by way of heritage sites and museums has become a regular practice for many, if not most people in contemporary urbanised societies. We have seen in Chapter 3 how the number of World Heritage sites grew rapidly in the period after 1972 to reach almost 1000 sites at the time of writing. As another indication of the sheer scale of heritage and its ubiquity in the contemporary world, the 2009 *Museums of the World* directory lists some 55,100 museums and museum associations in 202 countries. In the same year, it is estimated that museums and galleries in the UK alone registered over 100 million visits (Museums Association 2011) and over 70 per cent of adults in England had visited a heritage site of some kind in the previous year (English Heritage 2010a). We have already seen that it was possible for David Lowenthal to write in the 1980s of the phenomenon of 'creeping heritage' invading every aspect of public life in Britain and North America. Another of the early observers of the heritage boom was Robert Hewison, who coined the phrase 'heritage industry' (1987) to describe what he considered to be the sanitisation and commercialisation of the version of the past produced as heritage in the UK. In the late 1980s and 1990s, a number of authors across the UK, Western Europe and North America began to comment on what appeared to be a sudden, exponential growth in the number of visitors to heritage sites, historic attractions and museums, alongside the rapid expansion of sites being promoted as 'heritage' destinations (Wright 1985; Urry 1990, 1995; Walsh 1992; Samuel 1994; Mandler 1997; Lowenthal 1998; Dicks 2003; see Chapter 5).

But what evidence is there to suggest this late-modern boom in heritage? Statistics gathered across a range of categories demonstrate a rapid growth in the public interest in, and processes associated with, the identification, categorisation, conservation, management and exhibition of heritage in the decades around 1970, and its continued growth in the following decades. Similarly, they indicate a rapid growth in the number of visitors to heritage sites and museums, and the number of places that were managed and exhibited as heritage destinations over the same period. It is worth exploring some of the available data in more detail to get a sense of the scale of the expansion of the heritage sector over the last decades of the twentieth century. I will look at a range of data sources for England and the United States, to continue the regional foci of the examples discussed in Chapter 3. While data covering a comparable set of variables are not available from both these countries, I have tried to provide some indicative statistics that allow us to assess the various claims that heritage underwent a major period of growth in the later part of the twentieth century.

Growth in heritage presentation and visitation in England after 1970

In England, there has been some official interest in collecting information about heritage site visitation numbers, and a broader interest amongst historians in establishing indices to demonstrate the growth of the heritage 'sector' over the course of the second part of the twentieth century (Samuel 1994; Mandler 1997; Cowell 2008). National Trust membership has long been held as an appropriate index for measuring the collective public interest in heritage and conservation. This shows clear, exponential growth beginning after around 1970. Membership rose from 226,000 in 1970 to over 1 million in 1981, and doubled again by the Trust's centenary year in 1995 (Figure 4.1). The same source indicates that in 2008, over 50 million people visited the National Trust's (free entry) open-air properties, and more than 14 million people paid for entry to one of its ticketed attractions. Raphael Samuel documents the rapid growth in local amenity societies as another index of the growth in public interest in historic preservation over this period, pointing out that in the two decades between 1957 and 1977, the number of such societies saw a more than fourfold increase, growing from 213 in Britain to 1,167 in England alone (Samuel 1994: 237).

Records of visits to heritage sites in England have been collected by the various government departments responsible for heritage and tourism since the mid-1970s (Max Hanna Sightseeing Research 1998). Frustratingly, it is difficult to find earlier data than this; partially we can assume because it was only around this time that 'heritage tourism' became an issue that the government perceived was worth observing, although Peter Mandler records that visits to National Trust properties in England trebled to over 3 million between 1960 and 1970 (1997: 338). Figures published in the annual *English Heritage Monitor* show that by the late 1970s, historic properties were experiencing 54 million visits annually, and museums over 57 million visits.

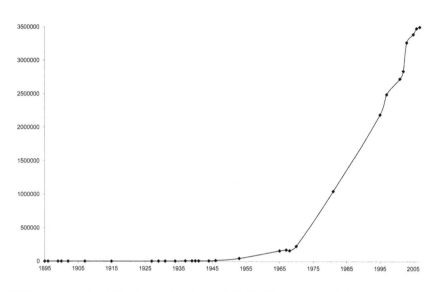

FIGURE 4.1 National Trust membership, 1895–2007. (Source: National Trust membership data, National Trust 2011.)

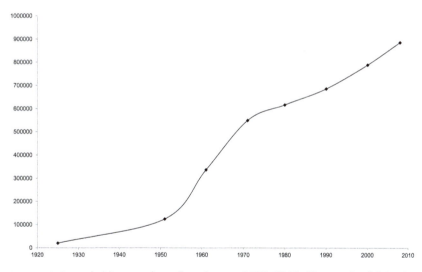

FIGURE 4.2 Annual visitor numbers, Stonehenge, 1925–2008. (Source: English Heritage 2011.)

This figure rose to a high point of over 71 million visits to historic properties by 1990, and a high point of museum visitation of 67 million in 1994, settling back to late 1970s levels by the mid-2000s.

In terms of visits to individual heritage sites, data published by English Heritage indicate that visits to the well known heritage site at Stonehenge almost doubled between 1961 and 1971 (Figure 4.2; note visitor numbers do not include solstice

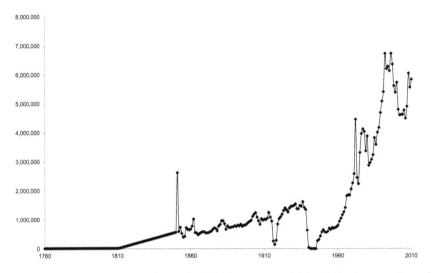

FIGURE 4.3 Annual visitor numbers, The British Museum, 1760–2010. (Source: Central Archive, British Museum.)

visits, which were discontinued for part of the period covered by these figures). In relation to museums, records relating to visitor numbers to the British Museum are available from 1760 to 2010. These indicate a slow rise in numbers into the twentieth century and an exponential jump in numbers after 1970 (Figure 4.3; note the major drop in visitor numbers over the period of the Second World War and the drop in visitor numbers that occurs in the late 1990s and early years of the new millennium).

Growth in heritage presentation and visitation in the United States after 1970

Similar trends are apparent in data relating to heritage sites and museums in the United States. Here, membership of the National Trust for Historic Preservation has tended not to be as high as in the UK, although it has been an important lobby group, playing a key role in the 1966 National Historic Preservation Act and the foundation of the Advisory Council on Historic Preservation in the same year, for example (Murtagh 2006: 56). Founded by congressional charter in 1949 to support the preservation of historic buildings and neighbourhoods, it printed the first edition of its members' magazine, *Preservation Matters*, in 1961. Since 1966, its membership has grown from 15,000 (Murtagh 2006: 56) to over 200,000 members at the time of writing (National Trust for Historic Preservation 2011b), an incredible proportional increase. As discussed in Chapter 3, the 1966 National Historic Preservation Act was significant as it established the basis for a national overarching historic preservation policy, a National Register of Historic Places, and a process for nominating and listing places on it. The Register automatically acquired a small number of existing National Historic Landmarks (Mackintosh 1985), but since 1966 more than 85,000 nominations have been added to the Register (at the time of writing, the Register had 86,255 separate listings composed of some 1,616,138 contributing properties; Historic Districts account for around 10 per cent of National Register listings).

There are no comparable national statistics on heritage site visitation, but the National Park Service keeps long and accurate historical records of park visitor statistics. Taking two examples, we can see a general pattern of increasing visitation to heritage sites over the course of the twentieth century, which mirrors the Stonehenge visitation data. For example, Colonial National Historical Park in Virginia (incorporating the first permanent English settlement at Colonial Jamestown, Yorktown Battle site, marking the final major battle of the American Revolutionary War and the Cape Henry Memorial at the landing place of the first Jamestown settlers) saw a massive jump in visitor numbers between 1959 and 1983, followed by a drop and subsequent slow rise to today's figures of around 3.5 million visitors (Figure 4.4). Chaco Culture National Historic Park in New Mexico, containing the archaeological remains of the ancient urban centre at Chaco Canyon, experienced a steadier rise in visitor numbers but with a noticeable acceleration after around 1960 (Figure 4.5). This is consistent with the increased visitor numbers experienced at one of the historic 'wilderness' parks such as Yellowstone or Yosemite NP (Figure 4.6).

This general pattern of an accelerated interest in, and visitation to, both natural and cultural heritage sites is also borne out by data relating to a growth in the number of museums and their visitors over this period. A 1978 survey sponsored by the Institute for Museum Services counted 4,400 museums in the United States; of those, almost half (47 per cent) had been founded after 1960, and only 9 per cent were founded prior to the beginning of the twentieth century (Leon and Rozenzweig 1989: xv). The survey estimated around 86 million visits had been made to museums in the

FIGURE 4.4 Annual visitor numbers, Colonial NHP, 1932–2010. (Source: National Park Service 2011b.)

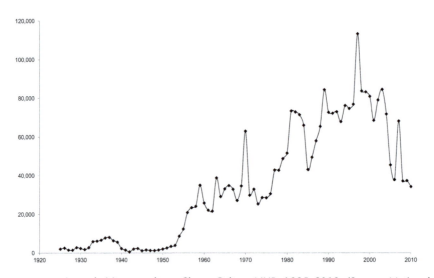

FIGURE 4.5 Annual visitor numbers, Chaco Culture NHP, 1925–2010. (Source: National Park Service 2011b.)

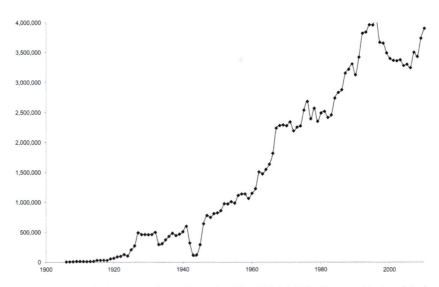

FIGURE 4.6 Annual visitor numbers, Yosemite NP, 1906–2010. (Source: National Park Service 2011b.)

previous year. Using slightly different criteria, the first *Official Museums Directory of the United States and Canada* listed more than 4,500 museums in 1961 'of which well over a thousand of them have been established since 1950, rising to almost 5000 by 1965, with the number of museums listed in the directory doubling to reach 9000 by the turn of the millennium'. The 2011 directory lists 13,400 museums. Similarly, visitor statistics relating to the Smithsonian Museums indicate that the number of visitors almost

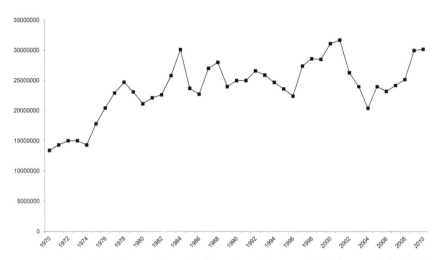

FIGURE 4.7 Annual visitor numbers, Smithsonian Museums, Washington DC, 1970–2010. (Source: Smithsonian Institution 2011.)

doubled between 1970 and 1978, and an overall trend (with some variation) for a steady rise in annual visitor numbers over this period.

Visitor statistics for England and the United States after 1970 compared

Although there is some variation in the data presented, there is fairly strong evidence to suggest that in the years around 1970 in England and the United States, there was a rapid expansion in the number of places exhibited as museums and heritage sites, the number and membership of heritage-related lobby and conservation campaign groups, and overall visitor numbers to heritage sites and museums. In some cases, these indices have shown a slight drop since the 1990s or early 2000s; in others they have continued to grow steadily. While to be truly accurate such data would need to take into account the increase in local populations and overseas tourist numbers over this period indexed against the number of new heritage sites being exhibited, nonetheless there appears to be a clear pattern of the intensification of a whole range of heritage-related activities that occurred in the years around 1970. The general trend seems to be borne out by data from Europe and elsewhere (Walsh 1992; Lowenthal 1998; Urry 1990; Graham et al. 2000; Dicks 2003; Davison [2000] 2008). The visitor data for the British Museum and Smithsonian Museums indicates that the growth in number of visitors to these well established national museums was not of the same scale as the overall increases in the number of new museums established over this period; indeed, both suffered annual drops in numbers over the 1990s and the early years of the new millennium. I suggest that this is largely due to the diversification of forms of heritage and 'culture on display' that occurred over this period, and the segmentation of the heritage market as a result of an increased emphasis on diversity, difference and the politics of representation in heritage and museums during this time. I explore these issues in further detail later in this chapter (see also Chapter 7). While a cluster of factors, including increased car ownership, cheap overseas package tourism, increasing disposable income and changes to the school curriculum, might all have contributed in various ways to the changes reported here, in the next section I explore various late-modern social, political and economic changes that occurred globally after 1970, which might help account for these changes in a more fundamental way.

Late-modernity

How can we account for this accelerated public interest in heritage at this time, and its continued significance over the following decades? In Chapter 2 I explored the relationship between heritage and the experience of modernity, and in Chapter 3 the ways in which the concept of heritage developed historically in what I have referred to as the first two 'phases' of modern heritage. Throughout the book, I have referred to a number of changes in heritage practices which came about in the period after 1970 in the wake of the World Heritage Convention. I have suggested that these changes are related structurally to a series of 'late-modern' shifts in economic, social and political practices (see also Walsh 1992). Many authors have pointed to the social changes in developed countries that have come about during the later part of the twentieth century as heralding a new and distinct period of history. In the same way that we are used to thinking of the modern age, or 'modernity', as relating to the outcomes of the Enlightenment and the industrial revolution, some authors have suggested we use the terms 'late-modernity', 'post-modernity', 'liquid modernity' and/or 'supermodernity' to define a distinct, recent historical period that can be seen as separate from modernity. They point to a series of phenomena that seem to mark the late twentieth century as separate from what came before it, including:

- the growth of new communicative technologies and electronic media
- the globalisation of technology and its association with altered patterns of production and consumption
- the widespread experience of mass migration and the associated rise of 'liquid' transnational flows (in terms of capital, technology, labour and corporations)
- new modes of capitalism involving more flexible forms of capital accumulation and distribution
- increased time available for leisure activities.[1]

In *The Postmodern Condition*, Jean-François Lyotard ([1979] 1984) suggested that modernity should be seen as a cultural condition characterised by constant change and the pursuit of progress, while postmodernity is the logical end product of this process, where constant change has become the status quo. Under such circumstances, the notion of progress fails to have any meaning, as everything is constantly in flux. Paul Virilio (1986, 2000) comments on the ways in which the late twentieth century has experienced an acceleration of time, or a sense of speed, which leads to a situation in which humans are so overwhelmed by the reversal, acceleration and simultaneous nature of time that space itself becomes an element of time (see also Tomlinson 2007). This produces a sense of 'time-in-flux', which comes to be experienced as a fundamental part of the urban and suburban landscape. The effect of this process in exacerbating modernity's sense of uncertainty is obvious. With an increase in the sense of speed comes an increase in uncertainty and the sense of risk, which we have already seen is a major motivating factor in the classification, categorisation, preservation and management of heritage.

I have characterised the late-modern period as a time in which various crises arose for heritage as a result of the application of old, nationalistic and canonical models of heritage to countries and communities with radically different perspectives on what heritage 'is', 'means' and 'does', by way of the World Heritage Convention. This was also a period that experienced what we might think of as a 'crisis in historicity', which had an important impact on the changing nature of the ways in which various publics came to relate to the past. The crisis in historicity related to an increasing inability to reconcile an understanding of history as presented (through history books, heritage sites, museums and the media) with the lived experience of everyday life. Fredric Jameson (1991) drew on Adorno and Horkheimer's analysis of the culture industry (Horkheimer and Adorno 1972; Adorno 2001) to suggest that this could be defined as the period in which the cultural sphere became entirely dominated by a newly organised corporate capitalism. He pointed to the frequent occurrence of pastiche, the imitation and mixture of styles or borrowing of aspects of other creative works in postmodern cultural forms such as art, architecture, film and literature, and suggested that this merging of all discourse into an undifferentiated whole was a result of this process by which the cultural sphere had become entirely colonised by the culture industry. He saw the widespread adoption of pastiche in postmodern creative arts as a reflection of this crisis in historicity, as it represents a form of juxtaposition without a normative foundation.

As Harvey (1990) points out, it is inaccurate to suggest this late-modern period represented a radical break with modernity, as the basic rules of the accumulation of capital remain the same. Nonetheless, the changes that occurred during the later part of the twentieth century can be said to have given rise to a distinct way of experiencing time and place.

> There has been a sea-change in cultural as well as in political–economic practices since around 1972. This sea-change is bound up with the emergence of new dominant ways in which we experience space and time ... there is some kind of ... relation between the rise of postmodernist cultural forms, the emergence of more flexible modes of capital accumulation, and a new round of 'time–space compression' in the organisation of capitalism.
>
> *(Harvey 1990: vii)*

This combination of new ways of understanding and relating to time and space and more flexible modes of capital accumulation has clearly been experienced in different ways by different people throughout the world during this period. Nonetheless, when considered as a global phenomenon, this phase of 'late capitalism', when more flexible forms of capital accumulation and distribution develop, characterised by increasingly flexible labour processes and markets, increased spatial mobility, rapid shifts in patterns of consumption, and a revival of entrepreneurialism and neo-conservatism (Harvey 1990: 124), can be understood to have produced fundamental changes in how people experience time and space in the period after about 1970 (see also Walsh 1992). This process can be argued to have stimulated an increased interest in the past, whilst simultaneously making people feel more distant from it, and opening up new markets for its exhibition and consumption.

Marc Augé argues that 'super'- or 'hyper'-modernity is a characteristic of societies in which the presence of the past in the present is so abundant as to overwhelm and clutter it. In such circumstances, the past and its traces are constantly recycled, and people are unable to distinguish between its original and subsequent manifestations.

> The presence of a past in a present that supercedes it but still lays claim to it: it is in this reconciliation that Jean Strabonski sees the essence of modernity ... the hypothesis advanced here is that supermodernity produces non-places, meaning spaces which ... do not integrate the earlier places: instead these are listed, classified, promoted to the status of a 'place of memory', and assigned to a circumscribed and specific position.
>
> *(Augé 1995: 75–78)*

He suggests that supermodernity, the experience of modernity *made excessive,* is characterised by three accelerations or excesses: time, space, and the individualisation of the point of reference. By the excess of time, Augé refers not only to our accelerated experience of time (as noted above in the discussion of Lyotard, Jameson, Virilio and Harvey; see further discussion in González-Ruibal 2008), but also to how we perceive and utilise time and a sense of the past.

> We barely have time to reach maturity before our past has become history ... the recent past—'the sixties', 'the seventies', now 'the eighties'—becomes history as soon as it is lived. History is on our heels, following us like shadows, like death ... time overloaded with events that encumber the present as well as the recent past. This can only ... make us more avid for meaning ... it is our need to understand the whole of the present that makes it difficult for us to give meaning to the recent past.
>
> *(Augé 1995: 26–30)*

This process is perhaps best exemplified by the development and exponential growth in the late-modern period of museums and exhibitions that relate to the histories of our own lifetimes. At the time of writing, the Victoria and Albert Museum in London is presenting a retrospective on 'postmodern style' from 1970–90, for example. We might also think of the many new museums of computing technology, which all selectively represent and exhibit the history of our own lifetimes in different ways. This has produced what is possibly the most pervasive phenomenon of having our own selves presented and narrated back to us through mass media since newspapers began circulating widely, and can be argued to have had as radical an impact on our sense of individual and collective identity. This also produces an abundance of the past, as new pasts are simply added to, rather than replacing, those prior representations of the past that have previously been exhibited. This leads to a sense of the 'abundance' of the past, which coincides with late-modernity's accelerated sense of speed and change. I consider the implications of this late-modern abundance of the past in Chapter 8.

In summary, a series of commentators have noted a variety of shifts and accelerations of modern perceptions of the relationship between the past and present, which could be argued to have informed the rapid growth of interest in the past that occurred in the years around 1970. I have elected to use the term 'late-modern' rather than 'postmodern' or 'super-modern' to describe this period and, by extension, its distinct qualities, to emphasise some of the continuities between the modern and late-modern periods, rather than draw too fine a line between them. As Jameson (1984; cited in Thomas 2004: 3) notes, the use of terms such as 'modernity' and 'postmodernity' has the tendency to establish a sense of homogeneity within, and heterogeneity between, those periods that may not exist. Like Thomas (2004: 3), I think it is more helpful to think of the terms modernity and late-modernity as social, economic and technological *processes* rather than entirely distinct time periods, to avoid making too clear a distinction between them and erasing the sense of continuity in certain longer-term processes that run through both periods, in particular the 'rules' that govern the accumulation of capital. Nonetheless, I think the various shifts in these processes are distinct enough to track their influence on various new projects and definitions of heritage that arose around this time. And yet, for all their significance in stimulating a renewed interest in and nostalgia for the past, such processes cannot on their own fully account for the changes in heritage that I have noted. The discussion so far has not taken account of the agency of the various publics involved in the creation and reception of these new, diverse and abundant representations of the past as heritage, which emerged in this period. In the next section, I suggest that these various conceptual shifts in the experience of time and space were accompanied by other social and economic shifts, which have reconfigured heritage in the late-modern period, including processes of deindustrialisation, reconfigurations of the tourist 'gaze', and the emergence of heritage as an element of a new 'experience' economy.

Deindustrialisation, decline and the rise of 'heritagisation': from museum to heritage site

My outline of heritage in the 'late-modern' period has so far avoided detailed discussion of the widespread economic and social shifts associated with processes of deindustrialisation that occurred over the course of the twentieth century in many industrialised nations. As early as the 1930s and 1940s, economists Colin Clark and Jean Fourastie had predicted that industrial societies would become 'postindustrial' societies, characterised not by the engagement of humans with raw materials, but by the work of humans on other humans, as part of an overall trend in the shift from agriculture to industry to service as the main areas of production and income generation. American sociologist Daniel Bell (1973) suggested that postindustrial societies could be characterised as 'knowledge-based' economies, a designation that persists in our discussion of contemporary societies as 'information societies'. Deindustrialisation is generally understood as a 'natural' process that occurs with the increasing efficiency of productivity in industry in advanced economies (Rowthorn and Ramaswamy 1997). However, as economist Daniel Cohen points out (2009), this is not the whole picture. The shift to a postindustrial society must be understood simultaneously as a *technological*, an *economic* and a *social* process in which the conceptualisation of goods (that is, the ideas behind their development) and the prescription of goods (that is, their marketing, promotion and sale) dominate over the cost of their production—a phenomenon in which the production of material things ironically comes to cost next to nothing and to have comparatively little or even no value, while the immaterial aspects of their development and promotion come to hold the greatest value. The increased productivity of industry and containerisation of goods transport ultimately makes manufacturing cheaper and more labour-efficient, leading to centralisation and reduction of the labour force (Rowthorn and Ramaswamy 1997). The globalisation and fluidity of capital, labour and transport networks also makes it easier to relocate manufacturing to cheaper locations and labour markets. Cohen notes that the break between the industrial and postindustrial eras might be seen to have been signalled by a series of interlinked social and material ruptures, beginning with the 1968 student and worker protests. In particular, he points to the ways in which the revolution in information technology has produced a trend toward flatter hierarchies of workers with multiple skills, and subcontracting and outsourcing have changed the nature of work. This has produced a new international division of labour, signalled by the economic rise of China, India and the former Soviet Union, and the negative economic effects of free trade on less wealthy and less politically powerful countries.

These global late-modern social and economic shifts have led, over a period beginning in the 1960s and leading up to the present day, to a widespread process of redundancy of former industrial sites, towns and infrastructure, as manufacture shifted from the old centres of industrial production to new ones. So, at the same time as the North American, British and European public's interest in the past was accelerating, so was a process of superfluity, abandonment and decline in the industrial centres of those same countries, which had a widespread impact on the economies of many former manufacturing and industrial centres and associated infrastructure. Ruined places and superfluous buildings began to multiply across North American and Western European cities and rural centres. Hewison (1987) has argued that heritage should be seen as a social response to the sense of decline that emerged as a result of the economic consequences of this shift in manufacturing and industry. But, in addition to perceiving this as a social response, it is possible to see the widespread 'heritagisation' of many new categories of place—in particular, 'industrial heritage' sites, largely unacknowledged prior to this period—as a pragmatic physical response to the problem of the *material excess of ruin*: what physically to do with the mine shafts, the ports, the factories, the vast material remnants of industry that were rapidly becoming defunct and lying derelict and useless, and how, in the words of Barbara Kirshenblatt-Gimblett (1998), to give them a 'second life' as heritage. We have already seen that categorisation and listing can be understood as a process concerned with the management of waste. During this particular conjuncture of issues and interests, museological notions of collection, documentation, conservation, and exhibition were extended beyond the walls of the museum to the preservation of places *in situ* as part of a process that has ultimately led to the extension of those same notions to living human beings by way of the concept of 'intangible heritage' (Kirshenblatt-Gimblett 2006: 161; see Chapter 6). This was partially made possible by extending the various modern museological processes of categorisation and cata- loguing to heritage 'sites', the lists themselves becoming the focus of the collection, which allowed the sites to be collected but to remain *in situ* (Harrison in press b). The World Heritage List itself operated as a model for such inventories, which, although they had existed for some years, grew rapidly in the decades following 1970. This shift in museological modes of collection from objects in museums to places on municipal, regional, national and international heritage registers can be understood to be an extension of a process which was largely concerned with the management of redundant objects, buildings and landscapes that were perceived to be too valuable to simply discard. Heritage had shifted from a process of the production of a public sphere in the eighteenth century to one of nation-building in the nineteenth and twentieth, to become concerned largely with the management of redundancy and waste in the late twentieth and early twenty-first centuries (see also Hetherington 2004; Chapter 8 in this volume).

In addition to the sense of decline that was instrumental in driving this process of the collection and preservation of defunct objects, buildings and landscapes, the late- modern period was haunted by an accelerated sense of vulnerability and risk. This was reflected in the number of 'heritage at risk' registers established during this period to draw attention to what was perceived to be the urgency of the need for pre- servation in the light of widespread processes of social and technological change. The international safeguarding campaigns in Egypt and Venice had drawn widespread attention to the vulnerability of heritage, and the 1972 World Heritage Convention established the principles by which the World Heritage Committee could inscribe on a 'List of World Heritage in Danger' properties whose protection required 'major operations … and for which assistance has been requested'. The first site was inscribed on the List of World Heritage in Danger in 1979, and the List grew slowly through the 1980s, with an increasing number of sites listed in the 1990s (Figure 4.8). Other international and national lists of heritage in danger that sought to draw attention to the vulnerability of different forms of heritage in the late-modern world were subse- quently established by various international NGOs following the UNESCO model. For example, the World Monuments Fund began to publish a biannual 'List of 100 Most Endangered Sites' in 1996, and ICOMOS began to publish a similar 'Heritage@Risk' list in 1999, with occasional thematic foci (e.g. special reports on underwater heritage and European modernist buildings in 2006). Similar lists, intended to highlight the

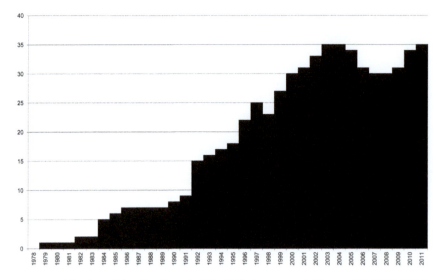

FIGURE 4.8 Number of sites listed on the World Heritage sites in Danger list, 1978–2011. (Source: UNESCO 2011c.)

vulnerability of particular heritage objects, sites and landscapes, also proliferated at the national level amongst states and heritage interest groups. In England, for example, English Heritage began to keep a 'Buildings at Risk Register' in 1998, listing Grade I and Grade II listed buildings and Scheduled ancient monuments believed to be at risk due to neglect or external threat. The Twentieth Century Society, founded in 1979 and the Victorian Society, founded in 1958 also established their own lists of buildings at risk as part of their campaigning activities. The growth in the number of such lists, as well as the number of objects, places and landscapes included, contributed to an accelerated sense of vulnerability and threat that added to the increasing sense of anxiety and obsessive, almost feverish approaches to the conservation of heritage that developed in this late-modern period.

However, it wasn't always enough simply to preserve these redundant places; they needed to be given a new function. Venice acted as the model 'museum city', and gained widespread attention as a result of the UNESCO safeguarding campaign established in the wake of major flooding that occurred there in 1966 (see Chapter 3). Soon, this museological model was to be applied to the recreation of a whole range of urban and rural sites, from former coal mines to factories, port cities made redundant by the growth of containerisation, and other buildings and places that were no longer profitable or were no longer required for the purpose for which they were constructed. In some cases, it was enough to designate the new function of such places as 'heritage', in which case the building or place would be refashioned in the model of a museum exhibit. Typical of such places are a series of sites associated with the industrial revolution in the UK, many of which are now listed as World Heritage sites, such as Ironbridge Gorge, New Lanark, various mining sites in Cornwall and Wales (Hewison 1987; Donnachie 2010), and other sites such as Albert Dock in Liverpool (Walsh 1992), which are all largely managed and exhibited as museum pieces on a monumental scale. In other cases, defunct buildings and landscapes were given other functions. 'Adaptive re-use' became a fashionable term for the reworking of existing heritage sites and buildings to give them a new, often commercial function secondary to their primary function of preservation as 'heritage'.

The state had a key role to play in the development of this new 'heritage industry' through the increasing forms of legislative control over heritage (discussed in Chapter 3), which provided a platform for neoliberal policies that shifted away from the idea of preservation for its own (or the 'public(s)') benefit and focused increasingly on the potential of heritage for local, regional and national income generation. Of course, various publics themselves had a key role to play in the process. The growth in local tourism had direct economic ramifications for communities, and the heritage and museum sector became a key revenue generator, creating an economically driven desire to maintain static stereotypical forms of 'culture' for tourist consumption. Tourists were active, too, in selecting those forms of 'culture' they were interested in consuming. The draw of the tourism economy began to challenge locals to produce 'new' forms of museum display that, where profitable, began to shift the emphasis in the forms of heritage exhibited, challenging the hegemony of the old 'high culture' museums and heritage sites. This activity provided a sense of regeneration and 'progress' even when it was clearly a response to processes of decline and redundancy.

One of the important early developments in this regard occurred in the adaptive re-use of Faneuil Hall Marketplace (Quincy Market) in Boston, Massachusetts, redeveloped by architect Benjamin C. Thompson of Benjamin Thompson and Associates and developer Jim Rouse of Rouse Company, who had previously been involved in building some of the first covered shopping malls in North America. The original Faneuil Market Hall was built in the early 1740s, and rebuilt after it burnt to the ground in a fire in 1761. In the early nineteenth century, the building was expanded to increase the capacity of its market stalls, and in the 1820s Quincy Market was built behind Faneuil Hall to provide additional undercover food and produce stalls. Throughout the twentieth century, Faneuil Hall became less and less important as suburban supermarkets became more common, and the area around the market became increasingly dominated by administrative and financial services. In 1960 Faneuil Hall was designated a National Historic Landmark, and it was subsequently added to the National Register of Historic Places some years later. By the early 1970s, the meat and other fresh produce markets had been moved out of the city and the buildings themselves were becoming run down. Threatened with demolition, a campaign to save the market buildings began. Drawing on public and private financing, Benjamin Thompson worked with developer Jim Rouse and Mayor of Boston Ken White to develop Faneuil Hall Marketplace as a retail, restaurant, fast food, entertainment and tourism venue in an attempt to revitalise not only the market buildings, but also the downtown area of Boston. Opened in 1976, the market was a great success, attracting local office workers and suburban and international tourists, and provided a model for other 'festival marketplaces' that Benjamin Thompson and Associates and Rouse Company would go on to develop: Jacksonville Landing in Jacksonville, South Street

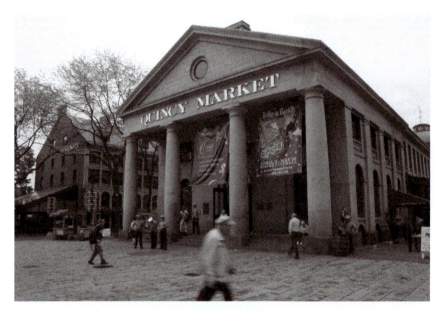

FIGURE 4.9 Faneuil Hall Marketplace (Quincy Market) in Boston, Massachusetts, rede-veloped by the architectural firm Benjamin Thompson and Associates and the developer Rouse Company and re-opened in 1976, formed the model for a number of other 'festival marketplaces' in the US and elsewhere that adaptively re-used buildings and structures made redundant by processes of late-modern deindustrialisation and urban and rural economic and demographic change. (Photograph by the author.)

Seaport in New York City, Harborplace in Baltimore, and Bayside Marketplace in Miami (Faneuil Hall Marketplace 2009; Fixler 2011; Krieger 2011; Padgen 2011; Schmertz 2011). Soon the 'festival marketplace' became one of the dominant strategies of North American urban revitalisation. Similar projects were also carried out in the UK and Europe, for example in the redevelopment of Covent Garden Market in London, which opened in 1980. These and similar adaptive re-use and heritage projects, which were rolled out in many different shapes and forms over the following decades, have had a major impact in creating and reshaping our contemporary international urban and rural landscapes.

Experiencing the past: heritage, 'visitability' and the experience economy

In addition to these processes of deindustrialisation and accompanying economic and demographic restructuring, the late-modern period is also associated with a series of social changes that would have major impacts on the importance of heritage in the contemporary landscape. Fundamental to these changes were shifts in leisure, tourism and travel, which saw the 'experience' of heritage become an important way in which redundant objects, places and practices could be marketed for commercial gain, alongside the exponential expansion of domestic and international travel and tourism amongst an increasingly wealthy Western middle-class elite. These changes relate in part to the rise of the culture industry and the corporate domination of the cultural sphere discussed earlier in this chapter. They are also closely associated with the 1980s venture capital boom and 1990s 'dot-com bubble', which saw a shift in investment towards the development and marketing of new 'knowledge' industries, and the various real-estate bubbles that were growing at the same time in many countries throughout the world, allowing large amounts of cash to flow into the tourism and service industries. One of the most distinctive developments in this period was the shift from the marketing and sale of 'services' to the marketing and sale of 'experiences' as part of a new economic model, described by Pine and Gilmore as a shift to an 'experience economy' (1999; see also Sundbo and Darmer 2008). This is an economic model in which goods and services have come to be valued not so much for their function, but in terms of their engagement of the senses and the experiences that surround their purchase and use. They see the origins of the experience economy in the opening of Disneyland in 1955, and urge their readers in business to consider the experiences they create as an integral part of the goods and services they provide. Similarly, Jensen (1999) has argued that the late twentieth century saw the emergence of a 'Dream Society', characterised by the commercialisation of emotion and the opening of new markets with which to exploit the economic potential of human emotions. Looking back on this language with the hindsight of knowledge of the early 2000s venture capital crash and the late 2000s global financial crisis, this language seems quaintly optimistic and frankly out of touch, but it is not possible to underestimate the impact this focus on 'experience' in the late twentieth century had on heritage and museums in this period, and its ongoing influence on the modes of exhibition and presentation of heritage that persist today.

Theme parks are generally considered to represent the most fundamental manifestation of the experience economy (Clavé 2007: 155), and are central to the discussion of the emergence of 'experience' as a commodity. Although there was a long tradition of amusement and trolley parks, which provided picnic areas, mechanical rides and other forms of entertainment (themselves evolving from a tradition of travelling fairs and expositions), the opening of Disneyland is considered to represent a watershed in that it represented one of the world's first fully themed amusement parks, which has subsequently acted as a model for the development of not only other theme parks, but themed attractions such as shopping malls, casinos, hotels and restaurants (see papers in Sorkin 1992; Mitrašinović 2006). Bryman refers to this process as the 'Disneyisation' of society, and notes that this process has several dimensions (2004: 2). The first dimension he refers to as 'themeing'—where institutions or objects are given an overall narrative that is unrelated to their history or function. Another relevant dimension is that of hybrid consumption—'a general trend whereby the forms of consumption associated with different institutional spheres become interlocked with each other and increasingly difficult to distinguish' (2004: 2). Both 'themeing' and the encouragement of hybrid consumption form key aspects of how heritage is marketed and consumed as an experience in late-modern societies.

Themeing and an emphasis on 'experience' had an important influence on the idea of heritage in the latter part of the twentieth century, which has persisted into the early twenty-first (see also Holtorf 2005, 2009, 2010a, 2010b; Baxter 2010; Silberman 2010). 'Experience' has emerged as an important focus for heritage in several ways. I have suggested above that the shift from processes of collecting and mobilising cultural relics (for example, in the form of museums and collections of antiquities) to one of *in situ* conservation of heritage objects, places and practices had an important influence on the changing nature of heritage during the later part of the twentieth century. Because heritage was perceived as best conserved 'in place', it became caught up in changing patterns of travel and tourism (see Urry 1990). As Bella Dicks notes, heritage was no longer about simply conserving the past, but about staging it as a 'visitable experience' (2003: 119).

> The desire to access the past can be seen as a manifestation of contemporary modes of representation which provide us with multi-sensory, multi-vocal, cacophonous places in which to experience it ... Modernity allows tradition to be disembedded from the constraints of situated and localized interaction, and to be 're-moored' in new and diverse contexts within the multiple forms of mediated spectacle ... What this means is that heritage is produced within the cultural economy of visitability in which the object is to attract as many visitors as practicable to the intended site, and to communicate with them in meaningful terms.
>
> *(Dicks 2003: 132–4)*

Heritage sites thus became places to which members of the public travelled to gain an 'experience' of the past (Gable and Handler 1996; Handler and Gable 1997; Otero-Pailos 2008). The second way in which experience has emerged as an important focus for heritage is through an increasing emphasis on 'intangible' heritage, either staged as an aspect of traditional culture (for example in the form of traditional dances, songs, food, and various other cultural 'performances' enacted 'in place'), or heritage re-enactments of various kinds involving actors and/or audience members in some aspect of fantasy role play.

Late-modern heritage and museum sites exemplify an 'experiential complex' (Hall 2006 after Bennett 1995), in which heritage is staged as a themed attraction combining interactive entertainment, simulation of the past, and the opportunity to purchase mementoes and souvenirs with which an individual's experience of the site can be subsequently revisited and remembered. The experiential complex is charac- terised by a strange self-reflexivity in which the past of the inhabitants of an area is repackaged for visitors in a way that forecloses that past and produces a rupture between it and the present. Many contemporary museums essentially operate as composite theme parks, producing simulated environments within which to stage themed heritage experiences (Holtorf 2005, 2009, 2010a; Hall 2006).

One of the implications of the commercialisation of heritage through adaptive re-use and an emphasis on 'experience' and heritage-based themes is the way in which it

FIGURE 4.10 Costumed actors awaiting the arrival of a school bus at the start of the Freedom Trail in Boston, Massachusetts. (Photograph by the author.)

came to occupy a space in the economy of those countries that were experiencing the largest economic and demographic shifts associated with processes of deindustrialisation. Heritage was no longer simply a symbol of civic society and a part of the educative apparatus of the nation-state, but became an important 'industry' in its own right. In 2010, travel and tourism directly contributed $759 billion to the US economy, and it is estimated that over 78 per cent of all travellers in that year participated in some form of cultural heritage activity or experience during their visit (National Trust for Historic Preservation 2011a). In the same year in the UK, it was estimated that heritage tourism accounted for approximately £12.4 billion of revenue and supported an estimated 195,000 full-time jobs (Heritage Lottery Fund 2010).

The important place heritage has come to occupy with regard to the tourism and service industries has transformed heritage in several key ways. Principal among these is the way in which heritage has been forced to diversify to market itself to distinct audiences. In its guise as part of the educative equipment of the state, it was perhaps enough for heritage to tell a single story of the origins of a nation, based on a single canon of heritage that promoted a clear series of messages about what constituted appropriate behaviours for its citizens. However, if heritage was to be profitable in an experience economy that was increasingly focused on individualised experiences, heritage would need to be able to diversify and appeal not only to those citizens who might traditionally have been left out of the national story, but also to a diverse range of international tourists, people of various different ages, backgrounds, religions and interests. Tony Bennett (2006) writes of how museums in the late-modern period became 'differencing machines' concerned with the representation of multiple constituencies, and the explanation for the origins of their differences. This shift occurred alongside another series of intellectual changes that gave greater emphasis to issues of the politics of representation, and saw heritage shift from the production of a single 'canon' to a concern with producing multiple forms of heritage that would be broadly representative of its various audiences. Museums, in particular, began to become interested in community outreach activities and in recording visitor statistics, which allowed them to consider the ways in which they marketed themselves to minority groups that they had traditionally not perceived as important audiences. This process led to a segmentation of the market and a diversification of forms of heritage and 'culture on display' over this period, which seems to have affected visitor numbers at more 'traditional' heritage attractions. This might account for the drop in visitor numbers to the British Museum and Smithsonian Museums noted earlier in this chapter, for example.

I have made reference to the close connection between the experience economy and the 1990s and 2000s venture capital, dot-com and real-estate bubbles. While 'experience' has persisted as an important element in the marketing and consumption of heritage into the period following the late 2000s global financial crisis, there has also been a notable re-emergence of the question of authenticity (e.g. Hall 2006), a rising focus on the really 'real'. In some ways, such an emphasis would seem inconsistent with the growing importance of 'virtual' forms of heritage and the increased emphasis on intangible heritage as a result of the 2003 UNESCO Convention for the Safeguarding of the Intangible Cultural Heritage. Gilmore and Pine (2007) refer to this focus on authenticity as a part of the 'consumer sensibility' of developed experience economies, but I think in the case of heritage, we might also see this as a reaction, following the global financial crisis, to the apparent decadence of certain forms of marketed experience and an increased focus on value. However, the form that this expectation of authenticity takes in relation to heritage is perhaps counterintuitive. As Holtorf (2005, 2009) points out, themed heritage experiences are very much a part of lived reality, and far from being 'duped' by heritage theme parks, people visit them to gain an authentic, affective and emotional connection with the past. Gaining emotional satisfaction from a themed heritage experience may not rely on the accurate presentation of factual material, even where the gaps between fact and fantasy are made clear to the consumer (Gable and Handler 1996; Holtorf 2009). What seems more important is that the various apparatuses and techniques by which the heritage experiences are created are made apparent so that the consumer feels empowered to make a judgement about the factuality (or otherwise) of the experience and information presented to them. The focus is on sincerity, rather than facts.

Heritage and globalisation: World Heritage as a 'brand'

We have seen how adaptive re-use projects sought to transform defunct objects, places and practices by placing emphasis on the values of heritage as a rare, threatened, non-renewable commodity that could be marketed, exhibited and made 'visitable'. Typical of this process was how World Heritage came to be used as a 'brand' in marketing destinations to international tourists. If heritage was a commodity, 'World Heritage' was the most marketable of this form of commodity, and in the years after 1972, governments and local businesses and interest groups would increasingly see World Heritage listing as an opportunity for revitalising and contributing to national, regional and local economies. While this has rarely been discussed (but see Ryan and Silvanto 2009, 2011), it would appear to be one of the reasons why the World Heritage List has expanded at such an impressive rate (see Chapter 3) and why States Parties were so keen to ratify the Convention. Tourist guidebooks began to list World Heritage sites as a series of 'wonders of the world', and the descriptions of World Heritage sites would often emphasise their picturesque aesthetic qualities and historical importance. World Heritage has become a mark of distinction; a symbol of wealth, status and cosmopolitan approach to urban planning and design; and a guarantee of a site's value as a visitable destination (Long and Labadi 2010).

The World Heritage Emblem itself has become a global brand (Ryan and Silvanto 2009, 2011; Poria et al. 2011), and is used to mark World Heritage sites clearly for visitors and tourists. The World Heritage Emblem was designed by Belgian artist Michel Olyff and adopted as the official emblem of the World Heritage Convention in 1978 (UNESCO 2011b). Guidelines for the use of the emblem were made an appendix to World Heritage Convention Operational Guidelines, which state that properties included in the World Heritage List should be marked with the World Heritage emblem jointly with the UNESCO logo. The guidelines recommend the use of plaques to commemorate the designation of a site to the World Heritage List, which it considers have a dual function of identifying the site as a World Heritage site and informing about its outstanding values, but also in providing information about 'the World Heritage Convention or at least about the World Heritage concept and the World Heritage List' (UNESCO 2011b). These plaques have thus become an important marketing tool not only for promoting tourism to individual sites, but also in promoting the World Heritage 'idea' as a universal, global principle.

The value of the World Heritage Emblem as a symbol for the World Heritage 'brand' is demonstrated by the variety of different ways in which it has been worked into local place branding. In addition to appearing on brass plaques, the symbol often occurs on street signs, posters and banners, and in other prominent locations in and around World Heritage sites to promote businesses and to highlight the presence of World Heritage sites to visitors. Although the take-up and use of the World Heritage 'brand' has varied considerably from site to site (Poria et al. 2011), it has nonetheless become an important symbol of place branding and a designation of a site's visitability.

This connection of World Heritage with domestic and international tourism cannot be overstated in terms of its importance in the globalisation of the World Heritage 'idea' and the popularity and growth of the number of World Heritage sites listed over the late twentieth and early twenty-first centuries (Di Giovine 2009). For sites to be designated as World Heritage, States Parties would have to ratify the Convention, prepare tentative lists, and generally sign up to the UNESCO 'approach' to heritage. Once sites were listed, they would be expected to be managed in ways that were consistent with the World Heritage Convention and, as universal

FIGURE 4.11 Brass plaque including the World Heritage Emblem and UNESCO logo recording the Renaissance fortified Upper Town's designation as part of the Ibiza, Biodiversity and Culture World Heritage Site in Ibiza, Spain. (Photograph by the author.)

FIGURE 4.12 Brass plaque in sidewalk showing the World Heritage Emblem at the Hospital de Sant Pau World Heritage Site in Barcelona, Spain. (Photograph by the author.)

FIGURE 4.13 World Heritage as a 'brand': UNESCO World Heritage Emblem containing schematic drawing of the 'Japanese Bridge' on a street sign in the Hoi An Ancient Town World Heritage Site in Vietnam. (Photograph by the author.)

FIGURE 4.14 World Heritage Emblem worked into design of iron gates at the Complex of Hué Monuments World Heritage Site in Hué, Vietnam. (Photograph by the author.)

heritage, exhibited for international tourists in some way. While the designation of World Heritage sites was clearly beneficial in terms of promoting tourism to particular regions, it also carried with it a series of assumptions about the ways in which these sites (and others in a region) would be managed. Its naming as a 'World Heritage

FIGURE 4.15 UNESCO emblem placed above gate to the old city in the Historic City of Trogir World Heritage Site, Croatia. (Photograph by the author.)

Site', its branding by way of signage and other interpretive apparatuses and media, and the various documents surrounding it 'create' it as a World Heritage site, and from this process a series of expectations flow about its appropriate conservation, management, curation and care. The friction that developed as a result of attempts to apply UNESCO's definition of heritage and its implications for its management to countries and communities with radically different ideas about the nature of heritage, its relationship with contemporary life, and the appropriate manner in which it should be managed, had far-reaching implications and would ultimately result in an important series of changes in how heritage was defined by UNESCO. These various instances of creative friction, generated by the awkward negotiations of the local and the global, form the focus of Chapters 6–9 of this book.

Conclusion

I began this chapter by asking how we might account for the dramatic growth in the public interest in heritage, which appears to have undergone a boom in the years around 1970. Following the Second World War, heritage and the past became an issue of broader public interest. I have suggested a number of reasons for this, including various late-modern accelerations and shifts in people's relationship with the past; a growth in the perception of vulnerability and uncertainty; shifting economic and demographic processes of deindustrialisation leading to widespread redundancy of many forms of buildings and sites; the development of 'experience' as a marketable commodity; the growth of domestic and international leisure travel and the accompanying restructuring of the tourist gaze; the diversification and segmentation of heritage to make it marketable to more varied audiences; and the widespread commercialisation of the past. It is not helpful to look for a single cause for these changes; instead, we need to consider them as the result of a cluster of interconnected influences, which varied across time and space, acting at different times and with different intensities in various countries across the world. These various shifts in popular understandings of the past and heritage combined with various developments that had occurred in relation to heritage in the previous decades to produce heritage as an important and pervasive area of public concern by the turn of the twenty-first century.

This series of changes occurred at the same time as, and partially facilitated, the globalisation of the World Heritage 'idea'. World Heritage became an important 'brand' for the marketing of international tourist destinations, and a way in which nations could compete internationally for prestige. The creative friction generated by the application of the rather limited definition of heritage embodied in the World Heritage Convention, which had developed largely in North America, Western Europe and Britain over the eighteenth, nineteenth and twentieth centuries, to countries and communities with radically different understandings of the relationships between people, their environments and the past, would have an important influence on the changing definitions of heritage that developed as a result of the work of UNESCO and its advisory bodies over the late twentieth and early twenty-first centuries. However, this was also a period in which heritage began to become an area of serious critical academic concern. Chapter 5 considers the development of a field of interdisciplinary critical heritage studies and the debates that have set the broad parameters of heritage studies as they are understood within the field today.

5

CRITICAL HERITAGE STUDIES AND THE DISCURSIVE TURN

Introduction

In the previous chapters we saw how heritage developed in Western Europe, Britain, North America and some of their present and former colonies as a set of official, state-led practices in the marriage of the Enlightenment idea of the public sphere with the notion that nature and historic objects need preservation in the light of widespread change in an industrialising world. This led to the view that places could be conserved and held in trust by public organisations and institutions for the future. This was underpinned by a series of modern philosophies that required the present to be defined in opposition to the past, albeit a past that was actively created out of the present.

From the outset, the idea that the 'best' examples of things should receive the greatest investment of money and energy was applied. The notion of what constituted the best varied across time and space, but in the case of cultural heritage, became increasingly caught up in the development of an art historical canon of objects and buildings. Throughout the twentieth century, heritage became increasingly controlled and defined by legislation and the state as part of the process of nation-building. At the same time, various global organisations put forward the notion that some natural and cultural places had value that was 'universal', and that their preservation was the interest of the international community. In the 1960s, and particularly after the World Heritage Convention in 1972, UNESCO facilitated the promotion of this philosophy amongst its member states, many of whom had quite different relationships with tradition and the past. In particular, countries and communities with more continuous traditions felt alienated by this set of cultural values around heritage, which emphasised the material, the monumental and the ancient. At the same time, official and unofficial heritage was experiencing a 'boom' as a result of various processes associated with changes in late-modern societies. Over the following years, heritage began to permeate almost every socio-cultural and economic sphere, and heritage began to be of critical interest to scholars and academic commentators.

This chapter describes the development of a contemporary field of interdisciplinary heritage studies. This field grew out of early academic studies of heritage in the critique of the use of heritage and the 'invention of tradition' by governments to produce a sense of nationalism, and the 'heritage debate' that arose in the mid-1980s in the UK. The chapter tracks various subsequent debates that have influenced the contemporary field of academic heritage studies, including debates in America and Britain on the public understanding of the past; the tradition of heritage interpretation in the USA, which developed in the work of the National Park Service; research on the relationship between tourism and heritage; and questions relating to the politics of representation, which developed separately in cultural studies/sociology, postcolonial studies, anthropology and within the context of the 'new museology', and were subsequently brought together in relation to debates about the ownership of cultural property. Finally, the chapter explores more recent discussions of heritage as a 'discourse' and the ways in which it is caught up in issues of knowledge/power alongside a broader critique of the World Heritage Convention. It is argued that these debates have set the broad parameters of heritage studies as they are understood within the field today.

Heritage, nationalism and the invention of tradition

The earliest academic debates that touched on issues of heritage were not framed as part of an interdisciplinary 'heritage studies', but concerned critical analyses of the use of the past by governments to build a sense of national identity. These debates on the uses of the past emerged separately from within the fields of history and archaeology. In the case of historians, this work was brought to the attention of the discipline by the publication of an edited collection, *The Invention of Tradition*, by Eric Hobsbawn and Terence Ranger (1983), and in particular its provocative and influential introductory essay (Hobsbawm 1983a). Hobsbawm argued that many of the 'traditions' of contemporary nation-states actually had a relatively shallow history, and pointed to the fact that many of these traditions showed an attempt to root a contemporary sense of nationhood in a distant, heroic past. While he suggested that all societies invented traditions, he noted that this process would accelerate under conditions of rapid social and technological change, and that it had done so over the previous 200 years in response to the rise of nation-states and colonialism.

> That comparatively recent historical innovation, the 'nation', with its associated phenomena: nationalism, the nation-state, national symbols, histories and the rest. All these rest on the exercises in social engineering which are often deliberate and always innovative ... because so much of what makes up the modern 'nation' consists of such constructs and is associated with appropriate and, in general, fairly recent symbols or suitably tailored discourse (such as 'national history'), the national phenomenon cannot be adequately investigated without careful attention to the 'invention of tradition'.
>
> *(Hobsbawm 1983a: 13–14).*

Contributors explored the invention of tradition in relation to the Highland tradition of Scotland, the British Monarchy, Victorian India and colonial Africa, amongst other examples; Hobsbawm's own contribution was an exploration of the 'mass-production' of traditions in Europe over the period 1870–1914 (Hobsbawm 1983b). In this essay, he introduced an important distinction between forms of tradition that were manufactured officially by the state, which he termed 'political', and forms of tradition that were unofficially manufactured by communities within society, which he termed 'social'. This distinction roughly maps on to the distinction between 'official' and 'unofficial' heritage introduced earlier in this book.

Research on the ways in which archaeology had been put to political use in nation-building developed separately over the same period (Trigger 1980, 1984, 1985, [1989] 1996), and received broad attention as an issue in the almost 'global' coverage of Phillip Kohl and Clare Fawcett's edited collection *Nationalism, Politics, and the Practice of Archaeology* (1995). This work emerged from an increasing interest within archaeology during the 1980s and 1990s in the social construction of archaeological knowledge, and the social, economic and political contexts in which this knowledge was formed. *Nationalism, Politics, and the Practice of Archaeology* (1995), and the work of others on this topic, drew attention to the many ways in which archaeology and 'the past' had been employed in nation-building and put to political uses, some positive but many negative, and mostly from relatively 'recent' twentieth century contexts, urging caution in examining the political uses to which archaeology was put by contemporary nation-states.

In his classic article on the topic, Bruce Trigger (1984) drew attention to the existence of various forms of archaeology—nationalist, colonialist and imperialist, and their knowledge/power effects. Nationalist archaeologies were the most dominant forms, and placed emphasis on tracing the strong connections between ancient peoples and the modern nation-state. Colonialist archaeologies were dominant in areas settled by Europeans, and sought to denigrate and dislocate Indigenous peoples from contemporary nationhood (see also Byrne 1996). Imperialist archaeologies were found to emphasise expansionist historical traditions and 'global' historical discourses. At the same time as Trigger was developing these ideas, Martin Hall (1984) was pointing to the inherent racism of early archaeological research in southern Africa, and Neil Silberman (1989) was pointing to the way in which archaeology had been employed in nationalist discourses in the Middle East. Meanwhile, these issues came to the fore within the context of the early World Archaeological Congresses, where a number of conference sessions focusing on debates around the politics of archaeology were held and subsequently published (Layton 1989a, 1989b; Gathercole and Lowenthal 1990), which added to a growing literature on the political nature of archaeology and 'the past'. All of this work contributed to the development of a critical attitude towards the relationship between the past and its use in nation-building, and an acknowledgement of the need to question the social and political contexts in which historical knowledge was produced using archaeology and heritage (Hamilakis 2007).

Academic responses to the late-modern expansion of heritage

Within the field of heritage itself, there was less critical, reflective comment on the relationship between the practical work of conservation and the social and political uses of heritage. As a field that was largely technical in its practice, and perceived to be something that was inherently natural or 'correct', publications written by preservation practitioners tended to be more often about 'doing', rather than thinking through the wider implications of that work. An example of this is the discussions that were captured in the International Charter for the Conservation and Restoration of Monuments and Sites (the Venice Charter) (ICOMOS 1964), which were agreed at the Second International Congress of Architects and Technicians of Historic Monuments in Venice in 1964. This essentially amounted to an agreement on technical standards without any critical discussion of the meaning of conservation practices. A critical, reflective commentary on heritage developed comparatively late when compared with the longer tradition of technical publications in the field. Nonetheless, the mid-1980s saw the emergence of a critical academic commentary on heritage within which most authors perceive the roots of contemporary critical heritage studies as an interdisciplinary area of research (Boswell 1999; Smith 2006; Carman and Sørensen 2009: 17; Harrison 2010a). This early critical literature was dominated by the publication of three books—*The Past is a Foreign Country* by David Lowenthal (1985), *On Living in an Old Country* by Patrick Wright ([1985] 2009) and *The Heritage Industry* by Robert Hewison (1987).

Lowenthal's book was an extended meditation on the place of 'the past' in the post-Enlightenment, Western tradition, and drew attention to the gap between the past as presented in heritage in contemporary Britain, Western Europe and North America, and the past as written by historians. Significantly, he pointed to the many economic, social and political motivations that lay behind the preservation of the past, and introduced a significant distinction between heritage and history. As he later pointed out in his follow-up to *The Past is a Foreign Country*—*The Heritage Crusade and the Spoils of History* (1998)—heritage is not history at all: 'it is not an inquiry into the past, but a celebration of it … a profession of faith in a past tailored to present-day purposes' (Lowenthal 1998: x). Lowenthal's apparent ambiguity towards heritage in *The Past is a Foreign Country* established a significant area of research within history that was concerned with exploring and uncovering the 'false consciousness' of heritage, and the gap between heritage as presented and history as lived and experienced. *The Past is a Foreign Country* was to have a significant influence on the work of historians in North America and the UK, as well as in Western Europe.

Debates about heritage in the UK in the 1980s and early 1990s

Wright's *On Living in an Old Country* and Hewison's *The Heritage Industry* differed from *The Past is a Foreign Country* in addressing themselves explicitly to the social, political and economic circumstances of Britain in the 1980s. Wright's book reflected on returning to Britain from Canada and finding the past being used explicitly as a tool for the production of a national identity by the newly elected Conservative government under Prime Minister Margaret Thatcher. It argued that various pieces of heritage legislation could be read as the revival of the patriotism of the Second World War, and connected this explicit 'manufacturing' of patriotism to the events of the Falklands conflict.[1] Like Hewison after him, he was critical of the 'timelessness' of the presentation of the past at various heritage sites, noting that:

> National heritage involves the extraction of history – of the idea of historical significance and potential – from a denigrated everyday life and its restaging or display in certain sanctioned sites, events, images and conceptions. In this process history is redefined as 'the historical', and it becomes the object of a similarly transformed and generalised public attention ... Abstracted and redeployed, history seems to be purged of political tension; it becomes a unifying spectacle ... the settling of all disputes. Like the guided tour as it proceeds from site to sanctioned site, the national past occurs in a dimension of its own – a dimension in which we appear to remember only in order to forget.
>
> *(Wright 1985: 69)*

Hewison's book, published two years later, took an even stronger stance against heritage. He suggested that heritage had developed into an 'industry', both drawing on Adorno and Horkheimer's notions of a 'culture industry' (Horkheimer and Adorno 1972; Adorno 2001) and reflecting on the (then) 'new' craze for the preservation and presentation of industrial heritage that had been growing at a dizzying rate as a result of processes of deindustrialisation and economic decline. *The Heritage Industry* drew attention to what Hewison considered to be the sanitised and commercialised versions of the past that were being produced as heritage in the UK, suggesting that heritage was a structure largely imposed from above to capture a middle-class nostalgia for the past as a golden age in the social, political and economic context of 'decline'.

The Heritage Industry was intentionally provocative, and derived from Hewison's belief that the rise of heritage as a form of popular entertainment distracted people from developing an interest in contemporary art and critical culture, providing them instead with a view of culture that was finished and complete (and firmly in the past). He pointed to the widespread perception of cultural and economic decline that became a feature of Britain's perception of itself as a nation in the decades following the Second World War:

> In the face of apparent decline and disintegration, it is not surprising that the past seems a better place. Yet it is irrecoverable, for we are condemned to live perpetually in the present. What matters is not the past, but our relationship with it. As individuals, our security and identity depend largely on the knowledge we have of our personal and family history; the language and customs which govern our social lives rely for their meaning on a continuity between past and present. Yet at times the pace of change, and its consequences, are so radical that not only is change perceived as decline, but there is the threat of rupture with our past lives.
>
> *(Hewison 1987: 43–5; see also Hewison 1981)*

The context in which both Hewison and Wright were writing was important in shaping their criticism of heritage as a phenomenon. *On Living in an Old Country* and

The Heritage Industry can be read as much as reflections on the changes that occur within a society—as a result of deindustrialisation, globalisation and transnationalism (in particular, the impact of rapid and widespread internal migration and immigration on the sense of 'rootedness' that people could experience in particular places in the UK in the 1980s, and the nostalgia that they saw as a response to this sense of uprootedness)—as criticisms of heritage itself. Hewison noted that the postwar period in the UK coincided with a period of growth in the establishment of museums and in a widespread sense of nostalgia, not for the past as it had been experienced 'in the past', but for a sanitised version of the past that was re-imagined through the heritage industry as a utopia, in opposition to the perceived problems of the contemporary world:

> The impulse to preserve the past is part of the impulse to preserve the self. Without knowing where we have been, it is difficult to know where we are going. The past is the foundation of individual and collective identity, objects from the past are the source of significance as cultural symbols. Continuity between past and present creates a sense of sequence out of aleatory chaos and, since change is inevitable, a stable system of ordered meanings enables us to cope with both innovation and decay. The nostalgic impulse is an important agency in adjustment to crisis, it is a social emollient and reinforces national identity when confidence is weakened or threatened.
>
> *(Hewison 1987: 47)*

This theme of decline was developed further by Wright in his subsequent book *A Journey Through Ruins* (1991). All three books can be read as a response to a series of Conservative government policies to develop heritage and tourism as alternatives to the heavy industries that were in decline in Britain, which were interpreted by both Wright and Hewison as much as cultural phenomena as economic ones (Wright 1985 [2009]: xiv).

On Living in an Old Country and The Heritage Industry became part of a lengthy debate amongst historians in the UK. The British Marxist historian Raphael Samuel noted in *Theatres of Memory* (1994) that the scale of popular interest in the past, and the role of that interest in processes of social transformation, argued against Hewison's and Wright's connection of heritage with Conservative interests. Samuel pointed out that heritage and 'the past' had been successfully lobbied as a catch-cry for a range of political positions and interests, and that heritage had served to make the past more democratic through an emphasis on the lives of 'ordinary' people. He also saw the roots of popular interest in the past as stretching back far earlier than the political era of 'decline' suggested by Hewison and Wright:

> The new version of the national past, notwithstanding the efforts of the National Trust to promote a country-house version of 'Englishness', is inconceivably more democratic than earlier ones, offering more points of access to 'ordinary people', and a wider form of belonging. Indeed, even in the case of the

country house, a new attention is now lavished on life 'below the stairs' (the servants' kitchen) while the owners themselves (or the live-in trustees) are at pains to project themselves as leading private lives – 'ordinary' people in 'family' occupation. Family history societies, practising do-it-yourself scholarship and filling the record offices and the local history library with searchers, have democratized genealogy, treating apprenticeship indentures as a symbolic equivalent of the coat of arms, baptismal certificates as that of title deeds. They encourage people to look down rather than up in reconstituting their roots, 'not to establish links with the noble and great'.

(Samuel 1994: 160)

Samuel was quick not only to emphasise heritage as a potentially democratic phenomenon, but also to see in the social practices surrounding heritage the possibility for promoting social change. An advocate of the potentially transformative power of history, and of the role of heritage in producing diversity and scaffolding multiculturalism in society, Samuel described heritage as a social process:

Conservation is not an event but a process, the start of a cycle of development rather than (or as well as) an attempt to arrest the march of time. The mere fact of preservation, even if it is intended to do no more than stabilize, necessarily involves a whole series of innovations, if only to arrest the 'pleasing decay'. What may begin as a rescue operation, designed to preserve the relics of the past, passes by degree into a work of restoration in which a new environment has to be fabricated in order to turn fragments into a meaningful whole.

(Samuel 1994: 303)

In this way, Samuel anticipated more recent discussions of heritage as a 'process' (Dicks 2000; Harvey 2001; Smith 2006; Byrne 2008; Harrison 2010c). This discussion was linked closely to important debates within the museum sector on issues of representation (Macdonald and Silverstone 1990) discussed below.

Debates about heritage in North America in the 1980s and early 1990s

While this debate framed important academic developments in the UK, due largely to its specificity to a British political context, it had less influence on North American scholars. While there was an important and burgeoning literature in North America within the field of archaeology relating to the political uses of the past, and within the field of history on heritage as 'false consciousness', these debates were not brought together in North America in the same way as in the UK. Much of the North American literature at this time was focused on technical standards for preservation work in heritage, and there was little sustained critical comment about the place of heritage in society. Nonetheless, it is possible to see parallel ideas to those of Samuel in the work of Roy Rosenzweig and David Thelen (1998), who also published an important account of the popular uses of the past in America around this time.

Rosenzweig and Thelen's (1998) book interpreted the results of a national phone survey of over 800 randomly selected Americans and another 645 African Americans, American Indians and Mexican Americans, who were interviewed during the early to mid-1990s. The authors found that almost all Americans had engaged in some form of 'past-related' activity in the previous year (within which they included a range of activities, from looking at photographs with family and friends to participating in a group devoted to studying or learning about the past). More than a third of all participants in the survey were found to have investigated their family history in the previous year, and two-fifths had worked on a hobby or activity associated with the past. Although many felt disconnected from the teaching of history at school, almost all were found to be interested in the past from a personal point of view in terms of how the past touched on their own lives and those of their family and community. Rosenzweig and Thelen noted how most Americans interviewed rejected the nation-centred accounts of formal histories that were taught at school, instead working from the basis of their more intimate pasts to connect with broader national historical themes. They tended to be less interested in academic histories and more interested in the authentic 'experiences' of the past, with which they could engage through museums and other historic sites. The authors also drew attention to the national counternarratives of history that circulated within the communities from which their African American and American Indian respondents were drawn, noting that 'the narrative of the American nation-state—the story often told by professional historians—is most alive for those who feel most alienated from it' (1998: 13). Wherever they looked, they found popular uses of, and engagements with, the past, concluding that popular history-making was thriving in North America in the final years of the past millennium, but that the communities involved in such pursuits felt alienated from academic history-making.

The management of public history at official heritage sites, and the ways in which particular versions of the past were presented to the public, formed the basis of Richard Handler and Eric Gable's important and frequently cited critical study of Colonial Williamsburg, *The New History in an Old Museum* (1997). Their ethnographic research, along with that of other scholars such as Michael Herzfeld (1991, 1997) and Sharon Macdonald (1997a,b, 2002), introduced anthropological methods to the study of heritage and its production and consumption by visitors. At the same time, other researchers were trying to engage with popular understandings of the past in less formal heritage contexts. For example, geographer Delores Hayden's influential book *The Power of Place* (1995) looked at the work undertaken by a non-profit organisation in downtown Los Angeles in documenting and celebrating the urban landscape history of African American, Latina and Asian American communities, and in doing so developed a model for the application of social history to urban planning in the production of public memory. Like Samuel (1994), Hayden raised questions regarding the representation of the working classes and ethnic minority communities through official heritage, and reflected on themes that were emerging from an increasingly professionalised field of 'interpretation' of heritage in North America. These issues of heritage and representation exploded into the public sphere at around this time in debates surrounding plans by the Smithsonian Museum to exhibit the Enola Gay as part of an exhibition commemorating the fiftieth anniversary of the atomic bombing of Hiroshima (Kohn 1995; Hogan 1996; Linenthal and Englehardt 1996; Laird 1998; Mayr 1998; Pretzer 1998; Roland 1998; Newman 2004). These debates were mirrored in what have been termed the 'Australian history wars' (Macintyre and Clark 2004), which centred on debates around the public presentation of Australian history following European settlement, in particular its impact on Indigenous Australians and Torres Strait Islanders, and its presentation within museums, including the new National Museum of Australia which opened in 2001.

Translating the past: heritage and interpretation

There had been a relatively long history in the United States of a professional field of interpretation of heritage sites, particularly archaeological sites, which grew out of the explicit nation-building educational programmes of the US National Park Service

FIGURE 5.1 'Scenes of the national parks and explanation of their scientific and historic wonders are unfolded by a Ranger at an illustrated campfire talk in Badlands NP', 1958. Mission 66 enabled the NPS to recruit more rangers and to expand its interpretive service to develop a coordinated educative infrastructure for the effective communication of national themes about history and the natural environment to US citizens. (Photograph by Jack E. Boucher. Courtesy of Department of Interior, National Park Service Historic Photograph Collection, Harpers Ferry Center.)

FIGURE 5.2 National Park Service Rangers erecting a sign, *c.* 1966. The sign reads 'NOTICE/Dogs and Firearms Prohibited on National Park Service Trails/ Park Boundary 12 miles ahead'. Note holder for interpretive brochures and/or map. (Photographer unknown. Courtesy of Department of Interior, National Park Service Historic Photograph Collection, Harpers Ferry Center.)

(Jameson 2008; West and McKellar 2010). The park ranger or guide assumed the role of an 'interpreter' who could 'translate' the material traces of natural and human history for park visitors. In doing so, this model reflected a modern Cartesian dualism in which 'nature' and 'the past' were perceived to be distant and separate from people in the present, and hence needed 'translation' for ordinary citizens to understand them. With the increasing development of 'visitor-led' tourism, in which the assumption was that tourists would not be guided directly but would 'self-guide' around national parks and heritage sites, a need developed for interpretive materials—signage, visitor centres, museums and other facilities. Many new visitor facilities in national parks were developed as a part of 'Mission 66', a massive decade-long programme of federally funded capital improvements to park visitor facilities, to be completed by the fiftieth anniversary of the US National Park Service in 1966. Mission 66 focused on upgrading roads and other transport connections to and within national parks, and saw a major building programme of visitor centres and accommodation facilities, which would act as an educational link between the national park system and the nation. Mission 66 became famous for introducing modernist architecture into the national park system (Allaback 2000), but it was also a coordinated attempt to develop an educative infrastructure for the more effective communication of the various national themes about history and the natural environment to US citizens.

Freeman Tilden's work on heritage interpretation for the US National Park Service in the years of these Mission 66 developments had a profound influence on

FIGURE 5.3 'History comes alive for young America at the visitor center at Yorktown Battlefield, Virginia', 1958. Interpretive diorama at Colonial NHP. (Photograph by Jack E. Boucher. Courtesy of Department of Interior, National Park Service Historic Photograph Collection, Harpers Ferry Center.)

the professionalisation of this field of heritage work, both in the USA and internationally. In his 1957 book *Interpreting Our Heritage*, he defined six principles of interpretation:

1. Any interpretation that does not somehow relate what is being displayed or described to something within the personality or experience of the visitor will be sterile.
2. Information, as such, is not Interpretation. Interpretation is revelation based upon information. But they are entirely different things. However all interpretation includes information.
3. Interpretation is an art, which combines many arts, whether the materials presented are scientific, historical or architectural. Any art is in some degree teachable.
4. The chief aim of Interpretation is not instruction, but provocation.
5. Interpretation should aim to present a whole rather than a part, and must address itself to the whole man rather than any phase.
6. Interpretation addressed to children (say up to the age of twelve) should not be a dilution of the presentation to adults, but should follow a fundamentally different approach. To be at its best it will require a separate program.

(Tilden 1977: 9)

Tilden's work was to have a lasting impact on the field of interpretation, which developed into an important educational apparatus that was inserted between the visitor and the heritage site (and helped identify and delineate the 'heritage site', which might otherwise be viewed as simply an ordinary place). This interpretive infrastructure manifested itself in a whole range of materials—perhaps most obviously in the form of interpretive signage at heritage sites, but also in guide books, films, audio recordings and other intermediaries intended to make the heritage site legible. Tilden's work also anticipated the increasingly active role of the visitor, and the emphasis on 'experience' that would develop over the coming decades (see Chapter 4). The heritage visitor could not be assumed to be a blank spectator, but the interpreter would have to assume that they would bring something of themselves to the experience.

Destination culture: heritage and tourism studies

The issue of various publics and their agencies in the co-creation of heritage was central to John Urry's (1990) criticisms of Hewison's *The Heritage Industry*, providing a useful corrective to the way in which Lowenthal, Wright and Hewison had criticised heritage as 'false' history. Focusing on museums, he suggested that tourists are socially differentiated, so an argument that they are lulled into blind consumption by the 'heritage industry' could not hold true. Urry drew an analogy with Michel Foucault's concept of 'the gaze' to develop the idea of a 'tourist gaze'. The tourist gaze is a way of perceiving or relating to places that cuts them off from the 'real world' and emphasises the exotic aspects of the tourist experience. It is directed by collections of symbols and signs to fall on places that have previously been imagined as pleasurable by the media surrounding the tourist industry. Photographs, films, books and magazines allow the images of tourism and leisure to be constantly produced and reproduced. The history of the development of the tourist gaze shows that it formed under specific historical circumstances, in particular the exponential growth of personal travel in the second part of the twentieth century.

Urry was interested in explaining the power of the consumer in helping 'create' heritage sites and museum. He suggested that the consumer has a major role in selecting what 'works' and what does not in heritage. It is not possible to set up a museum just anywhere – consumers are interested in authenticity and in other things that dictate their choices, and they are not blindly led by a top-down 'creation' of heritage by the state:

> Hewison ignores the enormously important popular bases of the conservation movement. For example, like Patrick Wright he sees the National Trust as one gigantic system of outdoor relief for the old upper classes to maintain their stately homes. But this is to ignore the widespread support for such conservation. Indeed Samuel points out that the National Trust with nearly 1.5 million members is the largest mass organisation in Britain ... moreover, much of the early conservation movement was plebeian in character – for example railway preservation, industrial archaeology, steam traction rallies and the like in the

1960s, well before the more obvious indicators of economic decline materialised in Britain.

(Urry 1990: 110)

The outcome of Urry's discussion of heritage was to shift the balance of the critique away from whether or not heritage was 'good' history to the realisation that heritage was, to a large extent, co-created by its consumers. Similarly, Dicks (2000) argued that heritage existed as a form of shared communication between museum and visitor. Heritage began to be framed within the context of consumer studies, and it became an area of recognised research within the burgeoning field of tourism studies (Rojek 1993; Rojek and Urry 1997; Timothy and Boyd 2003; Smith and Robinson 2006). Geographers and sociologists began to explore heritage within the context of new urban spaces of consumption and a new entrepreneurial model of cityscapes (Hetherington 1997, 2007; Ladd 1997; Miles 1997; Till 2005; Cronin and Hetherington 2008).

Barbara Kirshenblatt-Gimblett's *Destination Culture* (1998) and Bella Dicks' *Culture on Display* (2003, see also 2000) have been particularly important in bringing tourism and heritage studies more closely into conversation with one another, whilst simultaneously making reference to a robust literature on cultures of exhibition and display, which had developed separately within museum studies (Macdonald and Silverstone 1990; Karp and Lavine 1991; Bennett 1995; Macdonald 1997; see further discussion below). Both books were concerned with the processes by which museums and heritage sites created themselves as tourist destinations. Kirshenblatt-Gimblett argued that tourism stages the world as a kind of museum to create destinations out of what would otherwise simply be considered 'places'. Dicks termed this process the production of 'visitability', and saw it at work in a wide variety of settings in which 'place-identity' was produced, and culture was increasingly staged and exhibited for consumption. Kirshenblatt-Gimblett suggested that this process was a new mode of cultural production intended to give a second life to objects, places and practices that were no longer profitable due to the late-modern reorganisation of global economies.

Heritage, exhibitionary complexes and the politics of representation

I have mentioned above that one of the dominant themes of contemporary heritage studies concerns the politics of representation, by which I mean the issues raised by the production of meaning by way of the various images, texts, objects and practices that surround heritage and museums. These concerns grew in parallel in a number of different academic areas that have only recently come into conversation with one another within an interdisciplinary context of critical heritage studies. A concern with cultural representations in popular culture and the media was central to the development of the academic field of 'cultural studies' that emerged in Britain in the 1960s and 1970s, associated with the work of scholars such as Raymond Williams (1958) and Stuart Hall (1997). Hall, in particular, turned his attention to heritage and museums in a British postcolonial context, arguing the need for more inclusive modes of representation of British nationhood:

> the majority, mainstream versions of the Heritage should revise their own self-conceptions and rewrite the margins into the centre, the outside into the inside. This is not so much a matter of representing 'us' as of representing more adequately the degree to which 'their' history entails and has always implicated 'us', across the centuries, and vice versa. The African presence in Britain since the sixteenth century, the Asian since the seventeenth and the Chinese, Jewish and Irish in the nineteenth have long required to be made the subjects of their own dedicated heritage spaces as well as integrated into a much more 'global' version of 'our island story'. Across the great cities and ports, in the making of fortunes, in the construction of great houses and estates, across the lineages of families, across the plunder and display of the wealth of the world as an adjunct to the imperial enterprise, across the hidden histories of statued heroes, in the secrecy of private diaries, even at the centre of the great master-narratives of 'Englishness' like the Two World Wars, falls the unscripted shadow of the forgotten 'Other'.
>
> *(Hall [1999] 2008: 225)*

The widespread engagement of academics across various disciplines with postcolonial literatures which drew attention to issues regarding the representation of a colonial 'Other' in the wake of Edward Said's *Orientalism* (1978) began to have a serious impact on the work of museums during the 1980s, at the same time as a burgeoning literature within anthropology that took a critical look at the role of museums in the production of images and texts, which had important implications for the construction of Indigenous cultures in colonial contexts (Clifford and Marcus 1986; Clifford 1988, 1995, 1997; Greenfield [1989] 1996; Karp and Levine 1991; O'Hanlon 1993; Coombes 1994; Bennett 1995, 2004; Simpson 1996; Lidchi 1997; Barringer and Flynn 1998; Russell 2001). This literature was itself largely stimulated by an Indigenous critique of the role of anthropological and archaeological forms of expertise and knowledge production in processes of colonial governance, and the role of anthropological forms of knowledge in subjectification of Indigenous people (Deloria 1969; Tuhiwai Smith 1999; Nakata 2007). These debates received sustained scholarly attention in a North American context at the Poetics and Politics of Representation conference held at the Smithsonian Institution in 1988, the papers from which were subsequently published as *Exhibiting Cultures* (Karp and Levine 1991). James Clifford's widely known book *The Predicament of Culture* (1988; see also Clifford and Marcus 1986) and his subsequent work (e.g. 1997) also drew attention to the ways in which ethnographic knowledge was produced within museums, highlighting the processes by which museum displays were loaded with meaning and represented a form of 'contact zone'.

This work on the forms of representation associated with public museums, and the politics and knowledge/power effects they generate, found sophisticated exposition in sociologist Tony Bennett's *The Birth of the Museum* (1995), which drew on Foucauldian and Gramscian perspectives to show how museums should be understood as reformatory institutions that were engaged in programmes of governance aimed at regulating forms of behaviour and conduct. In doing so, he extended Pierre Bourdieu's (1984) discussion of the art gallery as a space for the performance of 'distinction' by elites. Bennett argued that the museum developed as a space of representation constituted by an 'exhibitionary complex' shaped by a series of historical sciences, which was ultimately concerned with making the population governable. Importantly, the museum was open to all individuals and social classes as a way of exposing the whole population to the 'civilizing rituals' (after Duncan 1995) associated with its new modes of exhibition of the 'order of things'. Based on evolutionary schema, Bennett argued that the modes of classification and ordering within the museum would act as a mirror for the state's production of a civilised social order.

Meanwhile, questions relating to the modes of exhibition within museums and galleries received attention from art historians, artists and archaeologists in relation to debates around what Vergo (1989) termed 'the new museology' (O'Doherty 1972; Horne 1984; Merriman 1991; Walsh 1992; Pearce 1994, 1995; Greenberg et al. 1996). These debates centred primarily on the relationship between curators of 'high culture' art galleries and museums and their relationship with their audiences. On the one side were those who felt that the museum's role was being eroded by its increasing consumption as 'entertainment'; on the other side were those who felt the museum should cater to broader (less 'elite') audiences by introducing new modes of exhibition, and address itself to alternative themes, allowing space for visitors to bring their own perspective to their visit. Curators had long understood their role as experts in determining the tasteful and 'correct' composition of objects collected and displayed within galleries and museums, but debates regarding the relativity of aesthetic value began to undermine the sense of a single 'canon' of artistic works or museum objects that could be determined by any individual, and the 'expertise' of the curator (Wright 1989; Macdonald and Silverstone 1990; see discussion in Benton and Watson 2010). The debates themselves were ultimately overtaken by the increasingly important economic role played by heritage and the desire to boost visitor numbers by creating for museums and galleries an increasingly broad target market, spawning a large literature on education and its role in the museum (Hooper-Greenhill 1992, 1994a, 1994b, 1995, 1997, 2007; Hein 1998; Falk and Dierking 2000; Black 2005).

A recognition that the ownership of heritage confers not only rights to control access to (and income generated by) cultural objects, but also the power to control the production of knowledge about the past, lay behind a series of increasingly vocal calls for the return or 'repatriation' of cultural objects and human skeletal materials to Indigenous people and other source communities and states over the last few decades of the twentieth century (Greenfield [1989] 1996; Layton 1989a, 1989b; Mihesuah 1995; Fforde et al. 2002; Kramer 2006). These calls were matched by equally vocal opponents of repatriation, who supported the idea that the 'universal' rights of access by the majority and/or the rights of academics to study those objects override those of source communities (Appiah 2007; Cuno 2008). Museums, and the curators, archaeologists and anthropologists who worked on Indigenous material culture, were at the centre of these debates. Perhaps most significant in this regard were the implications of the US Native American Graves Protection and Repatriation Act (NAGPRA) of 1990. The Act established a process for federally recognised Native American groups to apply for the return of affiliated human remains from federally funded museums, and for the return of remains found on federal lands (see discussion in Smith 2004); the wide-ranging implications of these and similar debates for the ethical practice of archaeology continue to be discussed (Scarre and Scarre 2006; Meskell 2009b). These debates ultimately drew on a notion of heritage as a 'cultural property' (Carman 2005), which derived from UNESCO's 1970 Convention on the Means of Prohibiting and Preventing the Illicit Import, Export and Transfer of Ownership of Cultural Property, and the subsequent discussion of 'cultural property' in the World Heritage Convention. Ethical debates went on to highlight a contradiction between the aspirations of the 1972 Convention to represent the universal values of heritage on the one hand, and UNESCO's support of the principle of the return of cultural property on the other (for example, through the work of the Intergovernmental Committee for Promoting the Return of Cultural Property to its Countries of Origin or its Restitution in case of Illicit Appropriation, established in 1978 at the 20th Session of the UNESCO General Conference). Questions of who 'owns' the past, and hence the right to control its representation, thus became central to the emergence of an academic interdisciplinary field of heritage studies.

Universal values, authorising heritage discourses and heritage studies' discursive turn

The other major series of questions that have driven the development of an inter-disciplinary field of academic heritage studies have come in the form of various critiques of the World Heritage Convention. These have coalesced around the notion of 'universal' value, and the global application of the Convention and its principles in relation to three main areas: the Convention's definition of heritage; the practices it suggests should be followed in managing such heritage appropriately; and the 'idea' of universal heritage value itself. Denis Byrne (1991, 1995, 2009) has noted that appealing to the universal or transcendent category of heritage is a means by which local stake-holders and communities with a particular interest in heritage places can be excluded from having a role in making decisions about managing them (see also Evans 2002; chapters in Harrison and Hitchcock 2005). Byrne drew on case studies from Australia, China and Thailand to suggest that notions of universal heritage value have been employed to operationalise Western notions of heritage management in the non-Western world, showing how these can conflict with local practices and living cultural traditions in such countries. Similar questions regarding the conflicts between local and universal values have been explored more recently in relation to concepts of cosmopolitanism and the ethics of heritage (see chapters in Meskell 2009a). Henry Cleere (2001: 22) sug-gested that the idea of a World Heritage List composed of a set of places that have universal value is inconsistent with the global spread of World Heritage sites, which is overwhelmingly biased towards countries with monumental architectural traditions

(Europe, Latin America, certain Asian countries) to the detriment of sites from countries whose cultures were primarily non-monumental (Oceania and sub-Saharan Africa, for example), a critique that UNESCO itself would apply in its own *Global Strategy for a Balanced, Representative and Credible World Heritage List* (UNESCO 1994; see also chapters in Labadi and Long 2010; Chapter 7 in this volume). This critique of the geographical coverage of the List has been matched with one that considers the representativeness of the List in terms of its themes, suggesting that the List emphasises the heritage of elites and excludes the heritage of minorities (Graham et al. 2000; Ashworth et al. 2007).

Laurajane Smith, who has perhaps made the most important recent contribution to the development of an interdisciplinary field of critical heritage studies through various publications and her work as editor of the *International Journal of Heritage Studies*, sees the principle of universality as part of the World Heritage Convention's Authorizing Heritage Discourse (AHD), which defines heritage in narrow and specific ways, through the lens of a Western European tradition of heritage:

> Part of the authority of the European AHD ... lies in its own legitimizing assumptions that it is universally applicable and that there is, or must be, universal cultural values and expressions. The whole discourse of universality is itself a legitimizing strategy for the values and nature of heritage that underline the AHD. The discourse of universality makes a moral plea to a sense of 'brotherhood' of 'mankind' ... this sort of appeal ... add[s] to its persuasive power.
>
> *(Smith 2006: 99)*

Smith's argument is that there is a dominant Western discourse or set of ideas about heritage, which she refers to as an authorised (or authorising) heritage discourse, or AHD. The AHD is integrally bound up in the creation of lists that represent the canon of heritage. It is a set of ideas that works to normalise a range of assumptions about the nature and meaning of heritage and to privilege particular practices, especially those of heritage professionals and the state. Conversely, the AHD can also be seen to exclude a whole range of popular ideas and practices relating to heritage. Smith draws on case studies from the UK, Australia and the USA to illustrate her arguments.

Smith suggests that the official representation of heritage has a variety of characteristics that serve to exclude the general public from having a role in heritage, and its bureaucratisation and professionalisation (see Chapter 3) has produced an industry in which heritage is perceived as something with which laypersons can engage only passively. While they may view heritage at historic houses or in museums, decisions about what constitutes heritage (and, perhaps equally importantly, what does not) are made by 'experts', and the representations that are produced from their select canon of heritage are thus exclusive of minorities, the working classes and subaltern groups. She sees the official discourse of heritage as focused on aesthetically pleasing or monumental things, and therefore largely on material objects and places, rather than on practices or the intangible attachments between people and things. She suggests that the documents and charters that govern heritage designate particular professionals as experts and hence as the legitimate spokespeople for the past; they act as 'interpreters' for heritage (see Chapter 4), and tend to promote the experiences and values of elite social classes, and the idea that heritage is 'bounded' and contained within objects and sites that are able to be delineated so that they can be managed.

Smith (2004) had previously drawn on Foucault's discussion of discourses as institutionalised ways of thinking, which describe forms of communication that require specialised knowledge, to explore the ways in which archaeological heritage management functions as a technology of government. In *Uses of Heritage* (2006) she draws on critical discourse analysis to chart the connection between power and the language of heritage more generally, showing how the discourses of heritage both reflect and go towards creating a particular set of socio-political practices. She suggests we can use the structure and messages embodied in the language surrounding heritage to understand the dominant discourse of heritage 'and the way it both reflects and constitutes a range of social practices – not least the way it organises social relations and identities around nation, class, culture and ethnicity' (2006: 16). It is this dominant discourse that she terms the AHD. Smith's work has been very important in drawing attention to the knowledge/power effects of heritage, and the concrete ways in which power is caught up and exercised through the exhibition and management of museums and heritage sites, an area of concern that has become central to the emerging interdisciplinary field of critical heritage studies. Smith (2006) and others (Harvey 2001; Dicks 2003) have criticised UNESCO's definition of heritage as residing in monumental, tangible 'things', suggesting that heritage should be understood as a process or series of discursive practices (see also Dicks 2000).

Beyond the discourse of heritage

While acknowledging its key role in producing a field of critical heritage studies, one criticism that could be levelled at this focus on the discourse of heritage is that it does not always produce an account that adequately theorises the role of material 'things'. I would suggest that the combined effect of a tendency within heritage studies more broadly to focus on issues of the politics of representation; an increasing emphasis on 'intangible' heritage in a reaction against UNESCO's early emphasis on the monumental and tangible; the marketing of heritage as 'experience'; the increased use of virtual media in the exhibition and interpretation heritage (Parry 2007); and the recognition that heritage often acts discursively as a governmental apparatus, has meant that heritage studies scholars have increasingly appeared to ignore the affective qualities of heritage. While Smith's advocacy of critical discourse analysis (2006; see also Waterton et al. 2006)—a development of discourse studies that explicitly attempts to move beyond the reduction of discourse to 'text'—cautions against such an approach, nonetheless it seems important to bring the affective qualities of heritage 'things' more squarely back into the critical heritage studies arena. Such an approach should not be viewed as inconsistent with a consideration of the discourse of heritage and its knowledge/power effects; indeed, I have already discussed Law's (2004) characterisation of ANT as a 'material semiotic' method. My intention is to consider how we might combine a critical approach to the discourses of heritage with a more thorough consideration of its material affects.

I have already implied that I see the material aspects of heritage, and the various physical relationships that are part of our 'being in the world', as integral to understanding our relationships with the objects, places and practices of heritage. Even in the case of 'intangible' heritage, the expressions and traditions that have been emphasised by World Heritage listing are practices that involve bodies, objects and landscapes in fundamental ways. So, while I see the discursive turn in heritage studies as very important, in the chapters that follow I want to explore not only the ways in which heritage operates as a discursive practice, but also its corporeal influences on the bodies of human and non-human actors, and the ways in which heritage is caught up in the quotidian bodily practices of dwelling, travelling, working and 'being' in the world. While heritage is not simply a collection of 'things', but instead constitutes the social 'work' that individuals and societies undertake to produce the past in the present, this process is not one that occurs only in the minds of humans, or one that functions solely in a discursive manner, but involves a range of material beings who co-produce heritage as a result of their own affordances or material capabilities. I explore the implications of more relational, dialogical models of heritage in Chapter 9.

Conclusion

This chapter has charted the development of an interdisciplinary academic field of critical heritage studies, which grew out of early critiques of the use of the past in nation-building, and subsequently developed into a field concerned with questions arising from the politics of representation and the idea of heritage as a series of discursive practices. While these issues are important, I have suggested that heritage studies has not adequately theorised the material affect of 'things', and that it needs to consider more comprehensively the interconnectedness of people, things and their environments in relation to heritage. In the chapters that follow, I explore a series of interlinked concepts. These include the *abundance* of heritage in the contemporary world, and its production as a result of a late-modern sense of *uncertainty* and risk. I draw on notions of *materiality* and *connectivity* to suggest that attempts to apply the World Heritage Convention globally have led to a series of crises that have had a major influence on the practice of heritage over the past few decades, and have fundamentally altered the ways in which heritage is defined, managed and understood in the contemporary world. These crises form the basis for the following four chapters, and in aggregate suggest the need for the development of a broader critical agenda for heritage studies in the future. My concluding chapter begins to outline this new agenda for heritage and its study in the twenty-first century, based on a *dialogical* model of heritage and a more democratic approach to heritage decision-making processes.

6

INTANGIBLE HERITAGE AND CULTURAL LANDSCAPES

Introduction

In previous chapters I have outlined the emergence of a late-modern understanding of heritage as a set of state-led practices concerned with the preservation of historic objects, places and practices (official heritage) as well as a broad set of public attitudes towards the past (unofficial heritage). This late-modern 'phase' of heritage was the third in what I identified as a series of historical phases. The first developed over the course of the eighteenth and nineteenth centuries in Western Europe, the UK and North America, and was dominated by private individuals and the demonstration of individual or familial philanthropy. It is associated with the emergence of the notion of the public sphere and a response to processes of industrialisation, in which objects from the past could be preserved for the future by being held in trust for public edification and benefit. In the second phase, throughout the late nineteenth and twentieth centuries, heritage became increasingly controlled and defined by the state, and the practice of conservation and preservation became progressively more professionalised and driven by issues of compliance. This period also saw nation-states invest heavily in heritage as part of the project of nation-building.

The third phase of heritage saw the emergence of 'world' heritage organisations and the idea of 'universal' heritage values. Models of heritage that had been developed in a Euro-American milieu began to be applied in very different cultural contexts, and this led to conflicts over the definition and ownership of heritage. A process of economic restructuring began in which heritage and other forms of culture 'on display' (after Dicks 2003) came to replace former manufacturing industries, and World Heritage came to define a global public sphere and a global cultural commons in which value was added to cultural 'assets' that would not otherwise be income-generating, and that were at risk of disappearing (Kirshenblatt-Gimblett 2006). At the same time, widespread changes in late-modern societies saw an intensification of public interest in the past, and various debates about the ownership of heritage and its functions in contemporary society. The emergence of academic heritage studies within the context of these debates was examined in Chapter 5.

However, even while this academic critique of heritage was emerging in the 1980s and over the intervening decades, the practice of official heritage was transforming in significant ways. In this and the following three chapters, I outline a series of conceptual 'crises' that arose as a result of the globalisation of the World Heritage Convention, and the subsequent modification and diversification of the concept of 'World Heritage' as a result of attempts to resolve these dilemmas over the later part of the twentieth and early twenty-first centuries. This period has seen the concept of heritage broaden to accommodate an increasingly large number of objects, places and, perhaps most importantly, practices, and the landscapes in which these occur. It has also seen heritage increasingly shift away from a concern with 'things' to a concern with cultures, traditions and the 'intangible'. Through the emphasis on the 'cultural spaces' of intangible heritage, the 2003 UNESCO Convention for the Safeguarding of the Intangible Cultural Heritage extended the commodification of heritage as 'visitable' spectacle, which had been initiated through the World Heritage List and its involvement in the reconfiguration of global tourism, to the spaces in which intangible heritage was performed. While this broadening agenda has been driven partially by economic interests and the need to appeal to increasingly diverse audiences (see Chapter 4), this has paralleled a movement in academic heritage studies away from a concern with the materiality of heritage to a concern with heritage as a discourse and a system of values. This broadening agenda emerged within the context of a multicultural and postcolonial critique in which heritage was seen to represent a limited number of interests, and new 'representative' models of heritage came to replace older notions of a single definitive 'canon' of heritage. It has also been a period in which almost anything could be defined as heritage, the implications in terms of the abundance of which are discussed further in Chapter 8.

In this chapter, I argue that these major transformations were driven by the World Heritage Convention's self-definition as a 'universal' principle—that these crises, many of which forced UNESCO and its States Parties to adopt broader and more inclusive definitions of heritage, were (perhaps counterintuitively) actually a result of UNESCO's own hegemony. In attempting to apply a model of heritage that had developed in Euro-American contexts during the nineteenth and twentieth centuries globally, to countries with radically different conceptions of heritage, the foundations and assumptions on which the Convention and its particular model of heritage rested would be challenged and ultimately transformed. These challenges and shifts in the definition of heritage and the practices associated with its preservation and management have had profound effects on the way in which heritage is defined, classified, managed and experienced in the contemporary world.

World Heritage and universal values

In Chapter 5, we saw that one of the major academic criticisms of the 1972 World Heritage Convention related to its claims to the 'universality' of the values it represented. This idea has been strongly criticised by Byrne (1991), Smith (2006) and others (e.g. Cleere 2001). However, I want to argue here that it was this very claim to universality that allowed the possibility for the Indigenous, minority, postcolonial and non-Western critique, that has ultimately been responsible for the transformations in heritage practice that have come about in the later twentieth and early twenty-first centuries. By expressing itself as a universal convention relating to the world's heritage, the World Heritage Convention is explicitly forced to confront the issue of *representation* whenever claims that run counter to its definition of heritage are made.

In Chapter 2, I argued that classification and categorisation are fundamental to the production of the experience of modernity, and that classificatory systems are not only necessary technologies for the management of risk, but are also universal, totalising systems that allow objects, people, plants, animals and other 'things' to be ordered in such a way that a series of familiar modern, Cartesian dualisms are produced. These dualisms represent apparently opposed pairings—objects and people, nature and culture, science and the arts, plants and animals, matter and mind. Mary Douglas (1966) has argued that because classificatory systems are supposed to function as universal systems, anomalies within classificatory systems are treated with distrust and are seen to represent potential sources of social disorder and threat. While one way of dealing with such anomalies is to sanitise them by ignoring them as 'myths', a more common response is to build more elaborate systems of classification that can take account of the anomalies. If the Convention had not been expressed as a set of universal values, there would have been no need for those who work with the Convention to consider any counter-claims or appeals to representation. But because of its claims to universality, the World Heritage Convention (and the model of official heritage it perpetuates) has consistently found itself subject to questioning and appeal, and the World Heritage Committee has constantly sought to redefine its definition of heritage since it was adopted in 1972. This process has had a profound effect on global practices of heritage management over the intervening decades, and on contemporary definitions of heritage.

It is important to distinguish two subtly different ways in which the Convention expresses its universality. You will recall that the Convention text defines World Heritage as having 'universal' value to all humans; hence its protection becomes the responsibility of the international community. But the principle of a 'World' Heritage List also implies that the Convention should be globally relevant and hence universally applicable. These two ideas contained within the Convention text mean that it expresses itself as a *totalising* discourse representing a *global* hierarchy of value (cf. Herzfeld 2004).

In making this argument, I draw on Tony Bennett's discussion of the history of the museum as an institution. He points to the contradiction inherent in the museum's claim to universality (based in turn on Paul Greenhalgh's [1988] discussion of the representation of women in the world fairs), and the ways in which this claim to be broadly representative of all human cultures meant that it could not ignore the demands of Indigenous minorities and marginalised social groups to receive equal representation with dominant cultures in museums.

It was ... only the museum's embodiment of a principle of general human universality that lent potential significance to the exclusion or marginalisation of women and women's culture, thereby opening this up as a politicizable question. The same, of course, is true of the range of demands placed on museums on behalf of other political constituencies as the space of the museum has been subject to the constant process of politicization in being called on both to expand the range of its representational concerns (to include artefacts relating to the ways of life of marginalized social groups, for example) and/or to exhibit familiar materials in new contexts to allow them to represent the values of the groups to which they relate rather than the dominant culture (... for example, Aboriginal criticisms of the evolutionary assumptions governing the display of Aboriginal remains and artefacts in natural history museums).

(Bennett 2005: 103)

If we replace the word 'museum' with 'World Heritage' in the quotation above, we are presented with a powerful rationale that helps explain why UNESCO has been constantly forced to revise and broaden the model of heritage with which it began in 1972. What I am suggesting is that it was only because the World Heritage Convention was expressed as a universal convention representing universal heritage values that the criticisms of minorities and marginalised peoples, and the question of representativeness itself, became a problem which it was important for the World Heritage Committee to address. Indeed, as a 'universal' document, the Convention text itself contained the roots of its own transformation over the coming decades. The engagement of UNESCO with the politics of representation in heritage has had far-reaching consequences, and has fundamentally shifted the official practices of heritage in the late twentieth century. This point is essential to understanding the ways in which heritage developed in the decades after 1972, and has had a profound influence on heritage practice throughout the world by (at least partially) shifting the focus away from practical issues of conservation to those of identity politics and representation.

As I show in Chapter 5, the principle of 'universal' heritage values embodied in the World Heritage Convention has previously been the subject of much discussion within the newly emerging field of interdisciplinary critical heritage studies. Smith (2006: 99) sees the principle of universality as part of the World Heritage Convention's authorizing heritage discourse (AHD), which both lists and defines heritage in narrow and specific ways, through the lens of a Western European tradition of heritage. She goes on to explain how this leads to the promotion of a particular, narrow set of Western assumptions about the nature of heritage:

The work the World Heritage Convention effectively ... does is to not only recreate heritage as universally significant, and in doing so authorize and legitimize the Western AHD within an international context, but also create a culture and discursive climate in which certain values and ideologies become dominant in defining cultural development and change.

(Smith 2006: 99–100)

Nonetheless, the expression of the World Heritage Convention and subsequent UNESCO conventions relating to heritage as 'universal' and 'global' instruments has not had the effect of closing off the definitions of heritage employed by UNESCO; on the contrary, it has opened up the question of heritage to debate and discussion. While I agree with these criticisms of the modernist, universalising underpinnings of the World Heritage Convention text, when we explore the ways in which it has been applied practically over the decades since 1972, what emerges is a model of heritage that is subject to constant criticism and that has been forced to adapt continually to incorporate a broader range of values around heritage. In this chapter, I explore this process in operation, in relation to the Indigenous critique of the separation of nature and culture and its influence on the development of the cultural landscape concept, and the ways in which alternative models of heritage were incorporated into UNESCO's definition of 'intangible heritage' and ultimately led to the development of the 2003 Convention for the Safeguarding of the Intangible Cultural Heritage. In Chapter 7, I explore the implications of this process of questioning the universal application of the Convention in relation to the issue of cultural diversity and the management of the nation-building programme of heritage in a globalised world.

Cultural landscapes, *Tjukurpa* and the Uluṟu-Kata Tjuṯa National Park World Heritage Site

The Uluṟu-Kata Tjuṯa National Park World Heritage Site is located in what has somewhat poetically been termed the 'dead heart' of Australia. It covers an area of approximately 1,400 square kilometres, and is located approximately 450 kilometres south-west of the regional centre of Alice Springs[1] in the Northern Territory. It is named for two important physical features, Uluṟu and Kata Tjuṯa, which represent physical manifestations of the actions of heroic creator beings/ancestors of contemporary Aṉangu people and nodes in a regional network of places which were formed by *Tjukurpa*, sometimes translated into English using the term 'Dreaming', but which represents a coherent landscape-centred ontology for Aṉangu people (Layton 1986), and a holistic philosophy that now forms the basis for park management (Australian Government 2010; Figures 6.1–6.2). In addition to describing the creation of the landscape, the concept *Tjukurpa* also refers to the rules that dictate the relationships between humans, animals, plants and the environment, the relationship between past and present, and the methods for the maintenance of these interrelationships in the future. Uluṟu is an immense sandstone monolith, which was given the European name 'Ayers Rock' by the explorer William Henry Gosse in 1872, after Sir Henry Ayers, then Chief Secretary of South Australia. It is also perhaps the most immediately recognisable natural symbol of Australia (Australian Government 2010: 2), and has featured prominently in national self-representations and materials produced by the federal government to entice international tourists since the 1970s. Kata Tjuṯa is a series of large sandstone boulders located approximately 32 kilometres to the west of Uluṟu that rise prominently above the flat surrounding

FIGURE 6.1 Uluṟu and Kata Tjuṯa at sunrise, Uluṟu-Kata Tjuṯa National Park. (© Parks Australia.)

FIGURE 6.2 Kata Tjuṯa at dawn, Uluṟu-Kata Tjuṯa National Park. (Photograph by Michael Nelson, © Michael Nelson/Parks Australia.)

area, which were named 'Mount Olga' in the same year by explorer William Ernest Powell Giles. This part of Australia was settled sparsely and relatively late by Europeans, and Aboriginal people maintained close connections with the area throughout the twentieth century, camping and hunting and gathering food throughout the area, which would subsequently be gazetted as a national park. In 1920, the Petermann Aboriginal Reserve was gazetted for the use of Aboriginal people in the area. In 1940 the Reserve was reduced in size to allow access for gold mining. Some Anangu people found work in the cattle- and sheep-ranching industries, but after 1964, following the revocation of large numbers of pastoral leases in the area, many of the people who had previously been employed in this industry returned to live more permanently in the area (Commonwealth of Australia 2010).

Tourism to Uluru began in the 1940s and grew rapidly in the late 1950s and 1960s with the increased availability of 4WD vehicles and the opening up of inland road routes to tourist buses. Conflicts inevitably occurred between traditional Aboriginal land-use practices and tourism. In 1958, what would become the World Heritage Area was excised from the Petermann Aboriginal Reserve as the 'Ayers Rock-Mount Olga National Park' and put under the management of the Northern Territory Reserves Board. While Anangu people continued to return to and use the Park over this period, they sometimes found themselves excluded from the Park by the Native Welfare Officers (Commonwealth of Australia 2010). During this period, Anangu people, like other nomadic Pitjantjatjara and Yankunytjatjara people in central Australia, were increasingly encouraged to remain on Aboriginal settlements, and found it progressively more difficult to maintain a nomadic lifestyle. Nonetheless, the Park remained an important part of the spiritual and economic life of Anangu people throughout the twentieth century.

Changes to government policies relating to the treatment of Aboriginal people in the 1970s saw Anangu people being encouraged once again to use the Park and to become more economically self-sufficient. In 1972, Anangu people established the Ininti Store within the Park (Commonwealth of Australia 2010). This offered goods and services to tourists, and became the focus for the development of a permanent Anangu settlement at Uluru. In the 1970s, plans were developed to remove the entire tourist infrastructure from the Park, and to build a new tourist village and airport at Yulara, outside the Park. In 1977 the 'Uluru (Ayers Rock-Mount Olga) National Park' became the first area to be declared as a national park under the new Commonwealth National Parks and Wildlife Conservation Act 1975, to be managed by the Commonwealth Director of National Parks. While official management passed to the Commonwealth, practical management of the Park remained a function of the Northern Territory's Park Service.

A major development for Anangu people occurred in the 1980s. In gazetting the Park under the Commonwealth National Parks and Wildlife Act 1975, the land had been alienated from the Aboriginal Land Rights (Northern Territory) Act 1976, a new piece of legislation which was the first Australian act to legally recognise Aboriginal rights to land based on traditional customary law. In the late 1970s and early 1980s, Anangu traditional owners and the newly formed Pitjantjatjara Council and Central Aboriginal Land Council lobbied Prime Minister Malcolm Fraser and Aboriginal Affairs Minister Fred Chaney to amend the Aboriginal Land Rights Act to allow them to lodge an Aboriginal land claim over the National Park (Australian Government 2005). A period of wrangling between the Commonwealth and Northern Territory Government ensued, in which the Northern Territory Government tried to have title transferred from the Commonwealth to the Territory, with an offer of reduced title to Anangu traditional owners. In 1983, newly elected Labour Prime Minister Bob Hawke announced an amendment to the Aboriginal Land Rights Act to allow for the return of the title for Uluru (Ayers Rock-Mount Olga) National Park to Anangu traditional owners. Under this arrangement, it was agreed that the land would be leased back to the Australian Parks and Wildlife Service and run under a system of joint management, an arrangement that had previously been put in place at Kakadu National Park (also in the Northern Territory of Australia). The Park would be managed at a day-to-day level by the Australian Parks and Wildlife Service, but would be overseen by a Board of Management, which would comprise a majority of Anangu members. Under the terms of the ninety-nine-year lease, Anangu people receive an annual rent and share of the Park's revenues (Figure 6.3).

Sir Ninian Stephen, Mr Holding and Mr Cohen (extreme right) with traditional owners, Mr Peter Bulla, Mr Peter Kanari, Mr Nipper Winmarti and his wife, Barbara Tjirkadu, with the special poster marking the handback of title.

FIGURE 6.3 Uluru (Ayers Rock-Mount Olga) National Park Handover/Leaseback Ceremony, Uluru-Kata Tjuta National Park (NT), 1985. Sir Ninian Stephen, Mr. Holding and Mr. Cohen (extreme right) with traditional owners, Mr. Peter Bulla, Mr. Peter Kanari, Mr. Nipper Winmarti and his wife, Barbara Tjirkadu, with the special poster marking the hand-back of title'. (Courtesy National Library of Australia/Uluru–Kata Tjuta National Park.)

At around the same time, the Australian Government began the task of putting together a nomination for the Park to be listed as a World Heritage site. The nomination was submitted to UNESCO in 1986. As Layton and Titchen (1995) point out, the 1986 nomination (Australian National Parks and Wildlife Service 1986) made the case for nomination of Uluru (Ayers Rock-Mount Olga) National Park on the basis of both natural and cultural criteria. However, the subsequent IUCN (World Conservation Union) evaluation recommended its inclusion on the basis of World Heritage Convention natural heritage Criteria ii and iii, that is, its demonstration of 'ongoing geological processes' and 'exceptional natural beauty and exceptional combination of natural and cultural elements'. ICOMOS, which would normally advise UNESCO on cultural criteria, provided no evaluation of the cultural heritage values of the Park at the time of the nomination (Layton and Titchen 1995: 176). The IUCN evaluation notes simply that 'cultural values of the area are being reviewed by ICOMOS' (UNESCO 1987: 9); however, this appears not to have occurred. Uluru (Ayers Rock-Mount Olga) National Park was subsequently inscribed on the World Heritage List in December 1987, at the eleventh meeting of the World Heritage Committee, as a 'natural' heritage site, despite IUCN noting 'the cultural values of the site are significant' (UNESCO 1987: 12).

The listing of Uluru (Ayers Rock-Mount Olga) National Park as a 'natural' site was met with concern by heritage professionals (McBryde 1990; Layton and Titchen 1995), as well as by the Anangu and the Park's Board of Management, who were pushing to receive more comprehensive recognition of the cultural values of the Park, and for these values to be better integrated with its management as a landscape. Since the early days of tourism to the Park, visitors had climbed to the top of Uluru to enjoy the view from the distinctive monolith—climbing the rock had become one of a series of heritage 'experiences' to be ticked off on the Australian tourist's agenda. A handrail to assist with the process of climbing had been installed in the 1960s. However, Anangu people had long expressed concern about tourists climbing Uluru. Anangu people themselves do not climb it because of its spiritual significance; the tourist track over the rock follows the route of Dreaming ancestors, which it is considered inappropriate to cross (Calma and Liddle 2003: 104). Anangu had requested closing Uluru to tourist traffic as one of the conditions of management of the site when they were lobbying for its handback in the 1980s. While this was initially agreed, continued access to allow tourists to climb Uluru would eventually form one of the conditions required by the Australian Government prior to agreeing to return the deeds to the Anangu in 1983 (Toyne and Vachon 1984). Trying to find ways to discourage tourists from climbing Uluru by educating them about its cultural values was an issue of ongoing concern to the Board of Management; the apparent lack of recognition of the Park's cultural values as part of the World Heritage nomination was thus a serious cause of unease and agitation for Anangu people. These protests over the lack of recognition by UNESCO of the cultural values of the Park were one of a series of related criticisms of the separation of natural and cultural heritage significance in the World Heritage Convention, which would result in fundamental revisions to the wording of the Convention text in 1992, alongside the introduction of the 'cultural landscape' as a distinct class of World Heritage place in the same year.

Problems relating to the strict delineation of natural and cultural heritage sites in the World Heritage Convention in relation to rural landscapes and 'mixed' natural and cultural sites were raised as early as 1984. At this time, the World Heritage Committee requested IUCN to consult with ICOMOS and the International Federation of Landscape Architects to put together a task force to consider the development of guidelines for the identification and nomination of mixed natural/cultural properties (Rössler 1995; Fowler 2003: 66ff). A meeting was held in 1985 and guidelines drafted; however, when the UK subsequently submitted a nomination for the mixed natural/cultural landscape of the Lake District National Park in 1987, the Committee did not feel able to make a decision on the nomination, with ICOMOS in favour of the nomination and IUCN undecided. The Committee ultimately decided to defer their decision until criteria could be developed specifically for the nomination of cultural landscapes.

In 1991, the UNESCO secretariat presented a proposal for the introduction of two new draft criteria for the nomination of cultural landscapes to the fifteenth session of the World Heritage Bureau in Carthage for consideration (Rössler 1995: 43). The Committee asked for further consultation on the revision of World Heritage Criteria, and an expert meeting was held in La Petite Pierre in France in October 1992 (Fowler 2004: 17–18). At this meeting, definitions of various categories of cultural landscape were proposed, and revisions to the World Heritage Operational Guidelines were suggested to allow for inclusion of cultural landscapes in the World Heritage List. These discussions were driven particularly by criticism of the separation of natural and cultural heritage that had been levelled by Anangu people in relation to the classification of Uluru (Ayers Rock-Mount Olga) National Park as a 'natural' site, and similar criticisms that had been raised by Māori in relation to the inscription of Tongariro National Park in New Zealand as a 'natural' World Heritage site in 1990. These criticisms of the World Heritage List, and the need to recognise the Indigenous values of cultural landscapes, were central to the discussions that occurred at La Petite Pierre (Rössler 1995: 44).

A number of participants with knowledge and/or direct experience of the Australian and New Zealand examples took part in the La Petit Pierre expert meeting (see UNESCO 1992: Annex A). Significantly, no new criterion was created, but recommendations were proposed for redrafting the World Heritage Convention's cultural criteria. These gave particular consideration to the need to recognise the cultural values of landscapes to Indigenous people, and the value of 'traditional' land management practices (it seems fairly certain that central Australian practices of managing the landscape using controlled burning were influential here). In this sense, the fundamental dualism between categories of natural and cultural heritage value was maintained; nonetheless, the revisions represented an important broadening of the concept of heritage as embodied in the Convention text. It is worth reproducing the proposed revisions in full as they demonstrate the strong influence of arguments based in the cultural landscape traditions of Indigenous people in relation to Uluru-Kata Tjuta and Tongariro on the participants in the expert meeting.

Paragraph 24(a)

(i) represent a unique artistic achievement, a masterpiece of the creative genius; or

(ii) have exerted great influence, over a span of time or within a cultural area of the world, on developments in architecture, monumental arts, town-planning or *landscape design*; or

(iii) bear a unique or at least exceptional testimony to a civilisation or *cultural tradition* which has disappeared; or

(iv) be an outstanding example of the type of building or architectural ensemble *or landscape* which illustrates (a) significant stage(*s*) *in human history*; or

(v) be an outstanding example of a traditional human settlement *or land use* which is representative of a culture (*or cultures*), *especially when* it has become vulnerable under the impact of irreversible change; or

(vi) be directly and tangibly associated with events or *living traditions*, with ideas, or *with* beliefs, *with artistic and literary works* of outstanding universal significance (the Committee considers that this criterion should justify inclusion on the List only in exceptional circumstance or in conjunction with other criteria);

Paragraph 24(b)

(i) meet the test of authenticity in design, material, workmanship or setting *and in the case of cultural landscapes their distinctive character and components* (the Committee stressed that reconstruction is only acceptable if it is carried out on the basis of complete and detailed documentation on the original and to no extent conjecture)

(ii) have adequate legal *and/or traditional* protection and management mechanisms to ensure the conservation of the nominated cultural property *or cultural landscapes*. The existence of protective legislation at the national, provincial or municipal level *or well established traditional protection* and/or adequate management mechanisms is therefore essential and must be stated clearly on the nomination form. Assurances of the effective implementation of these laws and/or administrative mechanisms are also expected. Furthermore, in order to preserve the integrity of cultural sites, particularly those open to large numbers of visitors, the State Party concerned should be able to provide evidence of suitable administrative arrangements to cover the management of the property, its conservation and its access to the public.

(Rössler 1995: 45, proposed revisions in italics)

The proposed changes, which were accepted at the sixteenth session of the World Heritage Committee held in Santa Fe, New Mexico in December 1992, demonstrate the clear influence of Aṉangu and Māori conceptions of landscape that had emerged in relation to debates surrounding the nomination of Uluṟu-Kata Tjuṯa and Tongariro as 'natural' properties. The recognition of multiple cultures and overlapping landscapes in changes to Paragraph 24(a)(v) and the emphasis on continuity of tradition in changes to Paragraphs 24(a)(vi) and 24 (b)(ii) appear to have been specific concessions to the Australian example. The meeting also defined three types of cultural landscape:

> The term 'cultural landscape' embraces a diversity of manifestations of the interaction between humankind and its natural environment.
>
> The most easily identifiable is the clearly defined *landscape designed and created intentionally by man*. This embraces garden and parkland landscapes constructed for aesthetic reasons which are often (but not always) associated with religious or other monumental buildings and ensembles.
>
> The second category is the *organically evolved landscape*. This results from an initial social, economic, administrative, and/or religious imperative and has developed its present form by association with and in response to its natural environment. Such landscapes reflect that process of evolution in their form and component features. They fall into two sub-categories:
>
> A *relict (or fossil) landscape* is one in which an evolutionary process came to an end at some time in the past, either abruptly or over a period. Its significant distinguishing features are, however, still visible in material form.
>
> A *continuing landscape* is one which retains an active social role in contemporary society closely associated with the traditional way of life, and in which the evolutionary process is still in progress. At the same time it exhibits significant material evidence of its evolution over time.
>
> The final category is the *associative cultural landscape*. The inscription of such landscapes on the World Heritage List is justifiable by virtue of the powerful religious, artistic or cultural associations of the natural element rather than material cultural evidence, which may be insignificant or even absent.
>
> *(UNESCO 1992: 4–5, original emphasis)*

The inclusion of the notion of 'continuing landscapes' that have an active role in contemporary society, and the category of 'associative cultural landscapes' that acknowledge the spiritual connection between particular groups and the landscapes they occupy, were directly influenced by arguments raised by Indigenous people in response to the 'natural' heritage nominations of Tongariro and Uluṟu-Kata Tjuṯa (Fowler 2004: 34), and the nature of those landscapes themselves, which were both rugged, remote and apparently undeveloped despite the complex spiritual connections and active regimes of landscape management which Indigenous people applied to them.

These changes had important implications, not only for Aṉangu people and the Park's Board of Management, but also in shifting and broadening the definition of heritage promoted by UNESCO. In 1993, at the request of Aṉangu and the Board, the name of the Park was changed to 'Uluṟu-Kata Tjuṯa National Park'. In the same year, Tongariro National Park was resubmitted for consideration under the revised cultural criteria as an associative cultural landscape, and became the first cultural landscape to be inscribed to the World Heritage List at the seventeenth session of the World Heritage Committee in December 1993. The following year, Uluru-Kata Tjuṯa National Park became the second cultural landscape to be included on the World Heritage List when it was resubmitted for consideration as a living and associative landscape. The ICOMOS evaluation noted:

> The cultural landscape … is of immense significance … a highly successful model of human adaptation to a hostile arid environment … also graphically demonstrates the intimate symbolic relationship between man and the landscape in this non-monumental culture … [The Park] is also worthy of commendation for its management system and policy … based on the perceptions and practices of the traditional owners of the land.
>
> *(cited in Fowler 2003: 107)*

In doing so, there was an explicit recognition of the value of *Tjukurpa* as an overarching philosophy in the appropriate management of the landscape, and the interrelationship of this system of management with the natural and cultural values of the Park and Anangu people's well being.

Uluru-Kata Tjuṯa National Park has consistently been seen as a model for the definition and management of cultural landscape values. In 1995 it won the Picasso Gold Medal, awarded jointly by UNESCO to Parks Australia and the Uluru-Kata Tjuṯa Board of Management in recognition of outstanding efforts to preserve the landscape and Anangu culture, and for setting new international standards for World Heritage management. Under the Park's Board of Management, it has introduced a 'Please don't climb' programme, which asks visitors not to climb Uluru out of respect for its spiritual significance to Anangu people as the traditional route of the ancestral Mala men on their arrival at Uluru. This has had a significant impact on the number of tourists who choose to climb Uluru. It 2009 it was estimated that around 38 per cent of tourists climb Uluru, down from 74 per cent in 1990 (Parks Australia 2009).

In this example, we see the ways in which the relationship between local actors and global processes create 'zones of awkward engagement' (Tsing 2005; Chapter 2 in this volume), creative spaces of friction that have long-lasting consequences for both local actors and global institutions. The debates surrounding the listing of Uluru-Kata Tjuṯa National Park as a 'natural' heritage site drew attention to broader issues relating to differences between the UNESCO World Heritage Convention's model of the separation and dualistic opposition of cultural and natural heritage, and alternative models of heritage in which natural landscapes might be conceptualised as 'cultural' ones. The Convention's self-definition as a universal convention representing all human heritage meant these alternative models had to be taken seriously and given equal consideration with existing ways of conceptualising heritage. The outcome of this process was a clear shift in the definitions employed in relation to World Heritage in the years that followed.

In the same way in which various individuals might be thought of as actors, the form of Uluṟu-Kata Tjuṯa and Tongariro as landscapes, and the relationships between these landscapes and their Indigenous custodians, had a major influence on the definition of 'cultural landscapes' adopted by the World Heritage Committee. These landscapes thus subsequently had an impact on the categorisation, preservation and management of a range of other landscapes in the world. As a result of the complex social and physical networks that were demonstrated by their Indigenous custodians in discussions about the form in which their nominations and management should take, these landscapes themselves might be viewed as exhibiting forms of agency that have had a long-lasting impact on how heritage is defined and managed in the contemporary world. We can think of Uluṟu as acting in these processes as an assemblage or collective agent that is composed not only of its human advocates, but also of the whole range of its physical characteristics—its biodiversity, its prominence in the landscape, and the various texts, images and other representations that had previously circulated to give it its sense of renown and visitability as an 'Australian icon'. All of these worked in tandem in influencing the specific form of the changes proposed by UNESCO in relation to the category of the cultural landscape.

Towards a global strategy for a 'representative' World Heritage List

The example of the category of cultural landscapes shows clearly how the rather limited definition of heritage, and the apparently binary opposition of the categories of natural and cultural heritage in the original Convention text, were forced to be revised as a result of claims to representation within a document that expressed itself as universally applicable. The failure of the World Heritage Convention and the World Heritage Committee to produce a comprehensive and representative World Heritage List, and hence the need to rework the definition of heritage and the various categories in the original Convention text to maintain its universal application, gained explicit recognition in the Report of the Expert Meeting on the 'Global Strategy' and thematic studies for a representative World Heritage List (UNESCO 1994), held at the UNESCO Headquarters in Paris in June 1994 and reported to the eighteenth session of the World Heritage Committee in Phuket, Thailand in November of the same year. In its introduction, the report noted

> Many high-quality attempts had been made over the past decade to consider the best ways of ensuring the representative nature, and hence the credibility, of the World Heritage List in the future, but they had failed to achieve a consensus among the scientific community, despite the fact that all the component bodies and partners of the Convention were conscious of its weaknesses and imbalances. Since the adoption of the Convention by the General Conference of UNESCO in 1972, moreover, the concept of cultural heritage had also developed considerably in meaning, depth, and extent.
>
> *(UNESCO 1994)*

The report emphasised the need for a balanced list to maintain its credibility as a representative 'World' Heritage List. It made significant acknowledgements of the shortcomings of the original World Heritage Convention, which directly mirrored those that had been raised by academic commentators, practitioners and local stakeholders in World Heritage sites such as the Anangu. It criticised the emphasis on individual monuments in the Convention text, for example, and argued for a more holistic definition of cultural heritage and human culture generally.

> It was apparent to all the participants that from its inception the World Heritage List had been based on an almost exclusively 'monumental' concept of the cultural heritage, ignoring the fact that not only scientific knowledge but also intellectual attitudes towards the extent of the notion of cultural heritage, together with the perception and understanding of the history of human societies, had developed considerably in the past twenty years … In 1972 the idea of cultural heritage had been to a very large extent embodied in and confined to architectural monuments. Since that time, however, the history of art and architecture, archaeology, anthropology, and ethnology no longer concentrated on single monuments in isolation but rather on considering cultural groupings that were complex and multidimensional, which demonstrated in spatial terms the social structures, ways of life, beliefs, systems of knowledge, and representations of different past and present cultures in the entire world. Each individual piece of evidence should therefore be considered not in isolation but within its whole context and with an understanding of the multiple reciprocal relationships that it had with its physical and non-physical environment.
>
> *(UNESCO 1994)*

This contextual model of heritage owed much to the new definition of cultural landscapes, and to a perception that the heritage of non-monumental cultures had been excluded from the List under previous interpretations of the Convention text.

The particular biases in the World Heritage List that were identified in the report included a *geographical* bias towards Europe; a *typological* bias towards historic towns and religious buildings in preference to other forms of historic property; a *religious* bias in the overrepresentation of Christianity in relation to other religions; a *chronological* bias in the emphasis on historic periods over prehistory and the twentieth century; and a *class* bias towards 'elitist' forms of architecture in relation to vernacular forms. Perhaps most significantly, it noted the gaps in recognition of *living* cultures:

> all living cultures – and especially the 'traditional' ones – with their depth, their wealth, their complexity, and their diverse relationships with their environment, figured very little on the List. Even traditional settlements were only included on the List in terms of their 'architectural' value, taking no account of their many economic, social, symbolic, and philosophical dimensions or of their many continuing interactions with their natural environment in all its diversity. This

impoverishment of the cultural expression of human societies was also due to an over-simplified division between cultural and natural properties which took no account of the fact that in most human societies the landscape, which was created or at all events inhabited by human beings, was representative and an expression of the lives of the people who live in it and so was in this sense equally culturally meaningful.

(UNESCO 1994)

The group recommended the development of a global strategy to increase the number of types, regions and periods represented on the World Heritage List, but also pointed to the need to take into account 'the new concepts of the idea of cultural heritage that had been developed over the past twenty years'. This is significant, and shows how the existence of broader conceptions of heritage in circulation in the global community, both official and unofficial, forced a reconsideration of the universal categories of the List to accommodate them, as well as the ways in which the World Heritage Convention was both an agent of globalisation, and itself subject to modification as a result of globalising processes. The List would shift from its original emphasis on typological categories of architectural monument in which heritage was conceptualised as 'dead' and removed from everyday, contemporary life, to incorporate non-monumental traditions, living expressions of human cultures, and forms of heritage that were more representative of humanity in its diversity. The global strategy would comprise a series of thematic and comparative studies to increase the breadth of the range of places represented on the List, as well as a parallel programme of expert meetings focused on underrepresented geographical regions. In addition, the World Heritage Committee would actively promote ratification of the World Heritage Convention to States Parties who had not become signatories to it, leading to ratification by a number of Pacific Island, Eastern European, African and Arab states in the coming years.

The global strategy represented an important acknowledgement of the failings of the original Convention text, and a watershed in opening up the question of representation while maintaining its totalising and universalising mission. This change in focus, coupled with its globalising mission, gave the World Heritage Committee renewed vigour in its influence on the globalisation and diversification of heritage in the later part of the twentieth century and the early part of the twenty-first. This new expansive definition of heritage not only would play a significant role in the work of the World Heritage Committee itself, but would have a proselytising effect amongst other national, regional and municipal heritage management agencies; ultimately, it would have an important influence on the way in which heritage was defined, conceptualised, managed and interpreted throughout the world. However, while this change was framed as motivated by a desire to be more inclusive of human diversity, it must also be seen as a process that expanded and strengthened UNESCO's field of governance by broadening the range of objects, places and practices over which it had authority, and the places and circumstances under which it could intervene in the activities of nation-states (Askew 2010).

Intangible heritage and the *halaiqui* of Jemaa el Fna Square, Marrakech

A similar process of expansion of the definition of heritage from the original World Heritage Convention text is apparent with regard to the category of 'intangible heritage'. We have seen how the call for a global strategy emphasised the gaps in representation of traditional and 'living' cultures on the World Heritage List. As in the case of the category of 'cultural landscapes', UNESCO adopted the concept of intangible cultural heritage as part of a programme of expanding its overall definition of heritage, and developing what it perceived to be more inclusive categories of heritage as part of a push to maintain its universal application during the later part of the twentieth century, as it was increasingly confronted with claims to represent forms of heritage that were outside its original definition. Once again, the specific circumstances of these claims would have an important influence on the ways in which 'intangible heritage' was defined and interpreted by UNESCO.

As early as 1973, Bolivia suggested to UNESCO that a protocol might be added to the Universal Copyright Convention in order to protect aspects of folklore (Aikawa 2004). In 1982 at the Mondiacult World Conference on Cultural Policies, held in Mexico City, UNESCO officially acknowledged these concerns regarding the importance of intangible cultural heritage and included it in its new definition of cultural heritage (UNESCO 2011e). UNESCO subsequently established a Committee of Experts on the Safeguarding of Folklore, and in 1989 the Recommendation on the Safeguarding of Traditional Culture and Folklore was adopted by the General Conference of UNESCO in Paris (Kurin 2004).

The Recommendation called on member states to develop a national inventory of institutions concerned with folklore, with a view to their inclusion in regional and global registers of folklore, and to establish national archives where collected folklore could be stored and made available. Moreover, the Committee made it clear that the preservation of folklore

> is concerned with protection of folk traditions *and those who are the transmitters*, having regard to the fact that each people has a right to its own culture and that its adherence to that culture is often eroded by the impact of the industrialized culture purveyed by the mass media.
>
> *(UNESCO 1989, my emphasis)*

It recommended that 'measures must be taken to guarantee the status of and economic support for folk traditions both in the communities which produce them and beyond'. How to put such preservation into action seemed harder to define, and recommendations were made, among others, to 'guarantee the right of access of various cultural communities to their own folklore by supporting their work in the fields of documentation [and] archiving', and to 'provide moral and economic support for individuals and institutions studying, making known, cultivating or holding items of folklore'.

It is worth pausing to reflect for a moment on the term 'folklore' and how it was employed by UNESCO in its recommendations. The term is most often associated with preindustrial societies, and its use seems to imply that 'traditional culture' cannot exist except in such contexts. It is clear that UNESCO's initiative was aimed primarily at the preservation of the non-material aspects of Indigenous/First Nations and developing peoples. In 1996 the Report of the World Commission on Culture and Development, *Our Creative Diversity*, noted that the World Heritage Convention is not appropriate for celebrating and protecting intangible expressions of cultural heritage such as dance or oral traditions, and called for the development of other forms of recognition (besides World Heritage listing) for the whole range of heritage found in societies across the world (UNESCO 2011e). An underlying principle of the report was that the diversity of world cultures must be protected and nurtured, but its emphasis on the threats to 'traditional' cultures seems to reflect the broadening, more anthropological focus of UNESCO on living cultures over this period.

Despite the Recommendation on the Safeguarding of Traditional Culture and Folklore, as Schmitt (2005, 2008) and Skounti (2009) have noted, as in the case of Uluru and Tongariro, it was not until significant external pressure developed around a specific set of local circumstances in relation to a particular place that there was sufficient impetus to get the development of a convention onto UNESCO's agenda. This place was Jemaa el Fna Square, and the nature of the heritage of Jemaa el Fna, as well as the work of campaigners (in particular the Spanish writer Juan Goytisolo) to highlight its significance, had an important influence on the final shape of the Convention. I draw on Schmitt's accounts of the Convention's 'back story' here to illustrate this point.

Jemaa el Fna is a square in the old city of Marrakech in Morocco. As Schmitt (2005) notes, although it is sited on the edge of the medina (historic old city) of Marrakech (itself a World Heritage site gazetted in 1985 under Criteria (i), (ii), (iv) and (v)), its layout owes as much to modern developments as to its medieval origins. As one of the main squares in the city, it hosts a changing suite of entertainers, drink sellers and restaurateurs. Snake charmers, monkey trainers, musicians and magicians perform for audiences in the open air, while herbalists, dentists and charm sellers set up temporary stalls on tables or carpets. In the evenings, the Square becomes more crowded, as the snake charmers and monkey trainers depart, and the Square is populated first by Berber or Arabic *halaiqui* (story-tellers), dancers and magicians, and subsequently with food stalls which are popular with locals and tourists alike.

Juan Goytisolo, who left Spain under Franco and has lived much of his life in self-imposed exile in Marrakech and France, had featured the Square in a number of his novels and short stories. As Schmitt (2005, 2008) recounts, in the mid-1990s he became concerned when he was made aware of local authority plans to construct a tower block with a glass façade and an underground car park immediately adjacent to Jemaa el Fna. He believed this would pose a serious threat to the tradition of oral story-telling by *halaiqui* in the Square, and after failing to convince local authorities of his concerns, he wrote to Federico Mayor, Director General of UNESCO, through his publisher, Hans Meinke. In his letter, dated 26 January 1996, he proposed that the

FIGURE 6.4 Jemaa el Fna Square in Marrakech, Morocco. (Photograph by Jane Wright, 1992. © UNESCO/Jane Wright.)

Square be placed under the protection of UNESCO as part of the oral heritage of humanity (*patrimonio oral de humanidad*), outlining the threats to the Square as he perceived them. Schmitt translates and reproduces the relevant part of the letter:

> Dear Federico,
> … yesterday your ears must have been burning, for Juan Goytisolo came to talk [to me] about taking action on behalf of the famous Jemaa el Fna Square in Marrakech, and about the possibility of persuading UNESCO to declare it as 'oral heritage of humanity'. According to Goytisolo, this square, with its story-tellers and reciters, is the only place in the Arab world where the tradition of oral literature is still cultivated. Apparently it is advisable to propose its protection by UNESCO in order to avoid it being destroyed by speculation.
>
> *(cited in Schmitt 2008: 98–9)*

Meanwhile, Goytisolo began a campaign to save Jemaa el Fna, which gained local support and spread to the international press, bringing international attention to the issue.

Schmitt goes on to demonstrate the ways in which the particular circumstances of this *local* problem created a *global* conceptual challenge for UNESCO, as no such category as 'oral heritage of humanity' existed. In a note he translates and reproduces in his article, he shows how the universalising logic of the World Heritage Convention was interpreted by the staff member who was asked to consider Goytisolo's request.

FIGURE 6.5 A *halaiqui* (story-teller) in Jemaa el Fna Square in Marrakech, Morocco. (Photograph by Jane Wright, 1992. © UNESCO/Jane Wright.)

The request submitted by the writer Juan Goytisolo is indeed a new and very interesting idea, but to implement it would be rather complicated. The concept of 'oral heritage' is not included among UNESCO's different categories of heritage. UNESCO will therefore need to define this new category, and then to propose its adoption by the States Parties. ... The act of declaring this square in Marrakech as 'oral heritage of humanity' might also cause offence to other countries where a rich oral tradition has been kept alive. This applies in particular to the countries of black Africa.

(cited in Schmitt 2008: 99)

Subsequent discussions around the formulation of a convention for the Safeguarding of the Intangible Cultural Heritage were strongly influenced by the specific circumstances of Jemaa el Fna, in particular through the emphasis on oral story-telling and on the 'cultural spaces' in which such story-telling occurs (Schmitt 2008). This was particularly the case when, in June 1997, the UNESCO Cultural Heritage Division and Moroccan National Commission organised an international consultation on the preservation of popular cultural spaces in Marrakesh, which was integral to discussion of the creation of an international convention to protect and draw attention to outstanding examples of folklore and popular culture. While the meeting agreed that defined 'cultural spaces' such as that of Jemaa el Fna were actually quite exceptional, and in the majority of cases the transmission and performance of oral culture was not confined to specific delimited spaces, the idea of the 'cultural space' of transmission as a category was maintained in subsequent discussions of a convention, and represented in the final wording of the definition of intangible heritage adopted by UNESCO (see below). However, despite the importance of the involvement of Goytisolo and other Moroccan heritage experts in this meeting, as Schmitt (2005, 2008) points out, the local *halaiqui* were not themselves involved in these meetings, and in this sense the definition of intangible heritage that derives from Jemaa el Fna is one which was very much filtered through the lens of the writer and the Moroccan conservation professionals who were involved.

In 1999, UNESCO and the Smithsonian Institution jointly organised a conference in Washington DC titled 'A Global Assessment of the 1989 Recommendation on the Safeguarding of Traditional Culture and Folklore: Local Empowerment and International Cooperation'. This was followed in May 2001 by the First Proclamation of nineteen 'Masterpieces of the Oral and Intangible Heritage of Humanity', which included Jemaa el Fna. Goytisolo himself acted as Chairman of the International Jury at the announcement, and made specific reference to the Square in his speech.

As I have learned from my custom of listening in the Square of Marrakesh, the halakis (story-tellers) perform in the framework of a changing society anxious for instruction and constantly looking over its shoulder at those who – outside an education almost exclusively linked to the practice of the competitive norms ruling the Global Village – preserve and memorise for the future the narratives of the past. ... the holders of oral knowledge can be and at times are more cultured than their compatriots versed only in the use of audio-visual and computing techniques. But in a world subjugated by these ubiquitous techniques, oral culture, whether primary or hybrid, is seriously endangered and warrants an international mobilisation to save it from gradual extinction.

(Goytisolo 2001)

In October 2003, the thirty-second session of the General Conference adopted the Convention for the Safeguarding of the Intangible Cultural Heritage, at which time the Second Proclamation inscribed twenty-eight new 'Masterpieces of the Oral and Intangible Heritage of Humanity'. A further forty-three were inscribed in 2005 (UNESCO 2011e). The ninety items on the List of 'Masterpieces' were incredibly diverse, and ranged from the language, dance and music of the Garifuna in Belize, Guatemala, Honduras and Nicaragua to the Slovácko Verbuňk Recruit Dances of the Czech Republic, and the Wayang Puppet Theatre of Indonesia.

The Convention for the Safeguarding of the Intangible Cultural Heritage (2003) defined intangible cultural heritage as

> the practices, representations, expressions, knowledge, skills – as well as the instruments, objects, artefacts and *cultural spaces* associated therewith – that communities, groups and, in some cases, individuals recognize as part of their cultural heritage. This intangible cultural heritage, transmitted from generation to generation, is constantly recreated by communities and groups in response to their environment, their interaction with nature and their history, and provides them with a sense of identity and continuity, thus promoting respect for cultural diversity and human creativity.
>
> *(UNESCO 2003c, my emphasis)*

While this definition is much broader than that which emerged from early discussions around Jemaa el Fna, it nonetheless bears a clear imprint of the particular circumstances of the original campaign to save the Square in its reference to 'cultural spaces' as integral to the conservation of intangible heritage. The Convention urged member states to establish inventories of intangible cultural heritage in their territories and to ensure recognition and respect for intangible cultural heritage, and directed UNESCO to develop a 'Representative List of the Intangible Cultural Heritage of Humanity ... [to] ensure better visibility of the intangible cultural heritage and awareness of its significance, and to encourage dialogue which respects cultural diversity'. Accordingly, in 2005 the List of Masterpieces was closed, to be replaced in 2008 by a 'Representative List of the Intangible Cultural Heritage of Humanity'. This was significant in shifting emphasis away from any single tradition as showing 'outstanding universal value', as in the case of the World Heritage List, recognising instead that the representativeness of a tradition might in itself make it important enough for inclusion. At this time, all of the existing 'Masterpieces' were moved on to the 'Representative' List. In addition to the Representative List, the Convention also made provision for the development of a 'List of Intangible Cultural Heritage in Need of Urgent

Safeguarding' and established a fund for the safeguarding of the intangible cultural heritage. These are now known collectively as the UNESCO Lists of Intangible Cultural Heritage. At the time of writing there are over 232 elements scheduled across the two lists.

Schmitt (2008) lists a number of factors that he believes were significant in generating a series of circumstances that allowed what was essentially a 'local' conservation issue to have a significant 'global' impact. He cites the fact that the Square was already well known and a popular tourist destination, that it was acutely at risk, and that the diversity of the forms of intangible heritage (story-telling, singing, performing) that were present allowed it to 'stand in' for many other forms of global cultural traditions. Similarly, Goytisolo's influence as an international intellectual and the fact that he was directly acquainted with the Director General of UNESCO, UNESCO's predisposition to the concept as a result of various other precursor documents and discussions about how to conserve oral heritage and tradition, and the support of the idea by Moroccan authorities seem to have been equally important. As in the case of Uluru, the various actors—individual stakeholders and local community members, heritage professionals, municipal, national and international organisations, and the places themselves—all seem to have played an active role in generating friction and conflict in this particular 'local' case, which subsequently had global consequences.

Both of these cases show how local issues have had significant global implications through their respective roles in reorganising the universal categories of World Heritage. However, it needs to be acknowledged that, in most cases, the structure of UNESCO has tended to make it difficult for individuals and minority groups to use the World Heritage List or the Lists of Intangible Cultural Heritage as strategically as they might in drawing attention to issues of local concern. This is a function of UNESCO's requirement that nominations are made via States Parties, thus prioritising the agendas of nation-states over those of minorities (and, somewhat contradictorily, the 'universal' principles on which it purports to stand). In this way, Indigenous and minority critique has often been marginalised as groups are subsumed within nation-states and representations of their culture employed within broader nationalist discourses (Benavides 2009; González-Ruibal 2009; Askew 2010). Nonetheless, some Indigenous groups have been successful in drawing attention to issues of local concern, even when they have been unable to overcome this problem in relation to the requirements of States Party compliance for nominations to be made to any of UNESCO's World Heritage Lists. For example, Lydon (2009) discusses the case of the international campaign led by Mirrar people in the Kakadu region of northern Australia, which successfully prevented uranium mining on the Jabiluka mineral lease, even though the World Heritage Committee's member states ultimately voted against listing Kakadu on the List of World Heritage in Danger, against the wishes of Mirrar Aboriginal people but in line with Australian Federal Government lobbying of other States Parties.

It is also worth reflecting briefly here on the operation of the new lists themselves, as apparatuses that accommodated a broader definition of heritage whilst simultaneously maintaining the universalising and modernist principles of the World

Heritage Convention. The criteria for inclusion on the Representative List, which were revised in June 2010, acknowledge explicitly the role of risk and threat in defining what is eligible for listing through the inclusion of a criterion that requires safeguarding measures to be outlined in any nomination received by the Committee. Similarly, the process of listing and categorising is maintained, despite the multiplication of the categories of heritage that are recognised to deal with the anomalies that its claims to universality exposed. Finally, in recognising intangible heritage as a specific category that stands in opposition to 'tangible' heritage, the Convention continues a separation of objects, buildings and places from the practices and traditions associated with them. This maintains the Cartesian dualism of matter and mind (see Chapter 9). In the same way, in the case of 'cultural' landscapes, the 'nature' and 'culture' dualism is maintained through the introduction of a new category, 'cultural landscape', which stands aside from the 'natural' landscapes. In this sense, this simply represents a reorganisation of the universal categories of World Heritage, rather than a fundamental revision of its classificatory system.

The Lists also began to operate as apparatuses in other significant ways. Through the emphasis on the 'cultural spaces' of intangible heritage, the Convention for the Safeguarding of the Intangible Cultural Heritage extended the commodification of heritage as 'visitable' spectacle, which had been initiated through the World Heritage List and its involvement in the reconfiguration of global tourism, to the spaces in which intangible heritage was performed. World Heritage was no longer simply confined to specific places, but would become mobile and hence easily stageable for the consumption of tourists and spectators. In many ways, this concept gave authenticity to forms of cultural performance that might in other decades have been perceived to be inauthentic, as performance of intangible heritage itself became a form of conservation activity, with spectators doing their own bit for the cause. At the same time, the new emphasis on 'intangible' heritage resonated with a broader global 'virtual' turn, and critical heritage studies approaches that emphasised a notion of heritage as a discourse. So, in addition to maintaining the universality of the heritage concept through the work of the World Heritage Committee, the category of 'intangible heritage' continued the movement away from the conservation of material things towards listing and archiving as an end in itself.

International heritage policy developed by UNESCO has a clear influence on the development of national, regional and municipal heritage policy. For example, the Council of Europe's European Landscape Convention, passed in Florence in 2000, owed much to the concept of cultural landscapes, and initiated a Europe-wide system of protection, management and planning for European landscapes and international cooperation on landscape issues. The US National Park Service began its national cultural landscape preservation programme in 1990, but it has expanded significantly since that time. While there still remain serious abstentions amongst the States Parties that have ratified the Convention for the Safeguarding of the Intangible Cultural Heritage—at the time of writing, the USA, UK, Germany and Australia, for example, are yet to ratify the Convention—nonetheless, the concept of intangible heritage now has wide acceptance. In the UK, for example, the UK National Commission for

UNESCO (UKNC) Wales and Scotland Committees are working with the Culture Committee to identify and record intangible cultural heritage practices within Wales and Scotland, and are working on an inventory of Scottish intangible cultural heritage practices, although, as Smith and Waterton (2009a) note, England has not formally engaged with intangible heritage. The abstention of certain States Parties seems in part to relate to potential issues to do with a clash between certain cultural traditions and human rights (see Chapter 7), and the perception that 'intangible' heritage is the preserve of 'traditional' and small-scale societies. Nonetheless, I would argue that the concept has had an influence on definitions of heritage and national heritage policy within all these countries. For example, a recent issue of English Heritage's *Conservation Bulletin* titled 'People Engaging with Places' (March 2011) contains a number of case studies that place a strong emphasis on the ways in which the practices and traditions of local people are a significant part of the country's heritage. While the increased emphasis on public inclusion in heritage in the UK arose as a result of late 1990s policy developments, it is possible to see how concepts of social value have influenced recent English heritage policy. Similarly, at a national and state level, Australia has long recognised the concept of social value, which has close connections with the concept of intangible heritage, as one of a series of values of heritage recognised in the Burra Charter. For example, the Victorian Department of Planning and Community Development lists a number of examples of intangible cultural heritage on its website, including Indigenous creation stories, community cultural events and festivals, and regional and rural agricultural shows (Department of Planning and Community Development Victoria 2011). In the USA, the Smithsonian Institution's Center for Folklife and Cultural Heritage has played an important role in the preservation of living cultural traditions as part of its annual Smithsonian Folklife Festival, which has been running since 1967, and the Smithsonian hosted the 1999 conference that was integral to the development of the 2003 Convention.

The other point here is that an acknowledgement of the process by which local actors and issues have been implicated simultaneously challenging and broadening the World Heritage Committee's operational definitions of heritage, whilst also upholding its hegemonic, universalising position, troubles and complicates various accounts of the 'top-down' hegemony of the World Heritage Convention (see also González-Ruibal 2009). Some scholars have attempted to account for this sort of anomaly in relation to Indigenous heritage and the alignment of local actors with state-sponsored models of heritage, using the notion of 'strategic essentialism' (cf. Amit-Talai 1996; Spivak 1996; see Byrne 2003; Meskell 2009b, 2009c; Harrison 2010b). However, what emerges from this analysis is perhaps closer to Michael Herzfeld's account of 'cultural intimacy' (1997), although in this case citizens do not align themselves with the state, but with an international body and its universal model of heritage. This suggests at the very least that the authority of the World Heritage Convention is co-created by local actors as much as it is by state officials. More detailed ethnographic investigations to understand how the relationships between local actors, heritage professionals, bureaucrats, objects, places and practices of heritage, and global institutions are formed and reformed through debates around specific heritage issues, would help refine and develop these models in productive ways (Smith 2007; Krauss 2008).

Conclusion

This chapter explored two conceptual crises that characterise the transformations in heritage practice over the past few decades, which have arisen as a result of the claims of the World Heritage Convention to represent a universal and representative series of categories of heritage. Drawing on Bennett's arguments relating to the claims of Indigenous peoples to be represented in the universal museum, I suggested that the categories and definitions of 'World Heritage' shifted as a result of challenges to the broadly Euro-American model of heritage, which was codified in the Convention text, as attempts were made to apply this model globally to people and places with radically different models of heritage. The examples of Uluru in relation to cultural landscapes, and Jemaa el Fna Square in relation to intangible heritage, show how actor–network approaches can reveal the ways in which the relationships between local actors and global processes produce creative spaces of friction that have long-lasting consequences for both local actors and global institutions. In this way, I have emphasised both the *materiality* of heritage and its affects, and the *connectivity* of heritage with people, objects and institutions. In Chapter 7, I explore another conceptual crisis for heritage that has emerged in relation to questions of human rights, diversity and cultural heritage.

7

HERITAGE, DIVERSITY AND HUMAN RIGHTS

Introduction

I have argued that one of the implications of the World Heritage Convention's assertion of universality was the inability of the World Heritage Committee to ignore the claims for representation that emerged as a result of the global application of a specific set of discontinuous, modern, post-Enlightenment ideas about heritage and the past, which had developed in Euro-American contexts over the nineteenth and twentieth centuries, to countries and communities with radically different conceptions of heritage. This, coupled with the abundance and globalisation of heritage in late-modern societies (as a consequence not only of the work of UNESCO and its advisory bodies, but also of broader processes of the restructuring of global economies, the growth of international heritage tourism, and the increasingly transnational flows of people, capital, ideas and images), generated a series of conceptual 'crises' for heritage that have seen radical transformations in how it is defined, managed and understood in the contemporary world. One of the major implications of this series of crises was a shift towards more 'representative' models of heritage, away from the 'canonical' model of heritage that emphasised aspects of high culture, and an attendant shift in the definition of heritage, which came to encompass a broader range of material and non-material entities (in particular, landscapes, traditional cultural practices, and the spaces in which they are performed) and the relationships between them.

In this chapter, I explore another of these conceptual crises, which has arisen as a result of the clash between the nation-building functions of heritage and the widespread commercialisation of the past as heritage in transnational, postcolonial and multicultural societies. On one hand, the increasing role of heritage in global economies pushes heritage to be more inclusive and to market itself (and make itself more directly relevant) to broader and more diverse audiences, a process that leads it to operate as a sort of 'differencing machine' (to borrow the term Bennett, 2006 uses to describe the work of contemporary museums). On the other hand, in the 'age of security' the more traditional role of heritage as part of the educative apparatus of the state seems to pull heritage in the opposite direction, towards the production of a single, dominant national narrative. These processes are themselves caught up in more complex issues relating to the changing politics of multiculturalism, cosmopolitanism and difference. My suggestion in this chapter is that the principle of cultural relativity that underpins the representative, 'values-based' approach to heritage, which I have argued characterises the major shift in direction for the management of heritage in the late twentieth and early twenty-first centuries, is fundamentally inconsistent with the principle of cultural diversity, and with the idea of universal human rights or a 'universal' World Heritage Convention. This conceptual crisis, although existing independently of it, has become well and truly entrenched as an issue for heritage as a consequence of the 2001 UNESCO Universal Declaration on Cultural Diversity, which suggests that cultural diversity *is itself* part of the common heritage of humanity; and the adoption of the 2003 Convention for the Safeguarding of Intangible Cultural Heritage and 2005 Convention on the Protection and Promotion of the Diversity of Cultural Expressions. This chapter traces the origins of this crisis and discusses its implications for heritage more generally as a key area of concern for interdisciplinary critical heritage studies. In making this argument, I draw particularly on Barbara Kirshenblatt-Gimblett's (2006) discussion of cultural relativity and diversity in the context of World Heritage and the global cultural economy.

Heritage and nation-building in a transnational world

In Chapter 3 I explored the origins of heritage in nation-building, and in Chapter 5 the earliest critical accounts of heritage in the exploration of this phenomenon. For example, Graham et al. (2000: 55–6) note

> The origins of what we now term heritage lie in the modernist nexus of Euro-
> pean state formation and Romanticism, which is defined in political terms by
> nationalism. While these nineteenth century European nationalisms evolved
> many different trajectories, they shared in the mutual assumption of modernity
> that all people of 'a similar ethical rationality might agree on a system of norms
> to guide the operation of society'.

The authors suggest that the canon of heritage developed as one of a set of discourses used to frame the idea that all members of a nation would share the same ideas and the same systems of norms. They continue,

> Hence nationalist discourses are sited within a sense of limitless change and
> advance which, in turn, demanded the creation of modernistic, progressive,
> linear heritage narratives that sought to subsume the diversity and heterogeneity
> of the everyday world. These were combined with assumptions of long-term
> continuities of culture, place and allegiance and constructed to lead directly to

the contemporary nexus of power, providing the precepts and traditions which underpin the legitimacy of that authority.

(Graham et al. 2000: 56)

Traditionally, nations are founded on the idea that citizens must hold shared cultural beliefs, with heritage as the foundation which roots those beliefs, and the structures of power and authority that underlie them, in the past. In doing so, nations connect these shared beliefs closely to the idea of racial and ethnic origins (Anderson [1983] 2006).

Another important aspect of heritage and its use in the production of nation lies in the construction of origin myths, which establish not only the norms of the current system of political and social power in individual societies, but also the series of behaviours and systems of class, gender and ethnic (or racial) inequalities on which such power rests (Hobsbawm 1983a). In the words of Stuart Hall, heritage is a 'discursive practice' which creates a sense of belonging to the nation.

> We should think of The Heritage as a discursive practice. It is one of the ways in which the nation slowly constructs for itself a sort of collective social memory. Just as individuals and families construct their identities in part by 'storying' the various random incidents and contingent turning points of their lives into a single, coherent, narrative, so nations construct identities by selectively binding their chosen high points and memorable achievements into an unfolding 'national story' ... Like personal memory, social memory is also highly selective, it highlights and foregrounds, imposes beginnings, middles and ends on the random and contingent. Equally, it foreshortens, silences, disavows, forgets and elides many episodes which – from another perspective – could be the start of a different narrative. This process of selective 'canonisation' confers authority and a material and institutional facticity on the selective tradition, making it extremely difficult to shift or revise. The institutions responsible for making the 'selective tradition' work develop a deep investment in their own 'truth'.
>
> *(Hall [1999] 2008: 221)*

Since the late eighteenth century, officially sanctioned forms of heritage have functioned as integral devices for the production of origin myths within which to root the histories, laws and traditions of nationhood, and for establishing a series of norms that explain the rules by which nation-states and their citizens should behave and interact with one another. Heritage and nationalism are thus fundamentally intertwined.

Heritage, multiculturalism and multi-'culturalism'

This model of the relationship between heritage and nationalism was developed primarily to explain the emergence and maintenance of monocultural nation-states between the eighteenth and early twentieth centuries. However, as noted in Chapter 4, the late-modern period is one in which many of the impediments that had contributed to the maintenance of isolation between nation-states have shifted or broken down. The (relatively) free flow of people (and capital) across national borders can be seen to be characteristic of the late twentieth and early twenty-first centuries, deriving from a series of global diasporas as result of various mid-century conflicts that continued to gather pace as modernity entered its late, 'liquid' (cf. Bauman 2000) phase. Many governments responded to these changes by developing policies that were explicitly targeted at managing the cultural and ethnic diversity of its populace. The term 'multiculturalism' came into popular use in the 1970s to describe the development of a series of government policies to manage the 'problem' of the existence of a wide number of different ethnic groups within a single nation (Ang 2005). It needs to be set against previous government policies of assimilation of different ethnic and racial groups into a single, monocultural nation-state, and it represents an acknowledgement not only of the failure of the assimilation project, but also of the positive aspects of cultural diversity. Multiculturalism was first officially adopted as government policy in Canada in 1971, in response to the 1963–69 Royal Commission on Bilingualism and Biculturalism, which had been set up to consider claims of injustice raised by the French-speaking minority located primarily in and around Quebec. The report of the Commission recommended the Canadian Government should formally acknowledge Canada as a bilingual and bicultural society, and should adopt policies to promote that diversity. Australia followed Canada in the adoption of formal policies of multiculturalism in 1973. Other contemporary countries with explicit or implicit bicultural or multicultural policies at the national or federal level include the UK, the USA, New Zealand and South Africa.

While multiculturalism emerged as a novel concept in the 1970s among Western industrialised nations, it had effectively existed in many countries (for example, India, Malaysia and Singapore) for decades, if not longer. Nonetheless, at the time of writing there are a number of nations, such as Korea, Japan and the Netherlands, that remain opposed to national policies which promote multiculturalism. Indeed, even in those countries where it has been adopted as formal government policy, there remains a significant critique of multiculturalism on both left and right sides of the political spectrum. Conservative political interests have traditionally been opposed to multi-cultural policies, particularly since '9/11'—the terrorist attacks on the US World Trade Center in New York and the Pentagon building in Virginia on 11 September 2001 (see Chapter 8). In the wake of these and other terrorist activities focused on Western countries and associated with radical Muslim extremist ideologies, many countries have hosted debates about the value of ethnic and cultural diversity, and many Muslims living in, or wishing to immigrate to, Western countries have been the target of calls to limit or halt immigration (Ang 2005). However, criticism of multiculturalism and its policies has also come from those on the left who support the principle of cultural diversity, who suggest that multicultural politics can mask real social, economic and political inequality beneath the rhetoric of political correctness (Wikan 1999, 2002; Grillo 2003). Multicultural policies have often been used by nation-states to disguise and avoid dealing with epistemic racism in circumstances under which social inequality comes to be relabelled as cultural difference. Multiculturalism is, at best, a contested topic, and one that is seen to have increasing significance in the early twenty-first century as governments struggle to maintain the nation-state in the absence of strict monocultural controls. It is now widely conceded that concepts of national identity, ethnicity and the role of religion in society must be rethought to give greater attention to the meaning and process of making culture in the late-modern world (Baumann 1999).

As noted above, multiculturalism is integrally linked with globalisation. Appadurai suggests we might think of the term 'culturalism' as an active term denoting 'identities consciously in the making' (1996: 15). He discusses the phenomenon of culturalism in the light of the widespread emergence of ethnic nationalism and separatism that characterised the last decade of the twentieth century (for example, in the Balkan states and post-Soviet nations), which was coupled with the phenomenon of globalisation. He suggests that the ethnic violence that accompanied this ethnic nationalism was not a rebirth of 'tribalism' from the past, but a new phenomenon relating to the employment of cultural differences to serve national or transnational political interests. Appadurai sees culturalism as linked closely to the idea of migration or succession of groups of people. These movements deliberately evoke aspects of history and heritage in the struggle between particular groups and the state. Appadurai links these developments with the experience of 'speed' and change in the late-modern period (see Chapter 4), and the state of mass migration and continual electronic mediation, which are a part of globalisation.

> What is new is that this is a world in which both points of departure and points of arrival are in cultural flux, and thus the search for steady points of reference, as critical life choices are made, can be very difficult ... as the search for certainties is regularly frustrated by the fluidities of transnational communication. As group pasts become increasingly parts of museums, exhibits and collections, both in national and transnational spectacles, culture becomes less what Pierre Bourdieu would have called a *habitus* (a tacit realm of reproducible practices and dispositions) and more an arena for conscious choice, justification, and representation, the latter often to multiple and spatially dislocated audiences.
>
> *(Appadurai 1996: 44)*

So when we think about contemporary global societies, it is perhaps better to think of multi-'culturalism', in the sense that all contemporary societies are composed of one or more groups actively using various forms of representation to imagine themselves and their relationships not only with other groups of people, but also with the nation-state. Thus culturalism embraces class divisions and other socio-economic distinctions. Similarly, the concept involves the work of the nation-state in imagining itself and its relationship with its citizens in particular ways, and the various economic and political implications of that work of imagination. While these issues are particularly pronounced in nations that have explicit multicultural policies, they are nonetheless international issues that flow from globalisation and the conditions of late capitalism (see also Kymlicka 1997).

Heritage as the management of different competing 'values'

This project of the increasing recognition of 'difference' has manifested itself in relation to heritage as a series of debates around notions of 'value'. While we have already seen that the concept of 'universal heritage value' was integral to the 1972 World Heritage Convention, the conservation of heritage as the management of different sets of 'values' did not receive critical attention until the 1980s or 1990s (Labadi 2007). The Australia ICOMOS Burra Charter, which was first developed in 1979 (and subsequently revised in 1988 and again in 1999), is generally considered to be the first formal heritage charter to foreground the explicit role of 'significance' and a value-based typology in heritage conservation management planning (Clark 2010). The Burra Charter suggests that the management of a heritage object, place or landscape should be determined by its significance according to a series of different categories of value—aesthetic, historic, scientific, social and spiritual (note the latter category was added in the 1999 revision)—themselves based on the forms of significance that were recognised in the 1964 Venice Charter. Clearly, any decision to conserve or not to conserve an object, place or practice from the past must be based on an assumption of value, but over the past few decades there have been a number of efforts to define the criteria on which conservation decisions are made, based on the recognition that the values of heritage are not inherent or intrinsic (Mason 2002; Smith 2006), but instead are established in the present according to implicit or explicit criteria. From the mid-1990s onwards, the notion of 'social' value has gained increasing importance in the determination of heritage significance (Labadi 2007: 149; Byrne 2008), alongside the recognition that the same heritage object, site or place may be attributed very different values by different stakeholders or members of society (Ashworth et al. 2007). This idea has been particularly transformative in terms of the narratives, exhibitionary practices and representational logics of new museums (see Message 2006).

This process of giving greater attention to social values, and the accompanying recognition that different people attribute different values to heritage, developed simultaneously with a series of other shifts, which I have referred to as the development of more 'representative' approaches to heritage. In general terms, this has meant an acknowledgement that, in a culturally diverse world, it is impossible to attribute a single set of positive values to a single 'canon' of heritage, and the recognition that different groups in society wish to see themselves, their values and their histories represented in the 'national story' of heritage. I have already noted the ways in which this has also been driven by the economics of heritage and tourism, the increased emphasis on individual 'experience', and the need to market heritage to an increasingly diverse set of consumers. What this has amounted to, more or less, is the development of a 'relative' approach to the question of heritage values, in which it is acknowledged that different cultural groups are entitled to value different forms of heritage and to attribute to them different forms of values. This constituted a major shift from the canonical approach to heritage, which insisted on absolute standards of significance and thus one set of norms, particularly around tangible heritage and aesthetic value.

Clearly, this relative approach would appear to be inconsistent with the idea of 'universal' heritage values in the World Heritage Convention, and this has been the basis for much of the critique of the Convention that has emerged from the inter-disciplinary field of academic heritage studies (see Chapter 5). It seems to make little sense, then, that at the same time that there has been a greater concern with recog-nising the different values of individuals and community groups, that there has also been a growth in the number of World Heritage sites (see Chapter 3) and the sig-nificance of the concept of World Heritage within the field of heritage management generally. How are we to account for this apparent contradiction? And what role has it played in weakening the connection between heritage and the nation-state?

Culture, heritage, modernity and 'difference'

Understanding the implications of multiculturalism and the weakening of the connection between heritage and the nation-state requires a consideration of the changing role of 'culture' in late-modernity. Bauman (2011) suggests that we might see three broad phases in the development of the principle of culture. The first was associated with the Enlightenment project and was transformative in intent, deriving from the idea that the educated classes could cultivate and communicate a set of universal values to the masses. The second saw the nation-state increasingly attempt to take control of this process for the education and governance of its citizens, to produce an 'imagined community'. This phase, which he argues was the one analysed and documented by Pierre Bourdieu in *Distinction* (1984), saw culture assume the role of stabilising the nation-state, of establishing a set of principles by which the classes defined themselves in opposition to one another, and by which nations did the same. In the final, late ('liquid') modern phase, Bauman suggests that culture is no longer a normative principle concerned with regulation, but exists primarily to seduce and drive consumption. He argues that the globalisation of capital, technology, labour and corporations and the accompanying mass-migrations and flows of people and information associated with the late phase of modernity have so weakened the power of the nation-state to maintain its borders that culture can no longer function towards the stabilisation of state power. Instead, he suggests that culture has been ceded to market forces and exists only to stimulate the desire for consumption, in which heritage forms an important com-mercial growth area. The ideological or cultural mobilisation of individuals under the banner of a sense of collective identity is thus relegated to the community level, where it tends to be enlisted only when the community feels a sense of threat.

Given that 'culture' draws so closely on 'heritage' to establish the origins of the forms that it takes in the contemporary nation, Bauman's three phases of culture in the modern period can be mapped almost directly onto the three phases of heritage identified in Chapters 3 and 4, themselves linked closely to various changes in the nature of capitalism. In the first phase, heritage is perceived as a set of positive qualities associated with philanthropic efforts to conserve aspects of the natural and cultural environment for the public good. In the second, heritage is increasingly caught up in processes of state regulation and bureaucracy and the nation-building project. In the third, heritage is increasingly commercialised and marketed as an experience, while it simultaneously adopts a 'representative' model based on an assumption of the value of diversity. As a consequence, it is broadened to include many different forms, which represent a number of different constituents, but which are also able to be marketed to different groups with different tastes. This helps to account for the development of representative models of heritage in the late-modern period, which are targeted to the interests and needs of particular community groups, and the shift away from singular national 'canons' of heritage.

There are a number of important implications of this weakening of the connection between heritage and the nation-state (see also Ashworth et al. 2007), all of which tend to assert themselves under conditions of threat of one form or another. Under certain circumstances, it appears that the state resists the dissolution of the link between nation-building and heritage and tries to reassert control of heritage as part of the development of a 'national story' when its authority is threatened, leading to attempts to develop strong singular national narratives. Similar circumstances may arise when an old political regime is overthrown and a new one is established, for example in the case of post-apartheid South Africa, which has experienced a period of accelerated nation-building using heritage (see Coombes 2003; chapters in Murray et al. 2007; and further discussion below). Under other circumstances, heritage comes to be managed at a community level, but might also be used to make strong boundary claims that exclude outsiders. These community level forms of heritage might simultaneously be exhibited and consumed by wealthy cosmopolitan elites for whom the 'experience' of cultural difference has become its own mark of 'distinction' (Bauman 2011). What makes tracking these different regimes of heritage difficult is the potential for apparently completely opposed processes to operate simultaneously within contemporary nation-states due to the dissolution of the power of heritage and culture as state-led regulatory regimes. I will briefly explore several examples that exemplify some of these different approaches, before moving on to consider the issues that might arise from the promotion of diversity as a value in relation to heritage in its own right.

Croatia and the management of a monocultural national heritage

The former Yugoslavian Balkan states provide good examples of countries that have strongly resisted the dissolution of the relationship between heritage and nation-building (Murzyn 2008). Since Croatia became an independent Republic in 1991 following the fall of Communism and the break-up of the former Socialist Federal Republic of Yugoslavia, it has pursued an active programme of nation-building, drawing strongly on historic imagery and ideas of a unified, heroic Croatian past rooted in the exhibition and interpretation of national sites and World Heritage sites (Goulding and Domic 2008). For example, the City of Dubrovnik, which was listed as a World Heritage site in 1979, was besieged by Serb-Montenegrin forces for seven months beginning in 1991, during which time it received heavy damage from shelling. The story of its recent siege and post-1995 reconstruction under the advice of

UNESCO is now emphasised in interpretive signage around the city walls, fusing the story of recent resistance to armed conflict with near neighbours with the monumental and historic values of the site (Figures 7.1 and 7.2). Since 1995, Croatia has been successful in having an additional four sites added to the World Heritage List, bringing its present number to eight World Heritage sites (seven cultural and one natural). Considering these new listings alongside those sixteen sites that, at the time of writing, have been nominated to the tentative list is informative. The cultural sites are dominated by fortified medieval and Renaissance cities, Roman imperial sites, and early churches and religious complexes. The emphasis on sites from these periods demonstrates a clear attempt to develop a national story that highlights periods of Croatian autonomy (through an emphasis on sites that date to the period of its kingdom and subsequent Hungarian union) and resistance to outsiders (through its emphasis on castles and fortified settlements), despite the very recent origins of the present Croatian sovereign state. The Roman sites are considered to pre-date the period of the arrival of Croats in the seventh century, but also connect Croatia historically with a tangibly monumental heroic Roman past.

These themes of national and local resistance to non-Croatian 'outsiders' also feature strongly in the nominations to the UNESCO Representative List of Intangible Cultural Heritage, which is another area in which Croatia has been very active in recent years

FIGURE 7.1 View across the Old City of Dubrovnik, Croatia from the city walls. The extent of bomb damage is apparent from freshly tiled rooftops and reconstructed walls, such as those in the centre foreground. (Photograph by the author.)

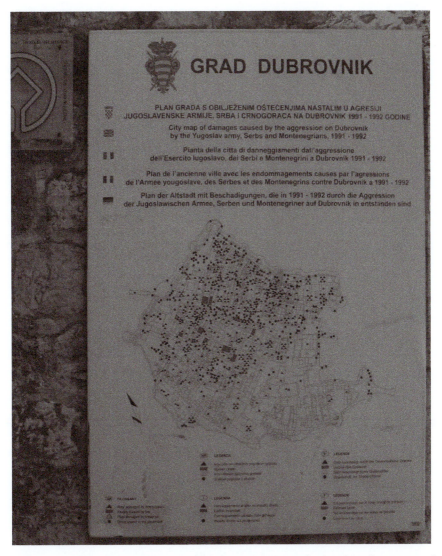

FIGURE 7.2 Interpretive sign in the Old City of Dubrovnik showing the extent of damage to buildings caused during the seven-month siege that took place during the Croatian War of Independence. (Photographer unknown.)

in making nominations to the World Heritage Committee. At the time of writing, it has ten practices or expressions of intangible cultural heritage listed on the Representative List of the Intangible Cultural Heritage of Humanity or the List of Intangible Cultural Heritage in Need of Urgent Safeguarding (Table 7.1). This is more than any other European country besides Spain, which also has ten (Croatia and Spain are

TABLE 7.1 Croatian practices or expressions of intangible cultural heritage listed on the UNESCO List of Intangible Cultural Heritage in Need of Urgent Safeguarding or Representative List of the Intangible Cultural Heritage of Humanity.

Intangible Heritage List	Practice or expression of Intangible Heritage	Year gazetted
List of Intangible Cultural Heritage in Need of Urgent Safeguarding	Ojkanje singing	2010
Representative List of the Intangible Cultural Heritage of Humanity	Gingerbread craft from Northern Croatia	2010
	The Sinjska Alka, a knights' tournament in Sinj	2010
	Annual carnival bell ringers' pageant from the Kastav area	2009
	The festivity of Saint Blaise, the patron of Dubrovnik	2009
	Lacemaking in Croatia	2009
	Procession Za Krizen ('following the cross') on the island of Hvar	2009
	Spring procession of *ljelje/kraljice* (queens) from Gorjani	2009
	Traditional manufacturing of children's wooden toys in Hrvatsko Zagorje	2009
	Two-part singing and playing in the Istrian scale	2009

themselves, at the time of writing, joint third only to Japan and China in having the largest number of listings of all of the 137 States Parties who have ratified the Convention). The practices or expressions of intangible heritage represented take a number of different forms, including festivals and processions, singing, and cooking and craft production.

The nomination documents for these practices or expressions of intangible heritage clearly emphasise themes of Croatian independence and national resistance. For example, the nomination document for the spring procession of *ljelje/kraljice* (queens) from Gorjani (Figure 7.3) notes:

> Since [the] 1990s, from the establishment of independent Croatian state, many local initiatives for renewal and safeguarding of ancient customs and other traditions appeared. It especially refers to those customs and traditions that were suppressed after the Second World War and during the communist rule due to their relation to religious holidays and the peasant segment of Croatian society. Kraljice were held sporadically during that time as well but their renewal in Gorjani village happened in the 1960s on the initiative and with the help of experts. In those years folklore festivals in Croatia, established in 1930s, were restored with the intention of encouraging the preservation of Croatian traditional peasant culture ... More recently, kraljice and similar customs are treated as cultural heritage of special value, so the state and local administration started

morally and financially supporting their performance. It is mostly done in the form of financial support to cultural-artistic societies that are training new generations of girls and representing kraljice on the stage and in their village on the traditional day. With the support of the state and the City of Zagreb, research and a folklore festival were organized in 2005. The festival included the performances of 11 kraljice groups from Croatia, Serbia, Hungary and the Czech Republic. The proclamation of kraljice from Gorjani as intangible heritage and also their inscription in the Register of Cultural Heritage of the Republic of Croatia has opened a path for inscription and safeguarding of other kraljice from Croatia.

(UNESCO 2009a)

The suppression of local 'Croatian' cultural traditions under the Socialist Federal Republic of Yugoslavia seems to be a particular theme that is emphasised as having threatened many of the traditions listed on the Intangible Heritage Lists. In this way, it could be argued that Croatia has actively pursued a monocultural nation-building programme, drawing on both tangible and intangible heritage, since it became an independent sovereign state in 1991.

Diversity as national heritage: South Africa's 'rainbow nation' and Malaysia's 'zoological multiculturalism'

South Africa provides an example of a country that has taken a very different approach to the problem of building a national story in the wake of significant changes that

FIGURE 7.3 Spring procession of *ljelje/kraljice* (queens) from Gorjani, Croatia. (Photograph by Vidoslav Bagur, 2009. © UNESCO/Vidoslav Bagur.)

have required an explicit political programme of nation-building in the post-apartheid era. Under the presidency of Nelson Mandela, post-apartheid South Africa quickly sought to establish itself as a new nation, in which

> each of us is as intimately attached to the soil of this beautiful country as are the famous jacaranda trees of Pretoria and the mimosa trees of the bushveld – a rainbow nation at peace with itself and the world.
>
> *(quoted in Manzo 1996: 71)*

In their important discussion of heritage in plural societies, Ashworth et al. (2007: 194) suggest that South Africa's construction of itself as a 'rainbow nation' demonstrates an attempt to develop a mosaic society in which a new past must be created to reflect the new political and ideological circumstances of the present. They point to the use of the heritage of apartheid in the post-apartheid era to contrast with the modern political regime, to develop a vision of history in terms of a linear narrative from 'bad past' regime to 'good contemporary' one, as well as to develop the theme of the struggle for freedom (see also Coombes 2003: 120).

An example of a heritage site that embodies both narratives is the District Six Museum in Cape Town, which has become an important space in which to negotiate new national identity issues whilst making reparations for past racial and social injustices. The museum explains its origins and meaning in terms of reparation and memorialisation of the clearances of large numbers of 'non-whites' from the mixed community of coloured and immigrant people that occurred in Cape Town in 1965 (more detailed analyses of the museum are presented in Hall 2001; Rassool and Prosalendis 2001; Coombes 2003; Rassool 2007):

> Up until the 1970s, District Six was home to almost a tenth of the city of Cape Town's population. In 1965, the apartheid government, as it had done in Sophiatown in 1957, declared District Six 'white'. More than 60,000 people were forcibly uprooted and relocated onto the barren plains of the Cape Flats. In the process, over a century of history, of community life, of solidarity amongst the poor and of achievement against great odds, was imperilled.
>
> The District Six Museum Foundation was established in 1989 and launched as a museum in 1994 to keep alive the memories of District Six and displaced people everywhere. It came into being as a vehicle for advocating social justice, as a space for reflection and contemplation and as an institution for challenging the distortions and half-truths which propped up the history of Cape Town and South Africa. As an independent space where the forgotten understandings of the past are resuscitated, where different interpretations of that past are facilitated through its collections, exhibitions and education programmes, the Museum is committed to telling the stories of forced removals and assisting in the reconstitution of the community of District Six and Cape Town by drawing on a heritage of non-racialism, non-sexism, anti-class discrimination and the encouragement of debate.
>
> *(District Six Museum 2011)*

The exhibition *Streets* has formed the core of the museum since it opened in 1994 (Rassool 2007: 119). *Streets* consists of a large floor overlain by family names hand-written by District Six former residents and showing the spaces where the people lived prior to being relocated (Figure 7.4). Bordering the map is a series of artists' prints and paintings, and hanging above are four banners with symbols representing the religions of Christianity, Islam, Judaism and Hinduism, 'an acknowledgement of the religious harmony and tolerance that existed in the neighbourhood' (District Six Museum 2011). A series of seventy-five original District Six street signs hangs in three tiers as a backdrop to the map—'a tangible reminder of "home", signposting nothing but our memories and treasured experiences of a past District Six' (District Six Museum 2011). Below the signs are boxes containing artefacts collected from archaeological excavations at District Six by the University of Cape Town. Further displays adjacent to the floor map focus on individual and family memories of indi-vidual places and streets in District Six through the use of photographs and oral recollections of the area. Temporary exhibits deal with other aspects of the history of District Six and other forced removals in South Africa's history.

The District Six Museum Foundation developed out of the 'Hands off District Six' campaign, one of a series of groups concerned with preserving the memory of District Six that grew up in the years following the forced removals and in tandem with the struggle for freedom from apartheid (Rassool 2007: 119). This local remit was itself already a significant one, but with the change of political regime South Africa has sought to re-imagine its national past, using heritage, in new ways. Central to the process has been the emergence of the victim of forced removal as a prominent figure in the perception of Cape Town's past and the national imagination.

> If the emblematic figure of African modernity in Johannesburg is the migrant worker, a figure that moves from the margins to the underground world of the mine, then in the case of Cape Town, with its history of (limited) racial cohabitation and subsequent segregation through apartheid, the emblematic urban figure is the victim of forced removal. The experience of forced removal has emerged as a key event in shaping communities of memory in the post-apartheid period, just as it has been central to public negotiations around heritage, identity and the transformation of urban spaces.
>
> *(Shepherd and Murray 2007: 14)*

District Six has thus emerged as a key part of South Africa's re-imagining of its past, and as a forum for discussion of the impact of forced removals on South African history and society more generally. This is reflected in the global attention that has been focused on the museum, and its place in academic commentary on the role of heritage in post-apartheid South Africa (Hall 2001; Coombes 2003; Shepherd and Murray 2007).

An overarching theme of the museum is compensation for past injustices—those in relation to apartheid more generally as well as injustices specific to Cape Town. This is in part a reflection of the growth of the museum in tandem with a movement that

FIGURE 7.4 District Six Museum interior, showing the *Streets* exhibition at the centre of the museum. (Photograph by Werner Dieterich. © Werner Dieterich/Alamy.)

called for land restitution for the victims of forced removals. The museum has explicitly articulated its mission as the recovery of lost memory (Hall 2001; Rassool and Prosalendis 2001; Rassool 2007). Through its emphasis on the histories of the poor and dispossessed, it seeks explicitly to place the history of subaltern people in the forefront of heritage and tourism in the city. By encouraging former residents to write themselves back on to the map of District Six, the museum attempts to recover for them the places from which they were forcibly removed (Coombes 2003: 128). It is a development consistent with the museum's involvement in the political struggle to secure land restitution for former District Six residents. Its focus on the recovery of memory and history can be seen as an attempt to counter the negative aspects of a past political regime and to create a new past to assist in the production of a new future.

Another reason for the museum's emergence as a place of national heritage importance is the way in which on the one hand it conserves the memory of apartheid, while on the other it celebrates a counter-memory of apartheid through its stories of harmonious relations among mixed communities, which existed for a time simultaneously with the regime. This sees the museum transform District Six into a popular symbol of the subversion of apartheid and part of the new national history of resistance to the regime, rooting the current national political agenda in the past and providing a set of foundation stories for a post-apartheid era.

Other countries, such as Singapore, Canada and Malaysia, have similarly promoted their culturally diverse make-up as an aspect of their history and heritage in an attempt to resolve the 'problem' of nation-building in an ethnically diverse country by rooting the relationships between different ethnic groups in the past (Ashworth et al. 2007; Tunbridge 2008; Hack 2010). The Melaka and George Town, Historic Cities of the Straits of Malacca World Heritage Site in Malaysia is typical of this process, in which diversity is made into a national possession by emphasising current multiculturalisms as a feature of the historic past. In George Town in Penang, the successive colonial and local cultural influences and historic co-existence of Chinese, Indian, European and Malay peoples is made into a mirror of a postcolonial, transnational present. The distinct inequalities that characterised the treatment of different ethnic groups at different points in Malaysia's history are largely ignored in the interpretation of the heritage of George Town, which instead focuses on the 'great variety of religious buildings of different faiths, ethnic quarters, the many languages, worship and religious festivals, dances, costumes, art and music, food, and daily life' (UNESCO 2011a) as if these were somehow all treated equally in the past.

Such an approach might be seen as a form of 'zoological multiculturalism' (after Bennett 2006, drawing on Hage 1998), in which the diversity of heritages of different ethnic groups are exhibited for tourists as part of the experience and consumption of multiculturalism. In Penang, the exhibition of multicultural heritage is explicitly linked with 'experiential' tourism, involving the consumption of different ethnic cuisines, the staging of various different religious and cultural practices, and the presentation of different museums and historic houses representing each of the main ethnic groups from the island. Bennett (2006), drawing on the work of Ghassan Hage (1998), argues that these practices of 'cosmo-multiculturalism' tend to address

FIGURE 7.5 The Pinang Peranakan Mansion House Museum in Penang, Malaysia, celebrating the recent inscription of George Town to the World Heritage List as
part of the Melaka and George Town, Historic Cities of the Straits of
Malacca World Heritage Site in 2009. (Photograph by the author.)

themselves to white, cosmopolitan, educated, urban elites, and may have little impact
in terms of opening cross-cultural dialogue at the local level. Observations of developments in the wake of the World Heritage bid suggest that it has done little to open
up the question of cross-class or cross-cultural inequalities in the city, and has tended
to foster a sense of civic identity, in which Penang emphasises its personality as a
'global' city and an international heritage destination, rather than questions of equality
and its civic responsibilities to its citizens (Nagata 2010). In this way, the promotion
of 'multicultural heritage' can also come to mask systemic racism and political, social
and economic inequality.

Universal heritage values and the right to cultural diversity

I have considered examples that demonstrate different responses to the 'problem'
of nation-building in the context of a weakening relationship between citizens and
the geographical boundaries of the state which characterises late-modernity. But
these examples raise a deeper conceptual conflict between the idea of 'universal'
values, human rights and the preservation and exhibition of cultural diversity. The
relationship between human rights and cultural heritage has not received explicit
academic attention until relatively recently (Silverman and Ruggles 2007; Logan
2008; Hodder 2010; Logan et al. 2010; Meskell 2010), despite the fact that many
appeals to rights associated with forms of cultural heritage have overlapped with

human rights issues, for example Indigenous land rights (Gilbert 2006). However, recent developments in relation to the 2002 UNESCO Universal Declaration on Cultural Diversity, the 2003 UNESCO Convention for the Safeguarding of the Intangible Cultural Heritage, and the 2005 UNESCO Convention on the Protection and Promotion of the Diversity of Cultural Expressions suggest the importance of considering these areas concurrently. The apparent conflicts between the management of intangible heritage and cultural diversity as part of a 'bundle' of universal human rights and heritage values suggests that there is significant potential for these different forms of rights to come into conflict with one another. Further, the focus on diversity as a universal human right has the potential to distract from the ways in which difference has almost always been used in relation to heritage in an exclusionary manner, in the unequal distribution of power and in claims to ownership over territory (be it geographic, cultural, ideological or historical territory). But before I consider these issues, I want to explore the interconnected history of universal human and cultural rights to attempt to unpick some of the issues raised by these more recent conventions.

In Chapter 3, I outlined the emergence of the UNESCO World Heritage Convention within the context of a series of post-war safeguarding missions, beginning with the Aswan High Dam campaign. But the foundation of the World Heritage Convention and its various advisory bodies needs to be set within a broader context of the idea of an international system of cooperation and regulation that emerged at the end of the Second World War from the 1944 Bretton Woods United Nations Monetary and Financial Conference, which established a series of organisations, including the International Monetary Fund, to regulate international financial security and aid postwar reconstruction and political stability, and with the establishment of the United Nations (UN) to maintain peace and promote international cooperation in addressing economic, social and humanitarian issues. The idea of promoting and upholding a set of universal human rights was central to the establishment of the UN, following the various humanitarian atrocities and genocide that had characterised the Second World War. The UN Charter, which was signed on 26 June 1945 in San Francisco at the conclusion of the UN Conference on International Organization, and came into force on 24 October 1945, obliges all member nations to promote 'universal respect for, and observance of, human rights' and to take 'joint and separate action' to that end. A Universal Declaration of Human Rights was adopted by the UN General Assembly on 10 December 1948 in Paris. Article 27 (1) declares the right to 'freely to participate in the cultural life of the community, to enjoy the arts and to share in scientific advancement and its benefits' to be a fundamental human right. Article 27 (2) notes that 'everyone has the right to the protection of the moral and material interests resulting from any scientific, literary or artistic production of which he is the author'. The Universal Declaration was followed in 1966 by the adoption of an International Covenant on Civil and Political Rights and an International Covenant on Economic, Social and Cultural Rights. The two covenants entered into force in 1976, after a sufficient number of countries had ratified them, and are now often referred to collectively as the International Bill of Human Rights (in which form they are bundled together with the Universal Declaration of Human

Rights). The International Bill of Human Rights is accompanied by a series of other international treaties and human rights instruments, including the Convention on the Elimination of All Forms of Racial Discrimination (adopted 1966, entered into force 1969); the Convention on the Elimination of All Forms of Discrimination Against Women (adopted 1979, entered into force 1981); the Convention on the Rights of the Child (adopted 1989, entered into force 1989); the Convention on the Rights of Persons with Disabilities (adopted 2006, entered into force 2008); and the International Convention on the Protection of the Rights of All Migrant Workers and Members of their Families (adopted 1990, entered into force 2003). These conventions have been concerned with establishing a series of fundamental *individual* rights, upholding principles of equality and protecting against discrimination.

Although its roots lie properly in the work of the League of Nations between the wars, the United Nations Educational, Scientific and Cultural Organization (UNESCO) was established in the months immediately following the San Francisco UN Conference on International Organization, at a UN Conference for the establishment of an educational and cultural organization held in London in November 1945. The Constitution of UNESCO came into force on 4 November 1946 after ratification by twenty countries. It immediately placed the questions of *collective* rights at the heart of its mission, suggesting that it is a misunderstanding of difference, and an ignorance of common humanity, that lies at the root of war, violence and mistrust between different groups of people.

> … ignorance of each other's ways and lives has been a common cause, throughout the history of mankind, of that suspicion and mistrust between the peoples of the world through which their *differences* have all too often broken into war … In consequence whereof … the United Nations Educational, Scientific and Cultural Organization for the purpose of advancing, through the educational and scientific and cultural relations of the peoples of the world, the objectives of international peace and of the *common welfare of mankind* for which the United Nations Organization was established
>
> *(UNESCO 2011f, my emphases).*

The first session of the General Conference of UNESCO was held in Paris from 19 November to 10 December 1946, with the participation of representatives from thirty governments entitled to vote. One of the most pressing issues on UNESCO's agenda revolved around the use of racial science by the Nazis to justify genocide; accordingly, a Statement by Experts on Race Problems was prepared on UNESCO's behalf, and signed by a series of anthropologists, including Claude Levi-Strauss, in July 1950. The statement confirmed 'the unity of mankind [*sic*] from both the biological and social viewpoints … to recognise this and to act accordingly is the first requirement of modern man' (UNESCO 1950: 4), and ultimately led to the 1978 Declaration on Race and Racial Prejudice. I have already shown how the World Heritage Convention emerged over this same period, and considered its implications in terms of the principle of universal heritage values.

So whereas the search for universal human rights emphasised the individual's right to difference, there was a sense in which the search for collective cultural rights was expressed less in terms of difference and more in terms of common humanity. This was certainly the case with the World Heritage Convention's notion of universal heritage value, in which the existence of certain common cross-cultural categories of value were assumed at the collective level. UNESCO's 1966 Declaration on the Principles of International Cultural Cooperation emphasised this notion of collective universal cultural rights by suggesting in its Article 1 that:

1. Each culture has a dignity and value which must be respected and preserved.
2. Every people has the right and the duty to develop its culture.
3. In their rich variety and diversity, and in the reciprocal influences they exert on one another, all cultures form part of the common heritage belonging to all mankind.

(UNESCO 1966)

The relationship between human rights and heritage was made more explicit by UNESCO in November 2001, following the recommendations of its World Culture Report titled *Cultural Diversity, Conflict and Pluralism* (UNESCO 2000), when it issued its Universal Declaration on Cultural Diversity (UNESCO 2002). The declaration, which the report itself notes was issued in the wake of the 9/11 attacks, makes a unique claim—that cultural diversity is itself part of the common heritage of humanity:

> Culture takes diverse forms across time and space. This diversity is embodied in the uniqueness and plurality of the identities of the groups and societies making up humankind. As a source of exchange, innovation and creativity, cultural diversity is as necessary for humankind as biodiversity is for nature. In this sense, it is the common heritage of humanity and should be recognized and affirmed for the benefit of present and future generations.
>
> *(UNESCO 2002: 13)*

Further, it suggests that the promotion of cultural pluralism is a key aspect of social cohesion in plural societies:

> In our increasingly diverse societies, it is essential to ensure harmonious inter-action among people and groups with plural, varied and dynamic cultural identities as well as their willingness to live together. Policies for the inclusion and participation of all citizens are guarantees of social cohesion, the vitality of civil society and peace. Thus defined, cultural pluralism gives policy expression to the reality of cultural diversity. Indissociable from a democratic framework, cultural pluralism is conducive to cultural exchange and to the flourishing of creative capacities that sustain public life.
>
> *(UNESCO 2002: 13)*

The declaration also makes a clear link between cultural diversity and human rights:

> The defence of cultural diversity is an ethical imperative, inseparable from respect for human dignity. It implies a commitment to human rights and fundamental freedoms, in particular the rights of persons belonging to minorities and those of indigenous peoples. No one may invoke cultural diversity to infringe upon human rights guaranteed by international law, nor to limit their scope.
>
> *(UNESCO 2002: 13)*

It attempts to tackle the problem of the requirement of different cultural groups to defend a common heritage in times of conflict or threat and the need to promote cultural diversity by expressing them as two sides of the same human impulse. In his introduction to the declaration, then Director-General of UNESCO Koïchiro Matsuura notes:

> The Universal Declaration makes it clear that each individual must acknowledge not only otherness in all its forms but also the plurality of his or her own identity, within societies that are themselves plural. Only in this way can cultural diversity be preserved as an adaptive process and as a capacity for expression, creation and innovation. The debate between those countries which would like to defend cultural goods and services 'which, as vectors of identity, values and meaning, must not be treated as mere commodities or consumer goods', and those which would hope to promote cultural rights has thus been surpassed, with the two approaches brought together by the Declaration, which has highlighted the causal link uniting two complementary attitudes.
>
> *(UNESCO 2002: 11)*

The declaration was followed by a convention on the Protection and Promotion of the Diversity of Cultural Expressions (UNESCO 2005). The Convention puts into practice the principles of the declaration and establishes the rights and obligations of member parties under the Convention. Its objectives, among others, are:

(d) to foster interculturality in order to develop cultural interaction in the spirit of building bridges among peoples; [and]

(e) to promote respect for the diversity of cultural expressions and raise awareness of its value at the local, national and international levels.

(UNESCO 2005: 3)

Besides the explicitly modernising intent of these various documents and conventions (Logan 2002, 2007; Langfield et al. 2010), it is also worth remembering the connection between the idea of universal values and modernity, mapped out in Chapter 2. The idea of a system of universal rights has generally been seen by anthropologists to sit uncomfortably with an acknowledgement of the cultural relativity and specificity of rights to different human societies; most anthropologists would agree on the need for a broadly pluralistic approach to the question of human rights, although there is disagreement about the extent to which cross-cultural perspectives might generate a sense of commonalities (Messer 1993; Goodale 2006 and comments; Goodale 2008). Many of the questions today seem to remain the same as those which emerged in relation to the concept of cultural relativism from Boasian anthropology, although anthropologists have played a major role working within human rights contexts to promote the cross-cultural study of rights and to bring the question of collective rights, in addition to individual rights, into the conversation.

It is helpful to consider the distinction Barbara Kirshenblatt-Gimblett makes between cultural relativity and diversity in relation to the global cultural economy of Intangible World Heritage. She suggests that the notion of intangible heritage creates an asymmetry between the diversity of those who produce cultural assets, and the humanity to which those assets belong as universal heritage. 'Diversity works centrifugally by generating cultural assets that can be universalised as World Heritage, a process that expands the beneficiaries to encompass all of humanity—your culture becomes everyone's heritage' (Kirshenblatt-Gimblett 2006: 162). By contrast, the notion of cultural relativity 'works centripetally by invoking tolerance of difference to protect, insulate, and strengthen the capacities within individuals and communities to resist efforts to suppress their cultural practices, particularly in situations of religious and cultural conflict' (2006: 162). She uses the terms 'descent heritage' and 'consent heritage' to distinguish between those who 'create' intangible heritage, and those who participate in the recognition of that heritage as part of the common heritage of humanity. These are clearly completely different processes. Designating something as 'intangible heritage' initiates a process by which museological values are applied to the practice or expression in question (and hence the individuals and communities who create it). This has the effect of simultaneously giving that practice or expression some importance in terms of its connection with tradition and the past, whilst also placing it in opposition to the values of modernity, which in contrast are claimed by those who determine what constitutes universal heritage and participate in its consumption. While the idea of intangible heritage is linked explicitly in the Convention with safeguarding and maintenance of tradition, nonetheless this delineation tends to have the opposite effect, of defining it as something in and of the past, and hence somehow less relevant to the present and future.

Kirshenblatt-Gimblett argues that World Heritage legislation has recast cultural relativity as cultural diversity (2006: 185), because relativity is logically opposed to universal standards, while diversity can be made consistent with a concept of universal value, as the Universal Declaration on Cultural Diversity does by asserting diversity as a universal value in its own right. Nonetheless, the existence of a list of practices and expressions of intangible heritage suggests that not all cultural expressions are equally valued (a principle that would seem to undermine the idea that diversity is a universal value), which implies that humanity does not wish to inherit *all* expressions and practices of intangible heritage, only those which meet certain thresholds of value (see also Nielsen 2011). In this sense, the Intangible Heritage Lists return to a model of heritage as a 'canon', despite their emphasis on diversity. What the implications of this process might be in terms of the ways in which heritage is managed in the future remains open to conjecture, but in many ways, this could be argued to represent a radical departure from the direction in which heritage has been developing as a concept over the past four decades.

Whither heritage and its relationship with difference?

One of the serious problems with the emphasis on diversity in relation to heritage in the 2002 UNESCO Universal Declaration on Cultural Diversity, the 2003 UNESCO Convention for the Safeguarding of the Intangible Cultural Heritage, and the 2005 UNESCO Convention on the Protection and Promotion of the Diversity of Cultural Expressions is that difference is treated in a way that assumes it is always interpreted as a positive value in its own right. There is a significant risk when reading these documents of forgetting how an emphasis on cultural, ethnic and racial difference has formed the basis for systemic prejudice and racism, and the primary means by which heritage has functioned for the *exclusion* and *persecution* of different minority groups in society throughout the twentieth and twenty-first centuries. We do not need to look very far to see clear examples of this in the recent past. Appadurai's *Fear of Small Numbers* (2006) considers the connection between globalisation and extreme culturally motivated ethnic violence in the genocides that occurred in the 1990s in eastern Europe, Rwanda and India, and in the new millennium in what was termed the 'war on terror'. He begins by noting that globalisation has produced a new level of uncertainty due to the speed and rate at which people, technology, money, images and ideas can cross national borders. 'Globalisation ... challenges our strongest tool for making newness manageable, and that is the recourse to history' (2006: 35–6). Under some circumstances, the existence of a new category of minorities within society becomes a focus for anxiety caused by such uncertainty:

> Minorities, in a word, are metaphors and reminders of the betrayal of the classical national project. And it is this betrayal – actually rooted in the failure of the nation-state to preserve its promise to be the guarantor of national sovereignty – that underwrites the worldwide impulse to extrude or eliminate minorities.
>
> *(Appadurai 2006: 43)*

He suggests that it is not the large size of the minority or a high level of cultural difference that creates the most anxiety for nations, but the small size of the group and the cultural gap between it and the majority that is most likely to cause friction and erupt into ethnically motivated violence, when one group begins to perceive itself as a threatened majority. He terms such threatened majorities 'predatory identities'

> whose social construction and mobilisation require the extinction of other, proximate social categories ... [which] emerge out of pairs of identities ...

which have long histories of close contact, mixture and some degree of mutual stereotyping ... [in which is involved] some degree of contrasting identification.

(Appadurai 2006: 51)

In other words, these forms of violence erupt against minorities under the very circumstances in which minority heritage is perceived to be threatened by the global community.

Predatory identities may seek to close the gap between majority and national identities by excluding minority 'others'. There is significant potential under such circumstances for expressions and practices of intangible heritage and other forms of heritage in its present guise as 'differencing machine' to be mobilised in the production of difference which the development of such predatory identities require:

> conflicts accelerated in the 1980s and 1990s, during which many nation-states had to simultaneously negotiate two pressures: the pressure to open up their markets to foreign investment, commodities and images and the pressure to manage the capacity of their own cultural minorities to use the globalized language of human rights to argue for their own claims for cultural dignity and recognition. This ... produced a crisis in many countries for the sense of national boundaries, national sovereignty, and the purity of the national ethnos, and it is directly responsible for the growth of majoritarian racisms in societies as diverse as Sweden and Indonesia as well as Romania, Rwanda, and India.
>
> *(Appadurai, 2006: 65)*

Appadurai suggests that the desire for 'completeness' is one of the main sources of inter-ethnic conflict and violence. Rene Girard's articulation of the relationship between mimesis and conflict in *Violence and the Sacred* ([1972] 2005) is important here. He argues that the 'Other' is the root of desire, and since we tend to imitate the desire of others (that is, it is contagious), the threat of violence and conflict is always present in the Other (see also Taussig 1991, 1993).

Discussion of universal rights in relation to minorities has focused particularly on the preservation of culture, language and heritage, which are perceived as threatened by their very existence as 'relics' amongst minority populations. This means that there is the potential under certain social, political and economic circumstances not only for such minorities to be perceived by the state as a threat to the maintenance of national sovereignty, but also for the same logics to be adopted by a majority population, who come to perceive their own culture as threatened by the existence of minorities. Importantly, in the same way that this perception of threat motivates the preservation of minority cultural tradition, it can also be used to justify culturally motivated violence and racial/ethnic cleansing *against* minorities to preserve majority cultures. There are a number of circumstances where diversity or difference might come to be seen as a threat to national sovereignty or majoritarian power. Where minorities within societies seek to use heritage as a tool to maintain effective links with groups of people and ideas existing outside national boundaries, the state may perceive this as a threat to its ability to reproduce an image of itself as a nation. Further, the maintenance of multicultural and minority heritage may create tensions within majority groups, which cause them to become predatory and seek to eliminate certain practices and expressions of heritage to close the gap between majority and minority heritage and culture. Indeed, it remains a fundamental premise that the strongest notion of heritage will always emerge amongst those individuals and communities who feel their sense of identity and community is most threatened, and who seek to empower themselves to resist this process in some way.

So, despite what we have seen in relation to the promotion of multicultural heritage by certain states in relation to national and World Heritage, and the fact that the professional classes and bureaucrats who manage heritage do not always follow the state agenda (and might be motivated by specific aesthetic or specialised interests; Herzfeld 1997), the issue of 'diversity' as a universal right remains a fundamental problem for heritage. Perhaps the only way in which this issue might be addressed is by uncoupling the sense of threat from the maintenance of diversity, in other words, to begin to perceive the maintenance of diversity not as a process of salvaging or preserving threatened relics of community from the past, but as an active, creative, negotiated process of seeking the basis for a common humanity in all of the forms which are available to us in the present. The reason for this suggestion should be reasonably clear—if both heritage and difference as the justification for violence against 'others' are similarly formed as a result of a perception of risk or threat, there seems little hope of uncoupling heritage and the forms of 'othering' on which racially and ethnically motivated violence depends. If, on the other hand, difference and diversity are conceptualised as the basis for an active negotiation of the content or nature of a series of universal human rights, only the forms of which are pre-determined, then the legacy of diversity comes to be conceptualised as a positive good, a series of practices and expressions of culture on which those who seek to negotiate a set of rights can draw. As Bauman notes in his discussion of the potential for 'culture' to unite a multicultural Europe:

> The recognition of such rights is nothing more and nothing less than an invitation to a dialogue, in the course of which merits and defects of the differences under consideration can be discussed and (with any luck) an agreement on their recognition can be reached. Such an attitude is radically different from that of universal fundamentalism, which rejects all other forms of 'being human', while granting only one form the right to an uncontested existence; but it is just as radically different from a specific kind of tolerance propagated by some strains of the so-called politics of 'multiculturalism', which assumes an essentialist character of difference, thus refusing from the outset any negotiations between different lifestyles
>
> (Bauman 2011: 94–5)

Despite the clear positive good of diversity in the world, the relationship between diversity and heritage needs to be managed carefully. Diversity and difference must be emphasised as *inherited* but not *inherent* or *inevitable*—rather as a series of qualities which are constantly chosen, recreated and renegotiated in the present. The current rise of far right organisations in Europe and their appeals to their own threatened heritage cautions against developing a cosmopolitan detachment or *laissez-faire* attitude towards the potential dangers inherent in this unholy trilogy of heritage, threat and the perception of difference. A notion of difference as inherent and inherited is almost always the basis for racism, conflict and prejudice.

Conclusions

If the basis for the connection between heritage and nationhood has traditionally found expression in the origin stories that account for the relationships between national cultures and citizenship, the acknowledgement of diversity as a universal human right has had far-reaching implications for heritage. We have seen how heritage has been used to establish multiculturalism itself as part of contemporary national origin myths, and the ways in which this has the potential to mask social, political and economic inequality by specifying these inequalities as a function of cultural diversity. While the issue of diversity has become more urgent as a result of late-modern changes in processes of globalisation and the associated flows of labour and capital, the systemic inequalities and forms of racism that often underpin the acknowledgement of diversity complicate any account of globalisation and its impact on the management and presentation of heritage. Within this context, difference and diversity must be presented not as inherent, but as something to be chosen and worked at; not as something that is simply rooted in the past, but as an active choice towards which societies work in the present for the future. Similarly, 'universal' rights must themselves also be viewed as negotiated and open to discussion and debate in response to the continually changing diversity of human cultures and their heritages. Our emphasis must remain on processes of constantly remaking culture *in the present*, and not on an easy recourse to tradition as an excuse for the maintenance of social, economic and political inequalities and/or for permitting the continuity of practices which are not humane or which harm or prejudice against others. The relationship between individual and collective human and cultural rights and diversity will remain a key issue for interdisciplinary heritage studies in years to come.

8

HERITAGE AND THE 'PROBLEM' OF MEMORY

Introduction

I have argued that the late-modern period has witnessed an exponential growth in the number of objects and places that are actively identified, listed, conserved and exhibited as heritage, alongside a rapid expansion in the definition of heritage to incorporate a large range of new forms of material memory; from cultural landscapes to intimate, everyday objects. In addition to the preservation of tangible forms of heritage, we have seen a global shift in the increased attention paid to intangible forms of heritage. This has led to the persistent and pervasive 'heritagisation' of society, in which the traces and memories of many different pasts pile up, constantly surfacing and intervening in our present. With all these factors contributing to the exponential growth of heritage lists and registers, we very rarely consider processes by which heritage objects, places and practices might be removed from these lists, deaccessioned from museums and galleries, or allowed to fall into ruin without active intervention. The implication of the abundance of heritage, and this process of the heterogeneous piling up of traces of the past in the present, alongside the increased conservation of intangible heritage practices and traditions, has not been widely considered by heritage practitioners or scholars (but see Pye 2010). If heritage is not a universal category of value, and if objects, places and practices are conserved according to criteria that are culturally determined, then it follows that certain aspects of heritage will at some point cease to be relevant and should be discarded. Instead, our approach has tended to be one that continually lists 'new' heritage without consideration of the values embodied in our past conservation decisions. I suggest that as a result of this, we face a coming 'crisis of accumulation' of the past in the present in the early twenty-first century, which will ultimately undermine the role of heritage in the production of collective memory, overwhelming societies with disparate traces of heterogeneous pasts and distracting us from the active process of forming collective memories in the present.

This chapter considers a number of parallel processes that have contributed to this developing crisis of accumulation of heritage. On the one hand, the increasingly wide definition of heritage employed by bureaucrats, governments and NGOs, and the shift to more representative models of heritage, have dramatically increased the number of heritage objects and places that are conserved. On the other hand, the increased attention to intangible and virtual forms of heritage, and the proliferation of what I term 'absent heritage' (see discussion below), has also contributed to a profusion of memorialisation, even in the absence of 'tangible' traces to commemorate. Nostalgia, and the transformation of outmoded political emblems into 'dark', 'dissonant' or 'conflict' heritage, coupled with the tumultuous political history of regime changes over the course of the second half of the twentieth century and the early twenty-first, has also contributed to this accumulation of heterogeneous, disparate and often conflicting, material and non-material memorials and mnemonic apparatuses in the present. Much of the literature on personal and collective memory suggests that the process of *forgetting* is integral to the process of remembering—that one cannot properly form memories and attach value to them without selecting some things to also forget. Remembering is an active process of cultivating and pruning, not one of completely archiving everything that may or may not be of value in the future. I argue that the same is true of heritage, and without closer attention to processes by which heritage might be deaccessioned or actively removed, and the values that underpin our conservation decisions, we risk being overwhelmed by memory and, in the process, making all heritage worthless. This is not to suggest that we should return to a limited notion of a single heritage 'canon', which would reverse much important work that has been done in making heritage more representative and diverse, but to argue instead that we must move beyond the dominant 'salvage' paradigm to focus on heritage as an active production of the past in the present, which must meet the needs of contemporary societies, rather than assuming that past heritage decisions are beyond question. This should be a key area of attention for critical heritage studies in the coming decades.

A present drowning in its pasts? Modernity's memory problem

The emergence of memory as a crucial concern in Western societies is one of the key cultural and political phenomena of late twentieth century modernity (Huyssen 2000: 57, see also 1995, 2003). Memory discourses first emerged in the West in the 1960s in response to the rise of new social movements, decolonisation and, after 1980, mobilised debates around the testimonial movement and 'remembering' the Holocaust. Richard Terdiman (1993) goes so far as to make note of modernity's 'memory crisis', while Kammen (1995) situates the roots of the postwar heritage movement in the development of a modern sense of nostalgia and an obsession with salvage and preservation; that is, with intentional collective acts of *not* forgetting (see also Otero-Pailos 2008). This has produced a boom in memory writing in the social sciences. Relevant here is recent work on history and memory (Darian-Smith and Hamilton 1994; Le Goff 1996; Nora 1998); memory studies in anthropology (Casey 1987; Olick and Robbins 1995; Teski and Climo 1995; Climo and Cattell 2002); and research on the role of 'remembering' and 'forgetting' in the study of material culture (Forty and Küchler 1999; Kwint et al. 1999; Hallam and Hockey 2001; Küchler 2003). Much of the work on memory in the late twentieth century has focused on the role of popular culture in shaping collective memory and representations of the past. Several historians have argued that in the post-war period, popular culture has become the principal site for the creation and contestation of memory and identity politics (Lipsitz 1990; also see Hamilton 1994). The globalisation of the public anxiety around memory in a media-saturated world, and its flip-side, a feverish obsession with not forgetting, needs to be viewed as one of the most important cultural developments of the past few decades (Huyssen 2003). This obsession with memory relates as much to the management of the memory of past conflicts, injustices and inequities as it does to the memories of 'positive' events and historical occurrences. The ways in which the past is actively produced in the present, and the form of this memorialisation, relate directly to contemporary moral and ethical perspectives on past events.

In Chapter 4 I outlined the dimensions of the late-modern heritage boom and the exponential growth of various official heritage registers, catalogues and lists at all levels—international, national, regional and local. These lists replicated at the same time as the numbers of objects, places and practices on each of them ballooned. The globalisation of what we might term 'the UNESCO approach' to heritage as a result of the spread of World Heritage played a major role in this, in the insistence that States Parties drew up their own national lists in addition to tentative lists prior to nominations being submitted for consideration by the World Heritage Committee. In Chapter 2, I showed how categorising and listing might be understood not only as one of the underlying modes of ordering of modernity, but also as a form of salvage, a direct response to the perception of risk and the vulnerability of heritage and the past, a concept that, I argue following Beck (1992) and others (e.g. Bauman 2000), has accelerated and played an important role in the globalisation of heritage in the late-modern world.

Many of these heritage lists and registers themselves have a long history, during which different, and sometimes conflicting criteria and value systems have governed their operation. And yet, very rarely at the point at which new criteria have been introduced have those lists been revised. There seems to be a general perception that, once objects, places and/or practices are gazetted and hence transformed into heritage, they will very rarely revert or transform into something else. The register comes to act as a sort of holding pen, a limbo. The World Heritage List itself provides a good example of this. Despite the various changes in the scope and definition of heritage employed in the operation of the World Heritage Committee and its States Parties and advisory bodies, a number of which are discussed in Chapter 6, the List has continued to grow annually (see Figures 3.11 and 3.12). Only two places have ever been de-registered from the List, and these not as a result of reconsideration of the criteria for their inscription, but as a result of changes that undermined those values for which they were listed. The first of these sites to be de-listed was the Arabian Oryx Sanctuary, listed in 1994 after the successful breeding and reintroduction of wild Arabian Oryx, extinct in the wild since the 1970s, into this Central Omani reserve. The site was de-listed in 2007 in consultation with the State Party following their reduction of the area of the reserve by 90 per cent and the decline in wild oryx as a result of loss of habitat and poaching (UNESCO 2007). The second, the cultural landscape of the Dresden Elbe Valley in Germany, was also listed as a World Heritage site in 2004. In 2006, the World Heritage Committee placed the site on its list of World Heritage in Danger, and threatened to remove it from the World Heritage List as 'plans to build a bridge across the Elbe would have such a serious impact on the integrity of property's landscape that it may no longer deserve to be on the World Heritage List' (UNESCO 2006). After protracted discussions between the municipal authorities and representatives of the World Heritage Committee, plans for the construction of the controversial four-lane Waldschlösschen Bridge subsequently went ahead, and the site was removed from the List at a meeting of the World Heritage Committee in 2009. Nonetheless, the Committee remained open to components of the landscape being re-nominated, as it 'recognized that parts of the site might be considered to be of outstanding universal value, but that it would have to be presented under different criteria and boundaries' (UNESCO 2009b). Despite these rare cases, which emerge very much as exceptions to the rule, the idea of de-listing any of the (at the time of writing) almost 1000 sites on the World Heritage List due to a reconsideration of the values for which they were listed in the first place seems extremely unlikely. This is also very much the case for almost all other national and regional heritage registers of which I am aware. For example, approximately 1,500 resources have been removed from the National Register of Historic Places in the USA (approximately 0.001 per cent of the more than 1.4 million individual resources presently listed according to a search of the National Register database at the time of writing), almost all as a result of loss of historic integrity by demolition, fire or other forms of damage. Similarly, properties may be removed from the statutory list managed by English Heritage, but only in circumstances where 'new evidence is available about the lack of special architectural or historic interest of the building, or a material change of circumstances, for example fire damage' (English Heritage 2010b). Unlike these examples, many regional or municipal heritage registers do not even make arrangements for de-listing. The assumption seems to be that the values on which criteria are established for designation are universal and will never change. It seems relevant here that the question of 'how many' World Heritage sites is an appropriate number has very rarely been discussed; instead, the focus is on increasing the representativeness (and hence the size) of the List, rather than reviewing the basis for past decision-making processes (Bandarin 2007).

Absent heritage: presencing absence

I have so far argued that the late twentieth and early twenty-first centuries have seen an exponential growth in the conservation of material traces of the past. Alongside this process, I want to consider another that contributes to the crisis of accumulation of memory which I have described. Absent heritage—the memorialisation of places and objects whose significance relates to their destruction or absence—has developed as a significant global cultural phenomena in which the visual and aesthetic language of heritage conservation is applied to the conservation of voids or absent spaces to maintain an 'absent presence' (cf. Hetherington 2004; see also Derrida 1994; Gordon

1997; Callon and Law 2004). These become spaces for the memorialisation of the destruction of a material symbol that remains significant to the present political regime or that becomes significant as a symbol of political action against a present political regime. The commemoration of absent heritage often follows an act of iconoclasm, in which physical memorials associated with a past religious, cultural or political regime are destroyed as a symbolic act of collective forgetting and deface-ment. I argue that this trope of 'absent heritage' emerged in response to the way in which the spectral traces of removed and defaced monuments developed throughout the twentieth century as a visual metaphor for the conquest of a former regime in which what had been removed continued to maintain an 'absent presence', a haunt-ing in which the maintenance of the defaced image held a double set of associations that involved both the former regime and its humiliation by the subsequent one.

The dialogics of conservation and destruction

In writing about heritage, we tend to approach the question of the destruction of buildings from a particular angle; that is, a concern with the creative possibilities present in the act of salvage or preservation, rather than a mediation on the meaning and implications of demolition or erasure. The modernist dream of progress has often been placed in opposition to that of heritage preservation, with self-proclaimed modernisers caricaturing preservationists as antiquated and anti-modern. Yet, throughout history, iconoclasm and destruction have often formed the preconditions for the realisation of new regimes of social and political power, and the setting for the creation of new collective understandings of the past, with which to recreate the pre-sent and re-imagine the future. Like preservation, such acts often involve judgements of value by majorities or political elites about what should be removed and what should be preserved. These are thus creative performances, which are underpinned (and in some cases haunted) by the tacit acknowledgement of the symbolic power of the image being removed. Despite this, discussion of the role of destruction has remained largely undeveloped in the critical heritage studies literature.

As Lynn Meskell (2002) notes, The Hague Convention for the Protection of Cultural Property in the Event of Armed Conflict (signed 14 May 1954) officially acknowledged the symbolic power of the destruction of cultural heritage sites in times of war, and established violence perpetuated against architecture as an analogue of the destruction of collective memory.

> ... cultural property has suffered grave damage during recent armed conflicts and ... by reason of the developments in the technique of warfare, it is in increasing danger of destruction ... damage to cultural property belonging to any people whatsoever means damage to the cultural heritage of all mankind, since each people makes its contribution to the culture of the world.
>
> (UNESCO 1954).

Iconoclasm, literally 'image-breaking', is a term that refers to opposition to the religious veneration of images. It is perhaps most closely associated with a Christian theological debate in the eighth and ninth centuries CE involving the Byzantine Church and state. The literal interpretation of Old Testament prohibitions against worshipping graven images led to the imposition of legislation that banned the production and use of figurative images in churches, and their veneration. In contemporary use, the term 'iconoclasm' has come to refer to any example of one political or religious regime erasing the images and symbol sets of an 'Other'. Modern examples include the destruction of both religious and secular images during the French Revolution, and the destruction of images in China as part of the Cultural Revolution.

Iconoclasm has a close connection with heritage, although it may at first glance be seen as its opposite; a form of 'anti-heritage'. But iconoclasm, like heritage, is a process by which people explicitly acknowledge the connection between particular objects, places and practices and collective memory. The process of destroying or removing an object, place or practice is not only a destructive process, but a process by which an attempt is made to clear the way for the creation of new collective memory (Benton 2010). However, while it is an active process of removal, it is also a tacit acknowledgement of the symbolic power of the image being removed—if the image had no symbolic power, it wouldn't need to be erased. Just as official heritage requires decisions about which objects, places and practices to conserve, so iconoclasm involves a decision of value about which places, traces and 'memories' to erase. The difficulty lies in understanding the motivations of such actions, and their impact on living communities. Andrew Herscher (2010) argues not only that architectural destruction is a symbol of violence, but that objects and places, and in this case, the built environment, form a necessary *context* for violence. His book *Violence Taking Place* reflects on the role of architecture and its destruction within the 1998–99 conflict between Serbia and the Kosovo Liberation Army, placing it within a much longer history of threatened, inflicted and remembered violence against architecture in Kosovo throughout the course of the twentieth century. Rather than concentrating on design as a form of inscription, Herscher revives violence and destruction as equally important forms of inscription and cultural production through a focus on the spatial and discursive sites where violence takes place, and where the subjects and objects of this violence are articulated. In doing so, he suggests that 'destruction' should be viewed as a form of 'construction', which aids in the production of the identities and agencies that would normally be viewed as violence's root cause.

Herscher suggests the role of destruction in cultural production has two dimensions. In the first, material things against which violence have been committed come to stand in for the violence itself. Herscher recounts how during the NATO bombing campaign on Serbia, images of damaged buildings obtained using US Defence Department satellites were used as a trace with which to represent ethnic violence. Similarly, during the trial of former President of Serbia and Yugoslavia Slobodan Milošević for war crimes, architectural damage became a manifestation of ethnic violence, which Herscher argues rendered other forms of violence—sexual, physical and economic violence, for example—invisible. The second dimension refers to the way in which the history of prior acts of violence against architecture prompts replication or mimetic destruction. Herscher describes the way in which the reversal of ethnicised violence in Kosovo following the war was a form of repetition, based on the reading of ethnicised violence against architecture that had emerged during the war and the years preceding it. The destruction of buildings that accompanied retributive violence helped focus and articulate that violence as ethnicised, and subsequent ruins acted as traces or mnemonics of ethnicised violence. In this sense, destruction of architecture can be understood as a form of cultural production that cannot be uncoupled from its cultural, political and geographic context. Architecture does not just symbolise political violence, but mediates and re-mediates violence, and emerges as central to the programme of political violence in Kosovo and the former Yugoslavia. Conquering states or dominant political organisations often express their domination in the form of buildings and monuments, and this way of understanding the relationship between architecture and political violence may also account for the targeting of particular buildings for destruction. This process calls to mind Kenneth Foote's (2003) discussion of four approaches to the management of sites of tragedy in the United States, which he suggests might be broken into one of four methods of sanctification, designation, rectification or obliteration. All four approaches represent different forms of cultural production in response to the traces of violence in the landscape.

The visual language of mutilation: iconoclasm as material trope

Drawing on these ideas about architecture, landscapes and symbolic violence, I want to suggest that, throughout the twentieth century, a particular visual language of iconoclasm was developed, on which what I distinguish as a genre of 'absent heritage' came to draw. It is well known that the Allied victory in the Second World War and the overthrow of the Italian Fascists and German National Socialists created an intellectual dilemma for new authorities and citizens regarding how to treat their respective monumental buildings and memorials of former regimes. Both Italy and Germany had experienced significant programmes of modernist urban development in the years preceding, as well as during, the Second World War, associated with construction of highly symbolic public memorials and buildings associated with each regime (Benton 1999, 2010; Macdonald 2009). Following the Second World War, an immediate flurry of demolition and removal of the most overtly symbolic buildings and political iconography often occurred in towns and cities throughout Germany and Italy. However, following the Allied return of control to municipal and state authorities, many were left with a dilemma—the symbolic designed landscapes and urban spaces of the old regime represented the spaces in which residents had to live, work and dwell. There followed a much longer period, in which certain symbolic spaces were ignored and allowed to fall into ruin, and others were modified for re-use, their original function and meaning actively ignored and 'forgotten'. For example, Sharon Macdonald (2009) describes the initial process of 'de-Nazification' which occurred in Nuremberg with the removal of swastikas and flags by US soldiers, and the staging of symbolic acts such as the draping of the central swastika on the Zeppelin building with the American flag prior to its partial demolition (Macdonald 2009: 54), an event that was widely publicised, and images of which circulated widely. The buildings associated with the Nazi

Party Rally grounds at Nuremberg remained, and were used during the period of US occupation for regular US military parades as a show of symbolic power. Nonetheless, following the Allied occupation of West Germany up until the 1970s, discussions regarding the future of the buildings and rally grounds were based on pragmatic considerations. Many of the buildings were adaptively re-used in an attempt to 'cleanse' them of their former associations (Macdonald 2009: 64), while the side galleries and end tower of the Zeppelin building, perhaps the most iconic of the Nazi buildings, were demolished to 'amputate' and hence symbolically 'disarm' it (Benton 1999, 2010). Significant discussions of the management of these spaces as 'heritage' did not occur until the World Heritage Convention era in the 1970s (Macdonald 2009, see discussion below on 'dissonant' and 'difficult' heritage).

Similarly, Tim Benton (1999, 2010) discusses the ways in which Fascist iconography in Italian towns and cities was managed through a process of initial removal of the most obviously political symbols, and subsequent processes of pragmatic 'forgetting' through adaptive re-use. Drawing on Freudian analogies, he suggests two processes in addition to outright demolition, which might operate in the management of material memories of former regimes. The first, *aestheticisation*, involves the transformation of political symbols into 'high' art, a process by which the political references are ignored in favour of the artistic merit of the work. The second, *mutilation*, involves the removal of the most obvious political symbols and the symbolic defacement or damaging of buildings and monuments. As an example of this process of mutilation, he cites the 'military castration' of Fascist sculptures through the removal of the blades from the axes of the fasces—symbols of Fascism represented by a bundle of wooden rods and an axe, which were on the flag of the National Fascist Party and built into sculptures and façades on many buildings throughout Italy. However, I want to push Benton's ideas a little further in suggesting that this process is one not only of removal or disarmament, but also of symbolic *humiliation*, in which the absent axe blade comes to symbolise and stand in for the act of military and political subjugation. In the same way as one could argue that these sculptures have been 'neutralised' (perhaps even 'neutered') by the removal of the axe blade, one could also suggest that they have in fact been transformed into something else, a *new* symbol of the defeat of a past regime, in which they refer not only to the old regime, but also to its defeat by the new one. I think such an interpretation would help account for what Benton (2010: 158) notes is the 'rather mediocre' quality of many of the sculptures that were preserved as a result of this process—they represent not only the neutralisation of old memories and the aestheticisation of objects to transform them into 'artworks', but also the simultaneous production of new memories of conquest and defeat. Such an interpretation is re-enforced by the other example Benton mentions, of Arno Becker's statue 'Readyness', which shows a naked youth reaching for his sword. This sculpture was given an 'artistic' credibility by cutting off the arms—as in many antique sculptures—and hence neutralising its political meaning.

The trope of the absent, mutilated or toppled statue or memorial appeared with increasing frequency throughout the twentieth century as a metaphor for a humiliated and overthrown political regime. Images of the acts of symbolic humiliation and mutilation of statues and buildings were often staged or recorded, circulating widely

FIGURE 8.1 Statue of a lictor, built 1939–40 on the Palazzo della Civilta Italiana, Esposizione Universale Roma, showing the removal of the axe blade after the war. (Photograph by Tim Benton.)

in print, film and later electronic media as part of what Macdonald (2009) refers to as the 'visions of endings' of discredited political regimes. In some cases the statues were immediately removed, but in others the mutilated statues remained as the focus for remembering the past regime in negative terms, or for its mockery. During the 'de-Stalinisation' that occurred in the former Soviet Union in the decades following the death of Stalin in 1953, many of the former dictator's statues were removed or defaced. In the 1956 Hungarian Revolution, for example, the eight-metre tall bronze sculpture of the dictator that topped the Stalin Monument in Budapest's Városliget City Park, which was completed in December 1951 as a gift for Joseph Stalin from the Hungarian people on his seventieth birthday, was cut at the legs using oxy-acetylene torches and torn down. Images of the event were disseminated widely and came to stand as a symbol of the Revolution itself. However, the boots remained attached to the limestone base and tribune, and the defaced memorial lingered in the central Budapest park for many years as a 'mockery' of the former dictator and the focal point for remembering the uprising that toppled the former regime. The site persisted as a space for the memory of this event, although what remained of the monument slowly deteriorated. More recently, the remnants of the monument were removed to make way for a new Monument of the 1956 Revolution, which was completed in 2006 for the fiftieth anniversary of the event. A copy of the sculpture of the broken boots standing on a brickwork dais was erected in the same year in 'Szobor Park', the Hungarian communist 'theme' park, in which many examples of communist era sculpture removed from public spaces are now displayed (see below).

FIGURE 8.2 Ruined statue of Stalin in Budapest. They put the Hungarian flag in what remained of Stalin's boots, and the head fell to the ground in Gyor, Hungary on October 23, 1956.' (Photograph by Reporters Associes/Gamma-Rapho via Getty Images.)

FIGURE 8.3 The reconstruction of the defaced Stalin memorial statue at Szobor Park, installed in 2006. (Photograph by the author.)

Throughout the twentieth century and into the twenty-first, the visual trope of the mutilated and humiliated monument continued to appear as a metaphor for defeat, re-enforcing absent parts of monuments and buildings as important 'intangible' memorials in their own right. The fall of Communism in 1989, in particular, was followed by the widespread mutilation and/or removal of statues of Lenin and other Communist leaders throughout the former Soviet Union. The removal of the large iron statue of Felix Dzerzhinsky, the first director of the Bolshevik secret police, from its location outside the KGB headquarters in 1991 was one well publicised example, but many others occurred throughout the former Soviet Union over this period. So it was perhaps unsurprising that one of the iconic images of the 2003 invasion of Iraq was the toppling of the large statue of Saddam Hussein in Baghdad's Firdos Square by a US M88 tank recovery vehicle on 9 April 2003. This image circulated widely as a 'symbol' of the fall of Baghdad to US-led coalition troops, and the fall of the regime. As in the case of previous examples, photographs and video images of the event, later described as 'the single image which came to define the war' (Wood 2004), were widely disseminated, and appeared for many days and weeks in constant circulation on rolling news coverage of the war. In undertaking this act of political iconoclasm, the soldiers involved drew on a history of the circulation of similar images and the power of the absent, defaced monument to represent the defeat and humiliation of a former regime. The empty space atop the plinth was later replaced by a new modernist sculpture designed by Iraqi artist Bassem Hamad al-Dawiri. Despite the replacement of the remains of the former sculpture, it could be said that the new one remains 'haunted' by the absent presence of the former, which persists as a

FIGURE 8.4 Photograph showing the toppling of the large statue of Saddam Hussein in Baghdad's Firdos Square by a US M88 tank recovery vehicle on 9 April 2003. Images of this event circulated widely as a 'symbol' of the fall of Baghdad to US-led coalition troops and the fall of the regime. (Photograph by Gilles Bassignac/Gamma-Rapho via Getty Images.)

memory of what had previously sat atop the plinth due to the saturation of the media with images of its defacement.

Shadow line: managing the spectral traces of the Berlin Wall

I have argued that the spectral traces of removed and defaced monuments developed throughout the twentieth century as a visual and spatial metaphor for the conquest of a former regime: what had been removed continued to maintain an 'absent presence', a haunting in which the maintenance of the defaced image held a double set of associations that involved both the former regime and its humiliation by the subsequent one. Hetherington (2002, 2005, 2007) suggests that ghosts in the urban landscape represent the traces of unfinished or unmanaged disposal, drawing on the theme of cultural and historical debt in Derrida's *Specters of Marx* (1994). Although many defaced monuments and absences were maintained only temporarily, it seemed natural that, in a period in which 'intangible' and 'virtual' heritage were beginning to become important concepts as part of the late-modern heritage 'boom', the preservation and conservation of such incomplete disposals and spectral traces would come to occupy the same feverish obsession as the maintenance of tangible heritage objects and places and intangible practices and expressions. These issues would be brought more thoroughly into the heritage arena by arguments that developed around the conservation of the remaining traces of the Berlin Wall, which had divided East and West Germany from 1961 until the 'Peaceful Revolution' of 1989, its demolition by protesters paving the way for the formal process of German reunification, concluded the following year.

The fall of the Berlin Wall, which is seen by many as the emblematic event of the collapse of Communism, began on 9 November 1989. In the wake of widespread mass protests against the German Democratic Republic (GDR) of East Germany and the mass exodus of many East Germans through Hungary to Austria, it was announced that the Politburo had voted to allow East Germans to go to West Germany directly through East Germany. Many East Germans swamped border guards, forcing them to open various border crossings at checkpoints along the wall. Soon crowds gathered on the wall itself, and in the days that followed, sections of the wall were dismantled by members of the public, and later by German officials, who opened a series of new border crossings. Although the wall continued to be guarded, and initially attempts to unofficially dismantle sections of it were actively discouraged by East German military officers, the official dismantling of the wall by the East German military began at Bernauer Strasse in June 1990.

Following unification in October 1990, the dismantling continued to be carried out by military units over the coming months, by which time only a few short sections and watchtowers were left standing as memorials. Although Gabi Dolff-Bonekämper (2002), a conservator at the Berlin Office for the Preservation of Historic Buildings during the period 1988 to 2002, reports that there had initially been some discussion about conserving the whole wall as a historic monument, the spontaneous destruction of sections of the wall, and the opposition of the general public and officials in Berlin to continuing to live with the wall (both as a barrier to movement and true reunification of the city, as well as a visual reminder of the former division of the city), meant that preservation efforts came to be directed towards the legal protection of four fragmentary sections—part of the border wall on Niederkirchnerstrasse; a 1.3-kilometre-long stretch of hinterland wall on the side of the River Spree on Stralauer Strasse known collo-quially for its graffiti art as the 'East Side Gallery'; a shorter stretch of hinterland wall on Scharnhorststrasse in Berlin-Mitte; and a 210-metre stretch of border wall on Bernauer Strasse, including the 'death strip' and hinterland wall—along with a watchtower at the Schlesischer Busch in Berlin-Trepnow and another on the Keiler Strasse in Berline-Mitte (these were listed later in 1992 and 1995, respectively) (Dolff-Bonekämper 2002: 239). The remaining sections bore many traces of its opposition and processes of destruction, including holes and broken sections, sledge-hammer peck marks and graffiti, some of which had become well known due to its political content and the widespread media coverage of the event. Dolff-Bonekämper recounts the way in which 'wall-peckers' focused particularly on sections of the border wall on Niederkirchnerstrasse, breaking it into small pieces for sale to tourists in the months that followed reunification. This section of the wall was subsequently fenced off and incorporated into a memorial site as part of the 'Topography of Terror' documentation centre, which was established in 1987 at the site where the headquarters of the Secret State Police, the SS and the Reich Security Main Office were located during the Third Reich (Figure 8.6). The traces of pick and hammer marks on the wall are now interpreted as important traces of the activities of Berliners

FIGURE 8.5 People atop the Berlin Wall near the Brandenburg Gate on 9 November 1989. (Photograph by Sue Ream/Wikimedia Commons.)

FIGURE 8.6 Sections of the Berlin Wall on Niederkirchnerstrasse which were conserved and incorporated into the 'Topography of Terror' documentation centre. Reconstructed wall in front, remnants of actual wall behind. (Photograph by Richard Honey.)

in demonstrating their opposition to it, and as symbols of opposition to the GDR more generally. The remaining section of wall at Bernauer Strasse became the subject of much debate due to its proximity to the Sophien community cemetery. Discussion around the thirtieth anniversary of the wall's construction saw the Berlin Senate agree to revised plans for the conservation of this part of the wall, in which the remaining 210-metre section would be cut into three discontinuous sections, and part of the wall demolished. Subsequently this decision was revised, and the wall was resurfaced and a memorial built alongside it in 1998, despite opposition to the plans from the Office for the Preservation of Historic Buildings (Dolff-Bonekämper 2002).

Karen Till characterises Berlin as 'a place haunted with landscapes that simultaneously embody presences and absences, voids and ruins, intentional forgetting and painful remembering' (2005: 8). The desire to commemorate the heritage of the wall, to force a remembrance of its impact on Berlin's citizens, meant addressing explicitly this question of conserving an absent presence. In addition to the remnants of the wall itself (which refer not only to themselves as remnants, but also to the absence of the whole), a double cobblestone line that traces the wall's former trajectory was installed during the 1990s along the entire former boundary (Cramer 2011: 6). Early initiatives to develop the 'shadow line' as a bicycle or walking trail and tour were realised as part of the development of a Berlin Wall Trail, consisting of the cobblestone 'ghost' of the wall itself, along with signs and information pillars along its length, which stand

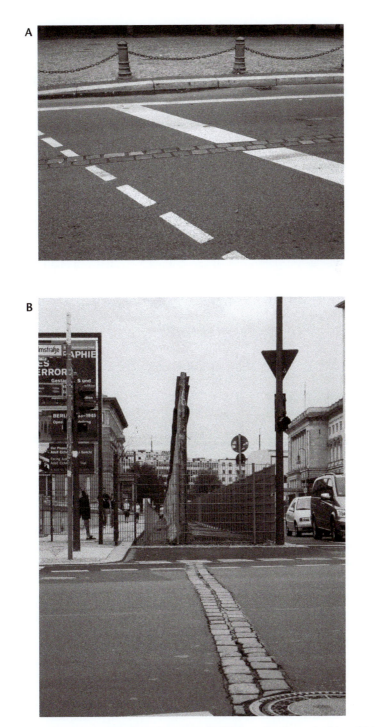

FIGURE 8.7A,B Spectral traces of the former Berlin Wall marked by a double cobblestone line. (Photographs by Richard Honey.)

12 feet tall to echo the height of the former wall (Cramer 2011: 7). These, along with a number of other official and private museums, memorials and displays, now contribute to the multi-layered material and spectral memorialisation of the Berlin Wall. Although the idea of the brick line was not in itself innovative, drawing as it did on other modes of heritage interpretation of demolished buildings which had been established in the 1970s, it demonstrates clearly the way in which the visual and spatial trope of absent heritage had begun to be adapted and adopted as a way of memorialising spectral or absent space in heritage practice.

Globalising absent heritage: the niches of the Great and Little Buddhas of the Bamiyan Valley, Afghanistan

'Absent heritage', the active conservation of spectral traces of defaced or demolished buildings and monuments, gained global recognition as a phenomena in UNESCO's responses to the destruction of the 'Bamiyan Buddhas', the Great and Little Buddhas of the Bamiyan Valley in Afghanistan, by Taliban forces in 2001. This event, and responses to it, had important implications which demonstrate how the accumulation of absent spaces has developed alongside the conservation of tangible objects and places, and expressions and practices of intangible heritage, in the early twenty-first century. This represents a significant development in relation to heritage in its own right, but is also relevant to discussions of the crisis of accumulation of heritage, to which I will return at the end of this chapter.

The Bamiyan Valley is located in the mountainous region of central eastern Afghanistan, approximately 230 kilometres (143 miles) north-west of the capital of Kabul. Sited in an area that formed a crossroads from China in the east, India in the south and Persia in the west, the valley was first occupied in the third century CE at the time of the height of Buddhist culture in central Asia, and soon became an important monastic centre for Buddhism during the fourth to eighth centuries CE. During this time, two enormous monumental standing figures of the Buddha, now known as the 'Great and Little Buddhas', were carved into niches in the limestone cliffs at Bamiyan. Standing 55 and 38 metres tall, respectively, these statues formed a striking monumental reminder of the Buddhist past of the valley, and were the largest standing Buddha carvings in the world. The monumental standing figures were accompanied by a series of seated Buddha figures, which sat in between them. In the Bamiyan, and surrounding Folodi and Kakrak Valleys, over 1,000 caves, grottoes and niches were also carved into the soft limestone of the hillsides. They functioned as shelters and temples for the Buddhist monks, and contained elaborate carved decoration and painted wall art (this section after Higuchi and Barnes 1995 and UNESCO 2003a). The caves were generally built in isolated places away from towns and villages, and were primarily used by monks for the private practice of Buddhism. Originally they would have had a wooden façade; however these have long since deteriorated. This series of archaeological sites, and the caves and frescoes associated with these valleys, document the area as a major urban centre associated with the practice of Buddhism throughout this period.

FIGURE 8.8 The Great Buddha at Bamiyan prior to its destruction by the Taliban. (Photographer unknown. © UNESCO.)

The Taliban, a Sunni Islamist movement, took Kabul by force in 1996 by over-throwing the regime of President Burhanuddin Rabbani (president 1992–96) and his defence minister Ahmed Shah Masood. They ruled most of Afghanistan until 2001, when their leaders were forcibly removed from government by a military coalition of the Northern Alliance (Afghanistan), USA, UK, Canada and Australia. The Taliban had originated in southern Afghanistan and western Pakistan, and were predominantly Pashtuns or ethnic Afghans. They first came to prominence in 1994 when their leader, village clergyman Mullah Mohammed Omar, promised to stamp out corruption, restore peace and re-establish *shariah*, or Islamic law, once in power. They extended their influence from south-western Afghanistan by targeting the *mujahidin*, feuding military leaders who had previously forced Soviet troops out of the country. By 1998 they were in control of approximately 90 per cent of Afghanistan (BBC News 2006).

Once in power, the Taliban established a hard-line, authoritarian government, and established a literal interpretation of traditional Islamic law, with punishments including public executions for those convicted of murder, and amputation of the limbs of thieves. Men were ordered by law to grow beards and all women were required when in public to wear the burqa. Television and music were banned, and girls over the age of ten were removed from school. On 17 April 1997, Mullah Mohammed Omar declared that the Taliban would destroy the Bamiyan Buddhas, as icons and religious imagery were forbidden by Islamic law. Following appeals by the UN Secretary-General and the UNESCO Director-General to political and military leaders in Afghanistan, urging them not to harm the Buddhas, the Taliban embassy in Islamabad, Pakistan, issued a statement on 28 April 1997 that the Taliban would not destroy the Buddhas and that they would conserve cultural heritage in accordance with existing international conventions.

However, on 26 February 2001, Mullah Mohammed Omar again stated that the Taliban would destroy the statues 'so that they are not worshipped now or in the future' as part of an edict to destroy all statues in Afghanistan which were considered to be non-Islamic. *The New York Times* reported the Taliban statement as follows:

> All the statues in the country should be destroyed because these statues have been used as idols and deities by the nonbelievers before ... they are respected now and may be turned into idols in future, too.
>
> *(Agence France-Presse 2001)*

The UNESCO Director-General responded by sending a telegram to Mullah Mohammed Omar, urging him to reconsider the decision to destroy all the statues of Afghanistan, and subsequently sought the support of representatives of other Islamic countries, including Saudi Arabia, the United Arab Emirates, Qatar, Iran and Tajikistan, as well as the President and the Secretary of the Organisation of the Islamic Conference. All agreed to do what they could to stop the destruction of the statues. However, by 3 March 2001 the Taliban stated officially that they had begun the task of destroying the statues and associated cave temples. The statues were destroyed over the course of several weeks. Anti-aircraft weapons and machine guns were used to shoot at the statues, and dynamite and land mines were placed strategically to bring them down completely. Ultimately, all that remained were the niches that had housed the statues. Some of the cave temples survived; however, these also sustained much damage. Video footage of the statues being blasted by dynamite and subsequent photographs

FIGURE 8.9 The empty niche of the Great Buddha at Bamiyan following its destruction by the Taliban in 2001. (Photograph by Mario Santana, 2011. © UNESCO/ Mario Santana.)

of the empty niches were released by the Taliban to the Western media to document the official process of their destruction.

Commentators have noted that the destruction of the Bamiyan Buddhas by the Taliban marked a turning point in the regime and influenced the decision by the US-led coalition to invade and overthrow it in October 2001. The act of destroying the statues came to be viewed as an explicit defiance of international conventions and a form of symbolic violence that was directed at the world's heritage, and hence at the whole world. Although early statements suggested that the destruction had been ordered on religious grounds, in a subsequent interview with *The New York Times* another possible alternative was offered by Sayed Rahmatullah Hashimi, who said that the decision had been made in an angry reaction to a foreign delegation sent by UNESCO to investigate the destruction of objects in the Kabul Museum, who had offered to provide funding for the statues' preservation:

> The scholars told them that instead of spending money on statues, why didn't they help our children who are dying of malnutrition? They rejected that, saying, 'This money is only for statues'. The scholars were so angry. They said, 'If you are destroying our future with economic sanctions, you can't care about our heritage'. And so they decided that these statues must be destroyed … If we had wanted to destroy those statues, we could have done it three years ago. So why didn't we? In our religion, if anything is harmless, we just leave it. If money is going to statues while children are dying of malnutrition next door, then that makes it harmful, and we destroy it.
>
> *(Sayed Rahmatullah Hashimi, quoted in Crosette 2001)*

The destruction of the Buddhas became subsumed within a global political discourse that focused on the refusal of the UN and other countries to give the Taliban official recognition, along with economic sanctions imposed in 1999 and 2000 by the UN Security Council due to alleged links with Islamic terrorism and allegations that the Taliban were harbouring al-Qaeda insurgents, including the al-Qaeda leader Osama Bin Laden. These remote political arguments must have played a role in this very political act of defiance. Only three countries—Pakistan, Saudi Arabia and the United Arab Emirates—recognised the Taliban as the legitimate government of Afghanistan, and in the months following the destruction of the statues, Saudi Arabia and the United Arab Emirates also withdrew their support. All three countries protested against the destruction of the statues.

While the heritage values of the Buddhist remains of the Bamiyan Valley were first made known to UNESCO when a nomination dossier for the archaeological sites and monuments was submitted by the Afghanistan Government in 1981, the property's inscription was deferred by the World Heritage Committee in 1983, due to the lack of definition of an appropriate boundary for the site to protect its archaeological remains. Throughout the period in which the Taliban were threatening to destroy the sculptures, they were thus not 'officially' part of the World Heritage List. It was not until 2003, well after Taliban forces deliberately destroyed the large

Buddha sculptures along with most of the Buddhist statues and wall paintings in the Bamiyan Valley in the spring of 2001, that the more secular and internationally oriented transi-
tional Islamic State of Afghanistan submitted a new nomination for urgent consideration by
the UNESCO World Heritage Committee. At the Committee's twenty-seventh session in
June 2003, the remains of the Buddhas' niches and other archaeological remains of the
valley were finally simultaneously inscribed on the World Heritage List and the List of
World Heritage in Danger. Ironically, it was the fact that the Taliban were not recognised
by the UN as the legitimate government of Afghanistan that made it impossible for them to
nominate the Bamiyan Buddhas to the World Heritage List while they were in power. For
this reason, the language of the appeals not to destroy the Buddhas in 1997 and 2001 is
noteworthy. At its eighty-third plenary meeting, the UN General Assembly adopted
Resolution A/RES/54/185, in which it

> Expresses its deep concern at reports of attacks on and looting of cultural
> artefacts in Afghanistan,
>
> Emphasizes that *all parties share the responsibility to protect their common heritage,* and
>
> Requests all Member States to take appropriate measures to prevent the looting
> of cultural artefacts and to ensure their return to Afghanistan.
> *(United Nations 2000; emphasis added)*

The idea of the Bamiyan Buddhas as part of the universal or common heritage of
humanity played an important role in how the media reported their destruction
(Colwell-Chanthaphonh 2003). This was an issue in which all people on Earth were
seen to have a stake or interest. Newspapers reported 'world outrage' at the decision
to destroy the statues. *The New York Times* quoted Rakhaldas Sengupta, the retired
former head of an Indo-Afghan team involved in restoration work at Bamiyan in the
1970s, who called it the destruction of the 'heritage of mankind' (Bearak 2001). The
abuses against 'World Heritage' were one of a series of issues (including alleged links
with terrorism and alleged human rights abuses) that can be seen to have lent a
position of 'global moral fairness' to the subsequent NATO military operation of
October 2001. It is arguable that these appeals against the destruction of the common
heritage of humanity facilitated the political position that allowed the coalition team
to invade and remove the Taliban from power. Such a suggestion sees the focus of
World Heritage move beyond a simple list of modern 'wonders' or the great canon
of heritage, to a global emblem used by the Taliban to draw attention to their feelings
of political oppression and exclusion on a world scale, and subsequently used by
NATO to direct the West's anger against them.

The Taliban, at least on an official level, defined the Buddha statues as icons, and
cited their destruction as a result of their particular interpretation of Islamic law in the
context of a widespread crack-down on images and icons throughout the country
(see further discussion in Flood 2002 and Elias 2007). But this must also be seen as an
action that resulted in the virtual erasure of the country's pre-Islamic past. It has been
suggested that the Taliban's decision to destroy the Bamiyan Buddhas is best viewed

as a form of iconoclasm aimed not at the statues themselves, but at World Heritage in general, and the UN in particular, as a symbol of global imperialism (Golden 2004). World Heritage, as a symbol of globalisation and the universalising cultural tendencies of the United Nations, would have made a tempting target for a political regime that was excluded from politics on a global scale. The attack on the Bamiyan Buddhas was not only an attack on the statues, but also an attack on what some would see as a very specific form of Western imperialism embodied by UNESCO's approach to heritage (Byrne 1991); that is, the imposition of a set of materialistic values on the statues by a world community that would not provide aid for Afghanis nor recognise the Taliban as its legitimate authorities:

> Like the emblem developed in the twentieth century to signal monuments worthy of special protection, the notion of world heritage, intended as a shield, may instead act as a target. This is hardly surprising. The history of iconoclasm shows abundantly that the act of symbolizing – tying certain objects to certain values – sometimes has contradictory effects. It recommends certain objects to the care of those who share these values but attracts the aggression of those who reject them or who feel rejected by them.
>
> *(Gamboni 2001: 11)*

The worldwide attention directed towards the demolished Bamiyan Buddhas saw them become symbols of the fragility of World Heritage and its role in conflict situations, as well as symbols of global terrorism, feeding the perception of the vulnerability of heritage and late-modernity's all-pervasive sense of 'risk' and its obsession with security. The poignant, hollow recesses that remained in the cliff walls of Bamiyan spoke to the absent heritage of the Buddhas in a way in which the presence of the Buddhas never had. The destruction of the statues, and their 'absent presence' as part of the niches that remained, came to be seen as part of the significance of the site. Among the criteria for inclusion on the World Heritage List is the statement:

> Criterion (vi): The Bamiyan Valley is the most monumental expression of the western Buddhism. It was an important centre of pilgrimage over many centuries. Due to their symbolic values, the monuments have suffered at different times of their existence, including the deliberate destruction in 2001, which shook the whole world.
>
> *(UNESCO 2003a)*

This statement is significant, as it demonstrates the way in which the absence of the statues became incorporated within its officially recognised heritage significance. Ironically, the destruction of the Buddhas by the Taliban, which was intended to undermine the principles of UNESCO and Western cultural materialism, has done more for the global hegemony of World Heritage and UNESCO than the Buddhas could have achieved if they had never been threatened. The Buddhas' empty niches have become a global symbol of UNESCO and World Heritage—a 'poster site', if you like, for the need for global heritage initiatives and the vulnerability of heritage to the risks posed by late-modern globalisation. The absent presence of the statues, emphasised by the physical shape of the carved niches, speaks not only of the memory of the statues themselves, but also of the circumstances of their destruction. A large amount of physical conservation work has gone into the preservation of what remains of the fabric of the statues, and this seems only to emphasise their obvious absence.

FIGURE 8.10 Scaffolding assembled inside the niche of the Great Buddha at Bamiyan. (Photograph by Ron Van Oers. © UNESCO/Ron Van Oers.)

FIGURE 8.11 Conservation works and recording of the remnants of Buddha images from one of the smaller niches at Bamiyan. (Photograph by Mario Santana, 2011. © UNESCO/Mario Santana.)

I have mentioned that the destruction of the Bamiyan Buddhas by the Taliban was one of a series of events that many see as cumulatively responsible for the (at the time of writing, ongoing) War in Afghanistan, which began with the US-led invasion of Afghanistan in October 2001. The primary motivation for the invasion was the series of coordinated attacks by hijacked aeroplanes on key symbolic locations in the USA, for which militant Islamist terrorist group Al-Qaeda claimed responsibility, on 11 September 2001. During the attacks, four planes were hijacked; two crashed into the Twin Towers of the World Trade Center in New York City, another into the Pentagon building in Arlington, Virginia, and a fourth crashed into a field near Shanksville, Pennsylvania, before it could reach its intended target in Washington, DC. Over 3,000 people died as a result of the 9/11 attacks. The images of the planes crashing into the Twin Towers were repeated for months on rolling news channels, in newspaper coverage and the electronic media. There has been a great deal written about the symbolism of the attacks and the reception and propagation of these images by the media (Baudrillard 2002; Virilio 2002; Žižek 2002), but even in the months that followed, the attacks on the World Trade Center were compared directly with those on the Bamiyan Buddhas. Meskell (2002) notes that the president and chairman of the World Monuments fund stated the symbolic significance of the World Trade Center building as a target and linked the attacks explicitly with other attacks on heritage:

> Our landmarks—the Mostar bridge, the Bamiyan Buddhas in Afghanistan, and
> the World Trade Center—have become prized targets for terrorists because
> they are what defines the cultures, ideals, and achievements of the people who
> created them, who use them, who live with them.
>
> *(Perry and Burnham 2001: 3, cited in Meskell 2002: 557).*

This statement not only claims all of these targets of conflict as common, universal
heritage, but also suggests that, in targeting them, we are all implicated in the forms
of symbolic violence which their destruction represents. As Meskell notes, this
demonstrates not only how common the language of heritage has become in
describing the impact of events, and the thorough heritagisation of late-modern societies, which I have tried to underline throughout this book, but also the way in which
this statement reconfigures the form of memorialisation that becomes appropriate for
the site. Before the design of the World Trade Center memorial site had been
finalised, Huyssen (2003: 161) had already suggested a symbolic link between the
after-image of the smouldering Twin Towers and the two destroyed statues in
Afghanistan. It seems relevant that the idea of absent presence, which has been
so pervasively demonstrated in the treatment of the niches of the Buddhas at Bamiyan,
is reflected so completely in the treatment of the National September 11 Memorial
and Museum at the World Trade Center site, designed by architect Michael Arad
and officially opened to the public on 12 September 2010. The memorial features
two square pools with water cascading into two voids in which the footings of
the Twin Towers originally stood. Meskell's insightful analysis of the symbolic connections developed between the two events (published in 2002), and the ways in
which each drew on notions of 'heritage' in particular ways, seem borne out in the
design of the memorial.[1]

Since the inclusion of the Bamiyan site on the World Heritage List and the List
of World Heritage in Danger in 2003, a number of projects have been initiated to
document the damage and consolidate the remaining archaeological sites. There are
ongoing discussions about rebuilding the Buddha statues, although this option is not
supported by UNESCO. A proposal has been put forward by the Afghanistan
Government to commission the Japanese artist Hiro Yamagata to project between
160 and 240 images of the Buddhas on to the Bamiyan cliff faces using coloured
lasers. Although scheduled for 2012, at the time of writing the project is awaiting
approval.

A number of other recent heritage projects also demonstrate the importance of
voids, gaps and empty spaces as part of the visual language of memorialising absent
heritage. The New Acropolis Museum, designed by architect Bernard Tschumi and
opened in 2007, includes an area in which the Greek Government wished to reinstall
the complete Parthenon frieze around a rectangular cement core that had exactly the
same dimensions as the cella of the Parthenon, which would allow visitors to view
the frieze in the manner in which it had originally been displayed. In response to the
failure of the British Government to return the Parthenon Marbles, it was originally
suggested that the spaces designated to them, and to other sculptures held by overseas

FIGURE 8.12 The 9/11 Memorial in New York City, showing the void in the footings of the former World Trade Center Twin Towers which has been incorporated into the memorial. (Photograph by the author.)

museums, should be left empty in protest. It was subsequently decided to insert casts, which are clearly marked as such in their correct sequence within the new museum alongside those original pieces already held by the Greek Government (Hellenic Ministry of Culture 2007), but it is nonetheless possible to see the influence of the concept of absent heritage here. Similarly, the Jewish Museum in Berlin includes a new wing, one of the first major public buildings designed in Berlin following German reunification, which incorporates a 'void' that slices horizontally through the entire building. Designed by the architect Daniel Libeskind, the museum opened to the public in 2001. The preservation, curation and exhibition of absences and spectral traces has developed throughout the late twentieth and early twenty-first centuries as an important focus for heritage production and collective memory-work.

'Difficult' and dissonant heritage

At the beginning of this chapter, I discussed Sharon Macdonald's (2009a) work on 'difficult heritage' in relation to the material remnants of regime change. As there is now a large body of work in critical heritage studies that explores 'dissonant' sites of heritage (Tunbridge and Ashworth 1996), a category that includes not only the heritage of oppressive political regimes, but also places associated with the experience and perpetration of massacres, atrocities and genocides, prisons and places of internment, and the heritage of former colonial governance (Tunbridge and Ashworth 1996; Ashworth and Hartmann 2005; Ashworth et al. 2007; Ashworth 2008;

FIGURE 8.13 A section of the void designed by Daniel Libeskind as part of the new wing of the Jewish Museum in Berlin, Germany, which opened in 2001. (Photograph by Carlos Neto. © Shutterstock Images/Carlos Neto.)

Jones and Birdsall-Jones 2008; Logan and Reeves 2009; Macdonald 2009; Benton 2010), I will not dwell on these issues here. Nonetheless, the idea of the management of the memories of the Holocaust clearly connects directly with the questions pursued in this chapter. While the idea of the formal conservation and presentation of such places as heritage can be seen to date back to the 1970s in the nomination of the Auschwitz Birkenau German Nazi Concentration and Extermination Camp to the World Heritage List in 1979, there has been an accelerated impetus and a growing market for the exhibition of such sites as heritage over the past few decades. While Tunbridge and Ashworth (1996) argued that all heritage is, by its very nature, 'dissonant', as the authority to control the stories told about the past makes it a conflicted resource, it is nonetheless obvious that the growth in the commemoration of atrocities has generated what Paul Williams refers to as a 'seemingly unstoppable [global] rise of memorial museums' (2007: viii). Logan and Reeves (2009) list a number of reasons for this, including the rise in 'atrocity tourism', citing the fact that more than a million tourists now visit Auschwitz Birkenau every year, and that many other sites associated with the Holocaust attract equal numbers of visitors. Besides the important commemorative and educative function of such sites, at least some of this visitor activity can be related to a broader growth in 'dark tourism' to sites associated with death and disaster, a phenomenon that is of increasing interest to tourism researchers (Lennon and Foley 2000; Ashworth and Hartmann 2005; Sharpley and Stone 2009). As already noted, there is a broad literature on this topic, and I refer readers to the references given here for more detailed discussions of these complex questions. Nonetheless, this area represents yet another horizon of expansion for heritage, which is seen no longer simply as a celebration of national identity, but also as a space for the remembrance of atrocity and disaster, and which has contributed to the process by which diverse and heterogeneous pasts are actively curated and thus accumulate in the contemporary world.

A present overwhelmed by the past? Absent heritage and its double

I have so far argued that a number of factors, including the increasingly broad definition of heritage, the growth of heritage tourism in the global economy, and the mnemonic or memorial function of heritage in late-modern societies has led to a proliferation of heritage in the contemporary world, which, when considered collectively, represents a 'crisis of accumulation' of memory. Before I discuss some of the issues this crisis raises, and some ways in which we might think about beginning to address it, I want to introduce a material metaphor—an object lesson, if you will—which helps to illustrate tangibly the form that this crisis has taken. At the beginning of this chapter, I mentioned Budapest's Szobor Park, the 'theme park' for removed and defaced Communist era memorials and statuary, in relation to the replica of the defaced statue of Stalin's boots erected there in 2006. The park, opened in 1993, contains the remains of forty-two Communist statues and memorials that were erected in Hungarian public spaces between 1947 and 1988, and that were defaced or removed following the 1989 Revolution and the fall of Communism. Designed by architect Akos Eleod, it contains an open air statue park and a series of mock 'Brutalist' brick walls and architectural follies which are intended to frame a space for reflecting on revolution and the fall of Communism. While the park is intended to educate the visitor about the 'fall of Communism, and not Communism itself' (Rethly 2008), it oscillates between irony and infamy in its presentation of historical detail, and appears as a jumble of mismatched memorials and statues, largely marketed to foreign tourists as an exhibition of Communist kitsch. Many visitors find humour in the stern or triumphant expressions of the statues themselves; others appear confused by what is effectively a large group of statues and memorials devoid of any context and displayed together in a designed landscape alongside a motorway in Budapest's urban–rural hinterland. As a *lieux de mémoire* (Nora 1996), it seems ambiguous at best, and confusing at worst.

It would be possible to argue that such ambiguities are necessary in ideologically divided communities, allowing for the celebration of contradictory perspectives on a shared history. However, Szobor Park raises for me two important issues, which I suggest are illustrative of the crisis of accumulation of memory in relation to late-modern heritage. The first is the way in which absent heritage replicates itself. If the spectral memory of Stalin's boots persists in the Városliget City Park in Budapest, it is also replicated here in Szobor Park on Budapest's outskirts. And—if the new Monument of the 1956 Revolution that replaced the disgraced Stalin memorial makes reference not only to itself, but also to the former statue of Stalin that stood in its place, and to the act of its defacement—the replica at Szobor Park acts as a mnemonic for all three of them, as well as their respective afterlives. Each of the forty-two dislocated statues physically present at Szobor Park has at least another 'absent

FIGURE 8.14A–B Relocated Communist era statues and memorials at Szobor Park, Hungary. (Photographs by the author.)

FIGURE 8.14C–D Mock Brutalist facades and relocated Communist era statues and memorials at Szobor Park, Hungary. (Photographs by the Author.)

presence'—a double referent in the space from which they were removed, if not others in the traces of their defacement and in the memorials that have replaced them. This replication and piling up of memories, material and spectral, constitutes a literal haunting of the late-modern present by the past.

Giving heritage a past

Secondly, and equally importantly, the uncanny piling together of this series of heroic, triumphantly posed statues, now disgraced, displaced and humiliated, also stands as a metaphor for the confusing jumble of material and intangible remnants from the past that can accumulate if we do not have the confidence to reconsider our heritages' histories and take the process of deaccessioning heritage seriously. I would argue that our general reticence to review previous generations' heritage decisions betrays a lack of belief not only in the values of previous generations, but also in our own. I have argued that one of the major shifts in heritage in the late-modern period came about partially in response to an increased recognition that heritage values are ascribed rather than intrinsic. Throughout the second part of the twentieth century, the increased recognition of the positive values of multiculturalism and cultural diversity and the impact of the postcolonial critique created a conundrum—how could a single canon of heritage represent the increasing numbers of diasporic communities that now made such a contribution to the character and make-up of society? This challenge, along with a recognition that heritage values could not be seen as intrinsic, and the influence of the nature conservation movement, led to the development of the concept of representativeness. This recognises that those in positions of authority cannot always anticipate the forms of heritage that diverse members of society will find important. By conserving a 'representative sample' of the diverse range of places, objects and practices which are of value to individuals and communities in the world, it is thought that we might safeguard the protection of a cross-section of places and things that may be recognised in the future as heritage. Representative heritage derives its values from the extent to which it can act as an exemplar of a class of place or type of object. The concept was largely borrowed from the idea of biodiversity conservation in natural heritage management, where representative samples of species and habitats are quantified statistically. But the concept of representativeness raises a broader question—what is to be represented? In the same way as the value of heritage has been recognised as ascribed and not inherent, the values on which we base decisions about what makes heritage representative (or not) must also be flexible and change with time. Although the concept was largely intended to avoid the complication of changing values, to reintroduce a scientific 'universalism' into heritage, it nonetheless stands on a concept of value as attributed, and hence malleable. This has important implications, which must be considered further.

During the 1980s, the phrase 'cultural resource management' became popular in many Western countries as a way of describing the work of cultural heritage preservation or conservation. However, I would argue that we have actually done very little at all to 'manage' heritage, as this would imply an active process of selecting, conscious pruning and judicious sorting. We have let heritage build up on registers without thinking about what work it does in the present as an ensemble or assemblage of places, objects and practices that are intended to reflect values from the past, which we might take forward with us into the future. Instead, like Szobor Park, we have ended up with a confusing jumble of memorials and mnemonics, much of which might be argued to be of little relevance to contemporary or future societies, as we rarely reconsider the basis for the decisions made to list them, and the values they represent. The fact that we rarely do this relates to an outmoded notion of heritage as a 'canon', which suggests that the values that inform our conservation decisions are universal and hence not open to discussion. However, this position is inconsistent with a late-modern 'representative' model of heritage, in which decisions are based on a consideration of the values of heritage to diverse and changing constituents, and the need to represent, and be represented by, the exhibition of official forms of heritage. Clearly, if the values on which conservation decisions have been made change, then we should reconsider those conservation decisions. Heritage that has been preserved using values-based approaches driven by the politics of representation cannot be treated as part of a universal canon, but requires regular revision and review to see if it continues to meet the needs of contemporary society.

Forgetting to remember, remembering to forget

Andreas Huyssen has argued that the late-modern period has become 'saturated' with memory, not only as a result of its peculiar conception of time (see Chapters 3 and 4), but also in response to a growing obsession with potential forgetfulness, which he sees as emerging from the temporal and spatial fracturing of globalisation processes and the emergence of the Holocaust as a cipher for the failure of the Enlightenment project and the violence of the twentieth century as a whole (Huyssen 2003). He represents the obsessive musealisation of the late-modern period as a sort of self-replicating apparatus, which develops as a response to an abundance of memory and mnemonic devices themselves. Paul Connerton (2008, 2009) suggests that the excessive memorialisation of the late-modern world can only exacerbate this obsession with social memory, as it ultimately leads to an inability to form collective memories.

> The paradox of a culture which manifests so many symptoms of hypermnesia and which yet at the same time is post-mnemonic is a paradox that is resolvable once we see the causal relationship between these two features. Our world is hypermnesic in many of its cultural manifestations, and post-mnemonic in the structures of the political economy. The cultural symptoms of hypermnesia are caused by a political-economic system which systematically generates a post-mnemonic culture-a modernity which forgets.
>
> *(Connerton 2009: 146–7)*

Marc Augé (2004) has put even more strongly the case for the importance of collective forgetting, or at least the active cultivation of some memories at the expense of others. As in the case of individual memories, societies must be able to forget to form memories properly. If we, as individuals, were able to remember everything, we would not be able to make sense of the information we could recall. Our minds would be saturated with information, and it would be impossible for us adequately to sort through the piles of memories to find the ones that were important to us. As Augé notes,

'Remembering or forgetting is doing gardener's work, selecting, pruning. Memories are like plants: there are those that need to be quickly eliminated in order to help the others burgeon, transform, flower' (2004: 17). Indeed, 'memories are crafted by oblivion as the outlines of the shore are created by the sea' (2004: 20). In the same way as individuals need to disregard certain memories to remember, Augé says we have a collective 'duty' to forget:

> Memory and oblivion stand together. Both are necessary for the full use of time ... We must forget in order to remain present, forget in order not to die, forget in order to remain faithful.
>
> *(Augé 2004: 89)*

The process of collective forgetting is thus not one that is opposed to collective memory, but an integral component of it, a work of actively returning to and revaluating the past anew (see also Forty 1999; Küchler 1999). This has important implications for the way in which we have treated heritage as a universal canon or, in our current more mindfully representational phase of heritage, our accepting past conservation decisions as beyond revisitation and revision, and simply adding new items to our lists, rather than considering whether any might more helpfully be removed.

Heritage needs to be perceived as part of a broader social process of consumption, use and disposal. Kevin Hetherington (2004) reminds us that disposal is integral to the process of consumer behaviour, 'disposal ... is not primarily about waste but about placing. It is as much a spatial as a temporal category' (2004: 159). Disposal is connected directly with concepts of value and processes of ordering and categorisation (Douglas 1966). Hetherington characterises museums as a conduit of disposal, as a space in which objects to which we attribute value are stored and held in a state of suspension so that they do not become rubbish (see also Hetherington 2010). The same, of course, is true for heritage, which gives dying objects, traditions, places and ways of life a 'second life' (Kirshenblatt-Gimblett 1998) through preservation, conservation and exhibition, holding the redundant in abeyance from jettison or discard.

The debates around the relationship between remembering and forgetting are paralleled by discussions that have emerged in relation to the preservation of digital data. Urry (2004) argues that digital technologies allow humans to inhabit multiple spaces, and hence are having a significant impact on changing patterns of absence and presence in relation to patterns of dwelling and communicating in the contemporary world. At an official level, UNESCO made a gesture of recognising forms of digital heritage as part of its Charter on the Preservation of the Digital Heritage (UNESCO 2003b). The charter defines digital heritage as follows:

> The digital heritage consists of unique resources of human knowledge and expression. It embraces cultural, educational, scientific and administrative resources, as well as technical, legal, medical and other kinds of information created digitally, or converted into digital form from existing analogue resources. Where resources are 'born digital', there is no other format but the digital object.

> Digital materials include texts, databases, still and moving images, audio, graphics, software and web pages, among a wide and growing range of formats. They are frequently ephemeral, and require purposeful production, maintenance and management to be retained.
>
> Many of these resources have lasting value and significance, and therefore constitute a heritage that should be protected and preserved for current and future generations. This ever-growing heritage may exist in any language, in any part of the world, and in any area of human knowledge or expression.
>
> *(UNESCO 2003b)*

Its definition of digital heritage is incredibly broad, and its take on the significance of digital heritage is perhaps even broader.

> The digital heritage is inherently unlimited by time, geography, culture or format. It is culture specific, but potentially accessible to every person in the world. Minorities may speak to majorities, the individual to a global audience.
>
> The digital heritage of all regions, countries and communities should be preserved and made accessible, so as to assure over time representation of all peoples, nations, cultures and languages.
>
> *(UNESCO 2003b)*

It goes on to describe the threat of loss of digital heritage as a potential loss of the 'memory of the world' (also the title of its programme for conserving documentary heritage).

> The world's digital heritage is at risk of being lost to posterity. Contributing factors include the rapid obsolescence of the hardware and software which brings it to life, uncertainties about resources, responsibility and methods for maintenance and preservation, and the lack of supportive legislation. Attitudinal change has fallen behind technological change. Digital evolution has been too rapid and costly for governments and institutions to develop timely and informed preservation strategies.
>
> The threat to the economic, social, intellectual and cultural potential of the heritage – the building blocks of the future – has not been fully grasped.
>
> *(UNESCO 2003b)*

The charter requires member states to develop and enforce legal and institutional frameworks to secure the protection of digital heritage. Its implications are far-reaching. At a time when museums and archives are increasingly having to recognise that it is impossible to conserve an example of 'everything', and are shifting towards a threshold-based system in which things must be assessed against a series of criteria to qualify for heritage status (and hence preservation), digital heritage presents particular problems. At the time of writing, new government initiatives are being developed in countries such as the USA, Canada, the UK and Australia to attempt to deal with the problem of how to archive digital publications such as websites, as well as government documents and electronic communications that form part of governments' remits as archiving institutions. Given the sheer volume of material being produced, this is pushing governments towards developing selection criteria to limit the material that is archived – to root out the 'treasure' from the 'junk'. Such selection criteria raise the same sorts of problems as the criteria that motivated the 'heritage as canon' model – principally, how one dominant group in society can decide what is significant and worthy of preservation for the future.

And yet, digital information scholars have expressed concern about the principle of 'total recall' of digital information. Viktor Mayer-Schönberger (2009) mirrors Marc Augé (2004) in suggesting that forgetting is a necessary form of cultural production, a vital decision-making process by which we choose to emphasise and memorialise events that have social value, and forget those that are irrelevant. Further, he exposes the real dangers in the development of a surveillance culture in which all of our actions are traceable and accessible, suggesting we need to put in place systems that give digital information expiry dates and engage in broader discussions of the value of different types of information and their storage. This debate clearly echoes the sorts of debate that I have suggested are necessary for heritage, in which we look closely at the history of our decisions about heritage and reconsider the values represented by what we have conserved in the past, for the future.

Whatever the outcomes of these discussions, it is important to acknowledge the responses of museums and other archives to a 'post-representativeness' model of heritage (e.g. see Message 2006). One of these responses is the increasing repatriation of materials from museums back to the communities from which they originated. While the push to repatriate Indigenous cultural heritage began with debates in the 1970s over who owns human skeletal materials held in overseas museums (see Chapter 5), the redistribution of materials to communities that have a stake in them is being seen increasingly as a solution to the problem of storage (and in this sense, connects directly with the issue of disposal discussed above). In some ways, this has had the effect of shifting the power balance from official institutions to the communities to which items have been repatriated. It is also leading to the development of new meanings and forms of significance for items of material culture that are in circulation once more – items both remembered and forgotten – as they are put to new uses in terms of the production of identity and locality in the communities that now hold them. Similarly, the question of deaccessioning objects for sale within the context of art galleries and museums is currently developing as an important and contentious topic. The American Association of Museums reviewed its Code of Ethics in 1991 to include a stipulation that proceeds from deaccessioning should only ever be used for acquisition or direct care of collections. In Europe, most objects in museums are held to be 'inalienable'; however, in France, debates are still occurring around suggestions made in 2007 that the law be changed to allow the deaccessioning of museum objects for sale. Within this context, museums and other heritage institutions are increasingly shifting focus from their object/place collections to media that do not present the same problems of storage and maintenance, in the form of 'virtual heritage' collections. This highlights the need for robust thinking about the appropriate processes by which existing collections of objects, places and practices that have been conserved as heritage in the past might be revaluated in the light of the histories of changing criteria used to evaluate them, and their value to the present and future.

Conclusion

This chapter has raised some provocative, perhaps even heretical questions. However, it seems that such questions flow naturally from a consideration of the ways in which the values that underpin our conservation decisions have changed since the 1970s (and in some cases even longer) in response to the challenges that have arisen as a result of the globalisation of official heritage practices, and the current crisis of the accumulation of memory that occurs as a result of the often indiscriminate piling up of heterogeneous traces, places and practices of the past in the present as heritage. I have identified several contributors to this process, including the fracturing and replication of memory that occurs in the conservation of absent presences as 'absent heritage', drawing on the double and triple referral of the statues of Szobor Park in Budapest as a visual and spatial metaphor. My intention in this chapter was not to suggest that we should not memorialise or conserve, nor that we should necessarily abandon or overturn the conservation battles that have been won in the past. I have argued that heritage, if actively cultivated, has an integral role to play in con-temporary societies. But this process of active cultivation also requires us to make brave decisions to prune those forms of heritage that are inconsistent with, or hold no continuing value for, contemporary and future generations, if heritage and its role in the production of social memory are to remain sustainable. To do this, we must open the canonical status of heritage registers and lists to debate, in the hope that this will promote a more informed engagement with the production of heritage in the future.

Underpinning this chapter is a concern that we distinguish between active and passive processes of remembering and forgetting, as well as the politics of collective memory and forgetfulness, and that we safeguard the work of making heritage more diverse and representative, whilst introducing an ethics of sustainability into con-temporary heritage practice. In the same ways in which some memories are actively cultivated by the memorialisation of absent space, some processes of forgetting are also actively pursued through the removal of traces that are not considered compat-ible with contemporary versions of history. And in the same way as some memories are actively cultivated by the preservation of traces of the past in the present, other traces persist and are ignored. Such traces might later re-emerge as significant sources for the creation of future collective memories, but it is the active process of the production of memory that remains most important in all of this. If conserved traces can behave as mnemonics, so can the spectres of their absence. As has been discussed earlier in this volume, all of these processes are embedded within unequal relations of power, which mean that they can be employed in both positive (or inclusive) and negative (or exclusive) ways. This draws us away from the idea that memory is passive or implied in the conservation of traces of the past in the present, to see memory as something that we must actively and mindfully produce in conversation with the traces of the past and their spectres. It is only through active engagement with the present that we can produce the collective memories that will bind us to the future.

Clearly, there is a danger in creating a kind of self-enclosed system of heritage, as if many of the problems of remembering and forgetting, conservation and destruction have not existed in societies for a long time. Buildings and artefacts were demolished before the late-modern heritage boom, and they were also conserved before this time. Destruction was sometimes a result of social change—such as the decline of the landed aristocracy from the mid-nineteenth century, or changes in religious observance— but it was mostly as a result of wealth, urban growth and land reform. Conservation was partly due to traditional practices associated with artefacts and buildings, but also partly due to the promotion of a series of aesthetic or cultural values enshrined in social structures, as discussed in Chapter 3. Nonetheless, the acceleration of processes of heritage conservation and management, the late-modern 'memory crisis' and the ever-broadening definitions of heritage have created a unique context in which questions about the sustainability of heritage require urgent, active engagement with the consequences of prior conservation decisions. The implications of a more effective engagement of people with heritage, and the obligations that might arise from a more relational, dialogical conception of the bond between people and the traces of the past in the present, form the basis of discussion in Chapter 9, as I look towards the future for heritage and heritage studies.

9

DIALOGICAL HERITAGE AND SUSTAINABILITY

Introduction

I have suggested that one of the main challenges to World Heritage and the concept of 'universal' heritage value has been the test of maintaining its very universality, meaning that it was forced to take seriously the claims to represent the various different ways of conceptualising heritage which it met as a result of the globalisation of heritage in the late twentieth and early twenty-first centuries. In Chapter 6, I suggested that it was the creative 'friction' between the particular set of Euro-American ideas about heritage embodied in the World Heritage Convention and alternative Indigenous and non-Western concepts of heritage that gave rise to the introduction of the concepts of cultural landscapes and intangible heritage, and their introduction into the work of the World Heritage Committee. However, I argue that the concepts of intangible heritage and cultural landscapes adopted as a result of this process are fundamentally at odds with the Indigenous ontological position on which UNESCO and other heritage professionals have often claimed to draw in broadening the definitions of heritage to include these categories, maintaining instead a modern set of Cartesian dualisms that hold nature and culture, and matter and mind, to be separate. In this chapter, I want to consider the final of the series of conceptual crises that I have suggested emerged for heritage in the late twentieth and early twenty-first centuries, in the form of the Indigenous ontological challenge to the concept of heritage expressed in the World Heritage Convention. In particular, I want to explore what it might mean to take seriously this ontological position, and the definition of heritage that emerges from it, as an alternative truth claim that might help us look at heritage and the world in a different way. In doing so, I propose a relational or dialogical model, which sees heritage as emerging from the relationship between a range of human and non-human actors and their environments. I suggest that this relational, dialogical model of heritage not only might be relevant in helping us to understand the friction between World Heritage and particular local traditions with which it comes into conflict, but also might help us connect heritage with broader issues of environmental, political and social concern. Further, I suggest it represents a way of thinking about heritage that might transform our troubled late-modern relationship with memory (Chapter 8) and allow us to emancipate and use heritage in more creative, transformative ways in the future. In developing these ideas, I draw particularly on the work of anthropologists Deborah Bird Rose and Eduardo Viveiros de Castro, and the symmetrical perspectives on culture and materiality that emerge from actor–network and assemblage theory and a consideration of heritage as apparatus or *dispositif*. I also argue that this dialogical model of heritage implies the employment of more dialogical models of heritage decision-making, drawing on Michel Callon, Pierre Lascoumes and Yannick Barthe's work on hybrid forums to suggest new procedures that challenge the traditional separation of specialists, politicians, bureaucrats and stakeholders in the identification, conservation and management of official heritage.

Modernist binaries: 'the Great Divide'

In Chapter 2, I suggested that the idea of heritage as it was expressed in the 1972 World Heritage Convention was an outcome of the experience of modernity and a particular way of thinking about the world that owed its origins to post-Enlightenment emphases on rationality, scientific reasoning and the concept of the public sphere. Fundamental to this way of thinking and being 'modern' are modes of ordering that rely on a pervasive series of opposing dualisms that are considered to structure the world (Law 1994). In *We Have Never Been Modern*, Bruno Latour (1993) summarises this way of thinking as the introduction of a philosophical 'Great Divide' between humans and non-humans, nature and culture, and mind and matter. The mind/ matter divide derives from the work of French philosopher René Descartes (hence 'Cartesian dualism'), who suggested that the mind is a non-physical substance that is separate from the body. The human/non-human dualism was important in the development of early anthropological thinking, and was advanced particularly in the work of Sir Edward Tylor, who contrasted primitive 'animism' with modern 'scientific rationality' in his theory of the origins of religion (see further discussion in Harvey 2005). Animism was defined by Tylor as the belief that beings or things other than humans had 'souls'; hence it is an ontology in which the Cartesian dualism of mind and matter does not exist, as there is no separation between the spiritual and material world. The nature/culture divide derived from the same constellation of Enlightenment thinking about what it meant to be 'modern' and 'human'. Philosophers Thomas Hobbes and Jean-Jacques Rousseau contrasted civilised 'culture' with the uncivilised 'state of nature'; this characterisation was fundamental to the development of unilinear theories of cultural evolution, which suggested that human cultures could be ranked according to their technology and culture from most primitive to most civilised (e.g. see Bennett 2004). Although Romanticism constructed itself as a reaction against the scientific rationalisation of nature, it nonetheless contributed to the construction of the divide between nature and culture in expounding a notion of wild,

untouched and uninhabited 'wilderness', which was contrasted directly with industrialisation, civilisation and 'culture'. This series of modern dualisms are integrally
bound up in the Euro-American notion of official heritage that developed over the
course of the eighteenth, nineteenth and twentieth centuries, and that ultimately
found expression in the 1972 World Heritage Convention (see Chapter 3).

These dualisms expressed themselves most directly in relation to the distinct categories of natural and cultural heritage which were to be assessed using separate criteria
in the World Heritage Convention. While the concept of cultural landscape was introduced in part to answer an Indigenous critique of the nature/culture dualism (Chapter
6), it could be argued that it actually continues to reinforce this dualism through its
maintenance of the separation of 'cultural' and 'natural' landscapes—in other words,
the 'really natural' landscapes are separated from the 'cultural' ones. Similarly, the
concept of intangible heritage was developed by UNESCO to address criticism
of the emphasis on 'monumental' heritage to the detriment of non-monumental
heritage, including the forms of traditional cultural practices that exist in small-scale
and Indigenous societies, and are integral to their sense of heritage and identity.
The introduction of a new category of 'intangible' heritage nonetheless preserved
the Cartesian dualism of mind and matter through its separation and opposition of the
concepts of 'tangible' and 'intangible' heritage. While these concepts reflect changes that
were brought about in response to an Indigenous, non-Western or minority critique of
the concept of universal heritage, they did not fundamentally transform the Cartesian
dualisms that underpinned it, but simply introduced a new series of concepts that
could be accommodated by its overarching 'modern' perspective. I've suggested that
it was forced to do this to maintain its illusion of universality. We might recall Mary
Douglas's (1966) work on categorisation (Chapter 2) and her description of the way
in which typological systems have two options when faced with examples which
are ambiguous and fall between existing categories, either to make them disappear
through rendering them mythological, or to reorganise the categories to accommodate
them. The introduction of the concepts of cultural landscape and intangible heritage thus
did not represent a fundamental overhaul of the system itself, but simply represented
a reorganisation of the categories used to describe heritage as either a material or
social phenomenon.

I want to pause at this point to consider what it might mean to take seriously the
non-modern worldviews and perceptions of heritage that gave rise to the concept
of cultural landscapes and intangible heritage as a way of reforming the concept of
World Heritage itself. Having undertaken to broaden the recognised categories and
definition of heritage to accommodate an Indigenous or non-modern worldview,
what would 'World Heritage' look like if we took this process to its logical conclusion?
I will draw closely on the work of Eduardo Viveiros de Castro on Amerindian ontological perspectivism to do this, as he has been one of the scholars to most eloquently
advance this non-modern ontological perspective and its theoretical implications for
understanding the relationships between people and the world. I should say at this
point that I recognise a great deal of variability in the worldviews and philosophical
systems of Indigenous people globally, and it is not my intention to characterise their

ways of being and thinking as homogenous or easily reducible to simple principles. Nonetheless, in speaking of Indigenous ontologies in general, and animism and totemism (Harvey 2005; see further discussion below) in particular, there are certain fundamental ways of thinking about 'being in the world' that emerge which are relevant to this discussion. So, in the same way that it is reductionist but often useful to speak about 'modern', Western worldviews and 'Euro-American' models of heritage, as I have done in several places in previous chapters, it is also helpful at times to gloss particular fundamental ways of thinking about being in the world as 'Indigenous ontological perspectivism'. I will explore this worldview in a more systematic way later in this chapter, but before I do, I want to make a short anecdotal detour to consider the path that has led to my posing these questions in this particular way, as it will help frame the discussion which follows.

Natural and cultural heritage: an artificial separation

I would like to draw on some anecdotal accounts that will not only help explain my approach in this section, but will also demonstrate the difficulties inherent in having to work with a heritage system that is premised on these modernist dualisms for Indigenous people, or those who hold what I have characterised as more 'continuous' traditions of heritage in a contemporary, globalised world. Since the mid-1990s, and particularly over the decade between 1996 and 2006, I have worked intensively on a range of cultural heritage projects with Indigenous Australians in a number of different urban and rural settings across the country, from the urban south-east to the remote north-western deserts, north-eastern rainforests and offshore islands. Over this time, I have been extremely lucky to work with a number of articulate and profoundly intelligent Aboriginal people who have taken the time to teach me about aspects of their culture and cosmology. My roles over this time have been diverse—I have worked variously as an independent researcher, a consultant to Aboriginal organisations and resource development companies, and as a government heritage manager and bureaucrat. In most cases, I have been employed as an archaeologist and engaged in the process of helping different projects comply with heritage planning and environmental impact legislation or guidelines. This sort of compliance work is very much the 'bread and butter' of contemporary heritage 'experts', and is a product of the intensive professionalisation and bureaucratisation of heritage that occurred over the course of the twentieth century, which I discussed in Chapter 3 (see also Smith 2006). This compliance activity would be familiar to a broad range of heritage specialists, including ecologists, architects, planners, engineers, public historians, interpretation specialists, geographers, biologists, and many others who are caught up in the apparatus of modern heritage management.

Much of the bureaucratic machinery of heritage in Australia (as it is elsewhere) is focused on the preservation and conservation of 'tangible' heritage (buildings, objects and landscapes), and for this reason the focus of most of my work was on 'archaeological' remains and their 'scientific' significance. And yet it became very quickly obvious to me, as it had to many of my colleagues, that most of what was of concern to the Aboriginal people whose interests I was at least partially supposed to be representing, was happening on the margins of the archaeology. It was in the process of walking through and visiting country that was known from childhood but had now become largely inaccessible. It was in hunting and gathering wild food resources on the surveys, and in recounting the stories, both religious and secular, that animated the countryside and bound together members of the community, both those still living and those who had passed. Sometimes it was in firing and 'cleaning up' the country to regenerate plant and animal species; at other times it was in undertaking ceremonial activities that aimed to do the same. Stories about historical events were often interspersed with 'Dreaming' narratives (see further discussion in relation to the concept of *Tjukurpa* in Chapter 6) or bush lore. Time and again, with all of the different Indigenous people with whom I worked, a consistent theme emerged of the interconnection of culture and the natural world. As a result of this, heritage was considered to be one of a number of broader 'regimes of care' (cf. Haber 2009) within which humans were implicated in their relationships with the natural and cultural world.

It was clearly impossible to distinguish between 'natural' heritage conservation and the processes of recording 'cultural' heritage in which I was engaged; these consistently formed part of the same discussions, and impacts on one would be impossible to distinguish from the other. While many aspects of the histories, cultures and traditional practices differed across the various Aboriginal communities I worked with, this was one consistent, overarching issue that arose in almost every situation I was involved in. For Indigenous Australians at least, 'natural' and 'cultural' heritage were inseparable, and their separation in contemporary heritage management practices was not only false and misleading, but was profoundly disempowering and undermined their capacity to fulfil their obligations to 'country' (see further discussion of this concept below), which they perceived as central to their heritage.

I was able to explore some of these questions regarding the ways in which archaeological heritage was intimately intertwined with contemporary political, social and economic issues and with natural heritage concerns in a more considered way as part of my Ph.D. research with Indigenous Jaru language speakers from Halls Creek in north-western Australia (Harrison 2002; see also Harrison 2005). I worked with a group of former pastoral labourers and their families who had moved in the 1970s into the town of Halls Creek from an Aboriginal pastoral labour camp on a cattle-ranching property at Old Lamboo Pastoral Station. When I started working with them in 1997, they had recently lobbied the federal Indigenous Land Corporation to provide financial support to their representative body, the Ngunjawirri Aboriginal Corporation, to lease Lamboo Pastoral Station for their community to operate. At the same time, members of the group were involved in preparing an Indigenous land claim that covered much of the historic property. Their sense of identity as a group was very much caught up in a heritage that fused traditional patterns of life with the seasonal rhythms of cattle-ranching work. So while we were engaged in remote archaeological field survey for weeks or months at a time, there was constant concern over the management of the station, which had become run down. Wells and water sources were running dry, and cattle stocks were low. There was concern that the younger men should be learning about the operation of the station from their fathers and uncles. The country's degradation was seen to be a direct result of the scattering of the families who had traditional custodianship for it. One of these custodians, Jimmy Button, noted in 1999:

> See these old people want their country back, so if me and my group of family from the Jaru tribe can get together, well, we'll soon have the country back … but see, we [are] all scattered everywhere. That's why I wanted [my brother] to come to a meeting, every fortnight or so, so we can get the place back that belongs to these old people. Doesn't matter who can manage the place, as long as we can get our family together.

The 'health' of the station was considered to be directly related to the well being of the country and its people. Another Jaru language speaker, Stan Brumby, explained the hybrid responsibilities of the Aboriginal pastoralists to their traditional country, saying the country made him 'sorry' because he was responsible for its management, but struggled against the bureaucratic machinery of government and the impacts of colonialism which had deprived him and his people access to it in the first place.

> How I got to get this country back, with the government? I bin get Lamboo. We gottem. That's Aboriginal station now. My country we got something, I got something bigger there, in that country, there. I don't want to losem, I got something there … That country make me sorry. Today. Today, make me sorry. I still thinking for my people, what bin happen langa my people. Today I think a lot. You know that people listen—while we standing, me and Jack [Ryder, his brother], we listen … I'm looking after that area … [1]

For Stan, it was important for him not only to ride horses through the country, to clear out the bores, and to stock the country with cattle, but also to fire the country so that wild flora and fauna are regenerated.

> Today, you got a book, bank book. Today. You got money in the bank now, today. You looking at television. You drive motorcar, today. Not me. I still walking foot. No motorcar. I can get motorcar, but my life is horse. I want to buy a horse, big mob horse, couple of horse. That's my life. I can fixem horse. Shoem up horse, breakem horse, that's my life. Me. Not motorcar. I can't fixem motorcar. I can't read and write. I never went to school, from start. I don't know what ABC. Gardiya [white person] callem ABC [laughs]. I want to take all this kid, takem out bush, teach [them] properly … story, word, country. Bushtucker, that's the good life for you, you never get sick … I light all the fire in my country. Burnim grass for goanna, and that frog, we callem *Gnangu, Gurnimganna*. Good beef [meat] that one. Cookem in the hot coals, that the good beef, sandfrog.

Understanding and revisiting the past was a way for this group of people to address contemporary issues about the running of the Lamboo lease, while reasserting their traditional and historical links to country. Country was understood dynamically as a concept that anchored past, present and future generations, and 'cultural' traditions concerned with maintaining the 'health' of the 'natural' environment were integrated with the contemporary responsibilities of pastoral land management. The basis of life and learning was in country, and in return for undertaking the activities that were necessary to maintain it, it would provide sustenance and knowledge. Working on the 'archaeological' project was as much a chance for them to fulfil their obligations to country as it was to record 'cultural' heritage sites (Harrison 2002, 2005).

These were not particularly unique observations, and they emerged as central issues over the period in which I subsequently worked for the Cultural Heritage Division of the former New South Wales National Parks and Wildlife Service (NPWS), during which time it instigated a number of different projects aimed at exploring the connections between natural and cultural heritage and their 'social' values to both Aboriginal and non-Aboriginal people in New South Wales (English 2000, 2001; Byrne et al. 2001; Veale 2001; Rose 2003; Rose et al. 2003; Harrison 2004; Byrne and Nugent 2004; English and Gay 2005). The NPWS was unusual in employing a number of Aboriginal staff, who were engaged in a process of trying to bring about structural and philosophical change within the organisation to acknowledge Aboriginal people's worldviews and explore how they might be used to transform the work of the organisation and its dual responsibilities for natural and cultural heritage management (some of this work is discussed in English 2000; Rose 2003; Rose et al. 2003; Kijas 2005 and Harrison and Rose 2010). During my time working for NPWS over the period 2000–04, I was fortunate enough to work on heritage projects with a number of Aboriginal sites officers and various Aboriginal community members, a process which convinced me that there were elements of Indigenous Australian cosmologies that had important implications for understanding and approaching heritage in an integrated, relational way, which might be beneficial not only to Indigenous Australians themselves, but more generally in approaching the question of the role of heritage in a contemporary, globalised world.

Typical of this work was a project undertaken by my colleague Anthony English to explore the role of wild resources in the social and economic lives of Gumbaingirr Aboriginal people at Corindi, a small town on the mid-north coast of NSW, where the collection of wild resources plays an integral role in the community (English 2001). This project involved interviewing members of the community about their use of wild food resources and medicines, recording oral accounts and mapping the locations of favoured wild resource gathering places. What emerged from the study was the way in which Gumbaingirr people associate 'cultural' value with the health of the environment. Social health and 'well being' is linked explicitly with environmental health, and access to wild resources is thus directly connected with cultural heritage issues (see also Rowlands and Butler 2007 and Butler 2011 on heritage and well being). The act of collecting wild resources is undertaken within a complex web of social and cultural practices that, while contemporary, have clear links to the past.

In mapping and recording wild resource-use places, frequent reference was made to their association with old camping places and other 'archaeological' sites, as access to particular wild resources had often ceased as a result of interlinked historical processes. While the values associated with collecting wild resources are generally what we would consider to be 'economic' values, the values of collecting wild resources to this community are also 'social' and 'cultural' ones, and lie in the way in which country and people, land and culture, are united through these uses of the landscape. My own work, undertaken with Muruwari and Dhan-gadi Aboriginal people in north-western and north-eastern New South Wales over this period, similarly challenged the idea that individual archaeological 'sites' could somehow be divorced from the significance of the landscapes in which they existed, suggesting that the management of 'cultural' heritage sites needed to be considered within a broader context of 'natural' landscape management (Harrison 2004).

For Aboriginal Australians, attachments to landscape form the basis for familial connections between humans and non-humans. Anthropologist Deborah Bird Rose has written of the work she undertook on a contractual basis for the NPWS over the period in which I was employed there, which aimed to explore the widespread concept of 'kinship' with the natural world that was held by Aboriginal people throughout New South Wales, and its implication for the work of 'natural' heritage management (Harrison and Rose 2010; see also Rose 2003; Rose et al. 2003). The concept of 'kinship' for Aboriginal people in New South Wales describes the individual and collective familial relationships that people have with particular plant and/or animal species as part of an overall system that organises relationships between all sentient beings, both human and non-human, in the world. Anthropologists generally refer to this concept as 'totemism'. While there are many different variations on the form of totemism throughout Australia and the world, with much variation even in contemporary New South Wales (Rose et al. 2003), individual and group totemism is

> expressive of a worldview in which kinship is a major basis for all life, in which the natural world and humans are participants in life processes. Relationships are based on the kin-concepts of enduring solidarity, responsibility and care.
>
> *(Rose et al. 2003: 3)*

One of the implications of this worldview is that humans are connected by bonds of kinship with particular plant and animal species, and with the 'natural' environment more generally. This explains why it becomes impossible to disentangle the 'cultural' from the 'natural'. Rose uses the term 'ecological connectivity' to describe this relationship. This is a term that is more often used in natural heritage management to describe the open space that surrounds ecosystems and links together different ecotones, but here it is broadened to include the 'social' relationships between people and the natural world. Totemism or 'kinship' relationships are closely linked with animism in Australian Indigenous ontologies through the concept of 'country'. Kinship structures the system of connection between people, group and country; but country is not only a place or an object, but is also a subject (or 'agent', see Chapter 2) in its own right. Indeed, it is perhaps the most important agent, as it is the source of the overarching principles that govern the world and the people in it. Elsewhere, Rose describes country as a 'nourishing terrain', 'a living entity with a yesterday, today and tomorrow, with a consciousness, and a will toward life. Because of this richness, country is home, and peace; nourishment for body, mind, and spirit; heart's ease' (Rose 1996: 7).

Rose (Harrison and Rose 2010) suggests that Indigenous Australian ontologies present a profound challenge to the idea of 'intangible' heritage and the definitions of heritage inherent in the World Heritage Convention more generally (see also Rose 2008, 2011). She begins by noting that, in their most abstract form, Indigenous ontologies destabilise Western anthropocentrism in its treatment of humans as pre-eminent over, or separate from, 'nature'. We have already noted the opposition between nature (the non-human) and culture (the human) as one of the under-pinning dualisms or 'Great Divides' of modern, post-Enlightenment thought. She suggests that, within an Indigenous ontology in which 'culture' is everywhere, not only is there no boundary between nature and culture, there is no mind–matter binary. This contrasts with a modern Cartesian dualism, which sees the mind and body as separate, and the mind itself as non-physical. Rather than mind being a strictly human property, leaving matter and nature 'mind-less', she notes that Indigenous Australian ontologies hold consciousness and sentience to be widespread amongst humans and non-humans, some of which would be classed as 'living' in a modern, post-Enlightenment way of thinking, but many of which would not. To illustrate this point, she cites a former colleague of mine, Phil Sullivan, a Ngiyampaa man and NPWS Aboriginal Sites Officer. He explains:

> The 'natural' and 'cultural' heritage of National Parks is not separate. This is an artificial white-fella separation. They are still boxing the whole into sections, we need to integrate management into a holistic view of the landscape.
>
> *(Harrison and Rose 2010: 251)*

In saying this, she suggests that Phil and other Indigenous Australians challenge the idea that heritage meaning is made only by humans. Indigenous ontologies challenge the tangible–intangible dualism that is fundamental to the definition of intangible heritage. Within this binary structure, she suggests that tangible matter is thought to be made meaningful by being brought into a world of intangible meanings that are the property of human culture and experience. In contrast, she suggests that Indigenous ontologies propose a philosophy of 'becoming', in which life and place combine to bind time and living beings into generations of continuities in particular places (Harrison and Rose 2010: 250). These generations are not only human; they also involve particular plants and animals, objects, and, indeed, whole ecosystems. These are associated by webs of connection that are not randomly patterned, but are structured by principles of kinship and established as part of the 'Law' or 'Dreaming'.

She goes on to quote another Ngiyampaa man, Paul Gordon, who explains the implication of this kinship system for the ways in which land management bureaucracies go about managing and protecting endangered plant and animal species. He uses the term 'meat' in place of 'totem' to refer to the 'flesh' that one 'is' as a result of being a member of a multi-species kin group. He notes:

> Some animals can't just be classified as fauna. Pademelon [a small, kangaroo-like marsupial] is my meat. They are my people, my relations … If National Parks has something going with pademelons, they should talk with us—it's our family.
>
> *(Harrison and Rose 2010: 252)*

The implication of this familial relationship with pademelons is that management decisions made with regard to pademelons will also affect Paul Gordon and other Ngiyampaa people whom pademelons recognise as kin; similarly, the connection between pademelons and other plant and animal species may mean that decisions made with regard to their management might also affect other entities that recognise them as kin. This connection between all things (remembering that some 'things' that might not be classed as 'living' in Western philosophies might be subjects in their own right, defined as such by their animation with spirit and ability to act on other 'persons') makes operating within a system of heritage management that separates natural and cultural heritage not only incredibly frustrating, but ultimately impossible for Indigenous Australians.

Indigenous ontological pespectivism and dialogical models of heritage

Eduardo Viveiros de Castro is one of a series of scholars whose work has been part of a broader 'ontological turn' (see discussion in Alberti and Bray 2009), which is at least partially related to the widespread discussion of the symmetrical or non-hierarchical approaches of actor–network theory and the recent interest in object-oriented ontologies in philosophy and the social sciences (Harman 2002; Olsen 2010; Bryant et al. 2011). He is one of many scholars who are involved in presenting Indigenous ontologies as serious alternatives to Western philosophies in understanding the nature of 'being in the world', as significant philosophical statements that might be the source for critical readings of modern, Western philosophies in their own right. His work on the question of subjects and objects in Amerindian ontology is directly relevant to this discussion of the implications for heritage of taking Indigenous ontologies seriously, and for this reason I want to work through it in some detail here, focusing principally on his article 'Exchanging perspectives: the transformation of objects into subjects in Amerindian ontologies' (Viveiros de Castro 2004). In particular, I want to focus on what he has to say about the various Western, modern mind/matter, nature/culture and human/non-human dualisms to help develop an alternative, dialogical model of heritage that emerges from the 'connectivity ontology' (see below) of Indigenous ontological perspectivism. Note that there are certain differences between Indigenous Australian and Amerindian worldviews (and, similarly, an enormous set of differences between these and actor–network theory and other symmetrical models of culture), which I do not intend to deny here, but there are also clear similarities that make their consideration together worthwhile in pursuing this goal. The point in this section is to consider the possibility that the world is patterned in quite different ways from those we have come to believe as a result of our reliance on Western dualisms, and to explore the ways in which alternative worldviews open up creative possibilities for thinking about heritage differently.

Viveiros de Castro (2004) begins by explaining that a fundamental Amerindian notion (as in Indigenous Australian worldviews) is an original state of non-differentiation between humans and non-humans, in which the common condition was one of humanity, rather than the other way around. Animals and other non-human agents are thus 'ex-humans', and for various reasons have come to acquire a bestial (or vegetable) form that conceals a common, human, socio-cultural core. Amerindian mythologies are thus concerned with the process by which animals (and other non-human agents) came to distinguish themselves from their original state of humanity—how spirits of the original jaguar-persons who had the bodies of humans, for example, came to inhabit the bodies of jaguars. The implication of this is that relationships between humans and non-humans come to be viewed as what we might otherwise term 'social' relations. These relationships are similar to the totemic or 'kinship' relationships with the natural world amongst Aboriginal people in New South Wales, discussed above. In Viveiros de Castro's example, cultivated plants might be conceived as blood relations of the women who tend them, game animals might be approached as relatives by marriage, and so on. Having once been people, non-humans continue to exist as people behind their everyday corporeal facade, thus reality is perceived from distinct points of view that are the product of the material perspective of the body.

> Animals see their food as human food (jaguars see blood as manioc beer, vultures see the maggots in rotting meat as grilled fish); they see their bodily attributes (fur, feathers, claws, beaks) as bodily decorations or cultural instruments, they see their social system as organized in the same way as human institutions are.
>
> *(Viveiros de Castro 2004: 466)*

Viveiros de Castro refers to this as a 'multi-naturalist', as opposed to a 'multi-culturalist' ontology.

> Where the latter are founded on the mutually implied unity of nature and multiplicity of cultures—the former guaranteed by the objective universality of body and substance, the latter generated by the subjective particularity of spirit and meaning—the Amerindian conception presumes a spiritual unity and a corporeal diversity ... culture or the subject is the form of the universal, while nature or the object is the form of the particular.
>
> *(Viveiros de Castro 2004: 466)*

This derives from an animist perception of the spirit as the universal quality that is held in common by all 'animate' things (see also Harvey 2005). It follows that 'reflexive selfhood, not material objectivity, is the potential common ground of all being' (Viveiros de Castro 2004: 467). It is the perspective or point of view that transforms the object into subject and gives it 'agency', as the perspective is a product of an embodied way of 'being in the world'. Differences are thus bodily (perspectival) differences, not 'cultural' ones. Animals perceive the world in the same way as humans, and in this sense we all share the same 'culture'; what varies on account of their different ontological state of being is the *world* that animals inhabit (2004: 472).

Viveiros de Castro goes on to explore the implications of this perspectivist ontology for understanding the relationship between artefacts and humans, drawing on shamanism, or the intentional crossing of ontological boundaries, as an example. While animism holds that non-humans are conscious subjects, they are not naturally perceived as such in everyday life, and it is necessary to *personify* them in order to know how to perceive them as persons. Personhood is defined as the capacity to occupy a particular point of view or perspective. This is why shamen, as humans who are able to cross ontological boundaries, hold such an important position of knowledge—they hold the power to assume different ways of *being*, which allow them to conceptualise and communicate with other animate object-persons as if they were human subjects. However, personhood is not a given, and is not evenly distributed throughout the world. Thus, in some cases, artefacts might be 'object-persons' or they might equally exist as 'material embodiments of nonmaterial intentionality' (2004: 471). Personhood, or 'perspectivity' is a matter of context and degree, and not an absolute (2004: 470).

The reader may feel that we have now moved a long way from the World Heritage Convention, and be wondering what the relevance of animism and ontological perspectivism might be to understanding heritage in the contemporary, globalised world. The first thing to note is that this is not simply a 'theory', but a worldview that insists on being treated seriously. To do so means to acknowledge it on equal terms with other ways of conceptualising being in the world. In this sense, it provides a profound challenge to the idea of Cartesian dualisms as universal, and thus to the modern notions that underpin the universal values of World Heritage. While this might be reason enough to acknowledge Indigenous ontological per-spectivism as an important counter to the World Heritage Convention's universalism, it also suggests an alternative way of thinking about the relationship between 'nature' and 'culture', which has significant implications in shifting the focus of heritage to the active relationships between humans and non-humans, none of which are necessarily privileged as the origin of meaning making, and all of whom are collectively involved in this 'dialogue' in different ways. We might also think here of the 'flat', symmetrical models of social and material relations that characterise actor–network theory, and the heterogeneous groupings of humans and non-humans of assemblage theory, as similarly describing alternative models of 'social' collectives, which include human and non-human agents or a 'federation' of actants, in which all material and non-material things are participants, which have been proposed as alternatives to tradition Cartesian dualisms (see Chapter 2). This way of thinking about being in the world has also been described as a 'connectivity ontology', a concept that draws on traditions from the humanities, ecology, philosophy and political theory, which suggests that being is inherently, inescapably, and necessarily relational. An ontology of connectivity entails mutual causality: organism and environment modify each other. Relations between organism and environment are recursive, meaning that 'events continually enter into, become entangled with, and then re-enter the universe they describe'.

(Rose and Robin 2004)

This connectivity ontology finds resonance in a range of other contemporary thinking. For example, Karen Barad (2007) has shown how quantum physics provides the basis for models of reality in which matter and meaning are fundamentally entangled. Her theory of agential realism suggests that the world is composed of phenomena that are natural–cultural processes, which arise as the result of 'intra-acting' agencies of humans and non-humans. New models of the fundamental connectivity of natural and cultural phenomena, which suggest that both people and 'things' are entangled and equally involved as agents in their production, are emerging from a number of different disciplines, including science studies, ecology and the humanities. Ontological perspectivism and its accompanying questioning of Cartesian dualisms thus provides us with some interesting angles from which to explore new relational models of heritage that have the potential to fundamentally challenge the underlying philosophies of the World Heritage Convention, rather than simply reorganising its existing principles to take account of new categories, as has previously been the case.

It is impossible to rethink the social or 'cultural' aspects of heritage without rethinking the natural. So what are the implications of Indigenous ontological perspectivism or a connectivity ontology for remodelling our ways of thinking about a 'universal' notion of heritage? One point that emerged from the review of Viveiros de Castro's work was the focus on perspective or 'relationality' as the basis for communication or dialogue. His articulation of Amerindian multinaturalism posits a common 'culture' as universal, and 'being' as the seat of difference. Drawing on similar concepts, Deborah Bird Rose suggests that Australian Indigenous ontologies propose that heritage is 'dialogical' (Harrison and Rose 2010: 264)—it is produced as part of a conversation between multiple subjects, some of whom might be human, but many others not. I have already described heritage as a process and a particular set of relationships with the past in the present (Chapter 2). This pushes the definition further by suggesting that the production of heritage emerges from the relationship between people, 'things' and their environments as part of a dialogue or collaborative process of keeping the past alive in the present.

A dialogical concept of heritage suggests that heritage making is interactive— meaningfulness arises out of encounter and dialogue among multiple subjects, some of whom are human. Place (construed interactively) may also be a subject in its own right … Communication runs through living systems, including land and people. The processes and practices of keeping the past alive in the present, like the practice and processes of keeping the future alive in the present, is collaborative.

(Harrison and Rose 2010: 264-5)

This idea of heritage as a relational dialogue between multiple subjects, positioned according to their particular embodied perspective, none of which is necessarily wholly privileged in dictating the terms of the conversation or in controlling the meanings attributed to the discussion, resonates harmoniously with a view of 'social' relations as distributed amongst human and non-human collectives and a broader 'connectivity ontology'.

Rose also notes the way in which such a view profoundly challenges what I have characterised as the 'discursive turn' in heritage studies.

> indigenous ontologies push us to rethink, and to move outside of, the tangible–intangible boundary. Rather than imagining a process by which human meaning makers engage in heritage practices by making meanings in or through physical realities, we are rather pushed to imagine that humans and other sentient beings bind time collaboratively. Heritage is thus both tangible and intangible, embodied, material, and equally mindful and emergent ... Defining heritage modestly as the processes and practices of keeping the past alive in the present, an indigenous perspective shifts the focus to local multi-species relationships that bind time, place and generations.
>
> *(Harrison and Rose 2010: 265)*

This criticism might be broadened to what I have suggested is the present dominance of questions of the politics of representation within the interdisciplinary field of critical heritage studies (Chapter 5) and within interdisciplinary museum studies (Harrison in press a). Heritage is not a world of images and texts, but a fundamental quality of experience of the material (and hence, social) world (cf. Olsen 2010). Heritage is not the inscription of meaning onto blank objects, places and practices that are produced in this process, but instead is produced as a result of the material and social possibilities, or 'affordances', of collectives of human and non-human agents, material and non-material entities, in the world. It is not primarily an intellectual endeavour, something that exists only in the human mind, but is one that emerges from the *dialogue*, or practices of people and things.

Dialogical heritage, environmental ethics and sustainability

A dialogical model of heritage pushes us to consider the relationship between heritage and other social, political and environmental issues, as it does not insist on seeing these various fields as separate, arguing instead that they are interconnected in fundamental and complex ways. In particular, it foregrounds issues of sustainability and the role of 'cultural' heritage conservation as part of a broader environmental agenda (see also Dibley 2011; Cameron 2010, 2011a, 2011b on the relationship between museums and climate change). Importantly, in the same way that I have argued that 'cultural' heritage issues are connected with 'natural' heritage concerns, 'the environment' comes to be seen as a 'social' issue as much as it does a 'natural' one. I want to explore briefly here some of the ways in which this opens up debates around the environment, global warming and 'natural' heritage conservation in challenging and potentially important new ways, and also to consider the question of ethics that is invoked by this discussion.

We live in an era in which 'environmental concerns' relating to anthropogenic activity dominate the media. Issues as diverse as climate change, land and soil degradation, species extinction, pollution, over-population and dwindling energy resources influence the lives of every human (and non-human) on the planet. A connectivity ontology implies not only connection between individual humans and non-humans, but also a level of connection that includes all of them as a natural-cultural assemblage. A flat notion of the social implies that all 'being' is interactive, and that all actors are simultaneously produced by other actors. Hence any damage to part of the world assemblage also damages other parts of it. This forces us to broaden the traditional scope of notions of the economic and political sphere to develop a more inclusive sense of ethics that acknowledges not only the universal rights of humans, but also those of non-humans—a category in which I include animals, plants, objects, places and practices—who must also be seen as having rights, which we have obligations to attempt to uphold. While it may not yet be clear what those rights precisely are, as we are not always attuned to communicating with these other non-humans as actors in their own right, it nonetheless forces us to consider how rights and interests in one sphere relate to, and interact with, rights and interests in another.

Bruno Latour (2004) argues that the concept of 'nature', not understood as a Cartesian opposite to culture or a specific domain that is used by way of contrast to construct another, but instead as a collective notion involving the whole community of humans and non-humans in their varied states of 'being' in the world, provides the basis for assembling a political order that breaks down our modern division of 'nature' and 'society'. He develops a notion of political ecology that sees 'nature' not as external, but as the basis for defining a multinaturalist 'social' collective composed of a number of insistent realities, rather than a multiplicity of idealised political and social models. This notion of multinaturalism (as opposed to multiculturalism) was similarly developed in Viveiros de Castro's (2004) work, discussed above as an alternative to the Cartesian nature/culture and mind/matter dualisms in which multiple lifeworlds or states of being are acknowledged in preference to a single state of being and multiple cultural 'takes' on it. The boundaries that are introduced in this concept between lived realities or worldviews require the introduction of a diplomat, who stands in the same position as Viveiros de Castro's shaman, to uphold the necessity of negotiation across worlds, which is required to maintain the unity of the collectives. Latour notes:

> To give new meaning to political ecology, we need to abandon Science in favour of the sciences conceived of ways of socializing non-humans and we have to abandon ... politics ... for politics defined by the good common world ... [which is] the provisional result of the progressive unification of external realities.

(Latour 2004: 235–9)

Natural heritage issues thus become cultural heritage ones, and the natural sciences become a way of communicating across different states of being to address issues of common concern. 'Environmental problems' are thus expanded and perceived simultaneously as natural and social issues requiring communication across multiple species and multiple states of being. Similarly, 'social problems' become 'environmental' ones. Such a position of multinaturalism also dismisses the questions that arise in relation to universal and relative values and multiculturalism raised in Chapter 7, as the question of the relativity of cultures disappears when the notion of an absolute 'nature' is removed. The diversity of 'culture', understood as multiple embodied ways of being, comes to be the rule rather than the exception, and is no longer something that has to be either 'worked at' or 'resisted'.

An ontology of connectivity is thus a call for action that empowers parts of the natural–cultural collective to influence the whole. It also requires an acknowledgement of our own vulnerability to changes that affect other parts of the collective. But this does not mean we are unable to act and that all things must be instinctively conserved 'just in case'. This is rather the situation I have argued we have found ourselves in with regard to the late-modern crisis of the accumulation of memory (Chapter 8) as a result of contemporary conservation policies, in which more and more objects, places and practices are listed and conserved, and little attention is given to whether we still agree with the cumulative impact of our past decisions to do so. Instead, connectivity ontologies and their accompanying dialogical model of heritage encourage us to take *action* and to consider the circumstances of each issue or problem on a case-by-case basis. As Rose argues, 'connectivity ethics are open, uncertain, attentive, participatory, contingent. One is called upon to act, to engage in the dramas of call-and-response, and to do so on the basis of that which presents itself in the course of life' (2011: 143). If certain objects, places and practices become important at particular times and in particular places for the maintenance of the past in the present, it follows that they may, like humans, come and go, live and die, pass from one state to another. This does not mean we should take an indiscriminate attitude to the conservation of things from the past for the future, but rather that we should develop more discerning and sustainable policies that consider heritage objects, places and practices as part of a range of actors in our environment, which we nurture and which in turn nurture us; that we recognise change as equally important as stasis. The notion of individual humans as part of a greater collective living system recognises the need for plural and diverse forms of knowledge and new modes of decision-making with which to take account of them (see further discussion in relation to dialogical democracy below).

Sustainability can be defined as the capacity to endure. A connectivity ontology and dialogical model of heritage helps us to characterise sustainability as an issue that is not simply concerned with the maintenance of human quality of life. The concept of sustainability has been important in broadening the 'environmental' field to consider a wider range of economic, social, political, ecological and 'cultural' issues. An ontology of connectivity forces us to broaden this field even further to include not only the endurance of our own species, but also the endurance of a range of other non-human actors. In relation to heritage, it forces us to question not only the capacities of various material heritages to persist, but also whether the pasts we are actively creating in the present could, or should, endure into the future.

Once again, we return to the relationship of forgetting to remembering, and the need actively to prune and cultivate heritage rather than to allow it to accumulate randomly. In thinking about this issue, I was reminded of a story I read recently in the newspaper on a cryogenic storage facility in Michigan, in which pet owners were paying to have their dead pets stored in cryostasis in the hope that some means of bringing them back to life might be found in the future. Thinking sustainably in relation to heritage not only means thinking about the connections between heritage and other environmental, social, economic and political issues, but also thinking sensibly about the pasts we produce in the present for the future. We should not think of heritage like a cryogenic freezer, in which we indiscriminately store things that we once valued but that have subsequently become redundant; instead, we should be active in cultivating and pruning the pasts we produce in the light of our obligations to the assemblage of actors with whom we share a common world in the present. This notion of obligation opens up the more specific question of our ethical obligations and responsibilities *to* heritage. What responsibilities and obligations arise from a consideration of heritage as something that is produced in the relationship between a series of human and non-human actors, who work together to keep the past alive in the present and to collectively build a common world? Such questions require urgent consideration in rethinking the sustainability and ethical practice of heritage-making in the contemporary world (Dibley 2011; also see Meskell 2010: 854 on the notion of obligations to heritage).

Museums, dialogical heritage and the ethical weight of 'things'

While I have been discussing heritage in broad terms, it seems apposite to consider the implications of this dialogical model of heritage to museum objects in particular, which, as 'inert' objects, might seem somewhat abstract from these broadly inter-species-based 'environmental' issues and the discussion of the nature/culture divide. I would like to frame this discussion by posing two questions that arose as part of an Advanced Seminar I co-organised at the School of Advanced Research in 2010 (see Harrison et al. in press). What are the curatorial responsibilities that emerge from a serious consideration of Indigenous ontologies, in which museum pieces might be considered to be 'object-persons'? And what are the implications of a dialogical model of heritage and an increased sensitivity to the 'ontology of things' (Olsen 2010), or to the alternative ways of 'being' implied by a flat notion of a social/material collective involving humans and non-humans, to contemporary museum practices more broadly? I consider the implications for the management of Indigenous museum objects first, then broaden the discussion out to consider the issues for museums and heritage more generally.

While debates between Indigenous peoples (and their supporters) and museums have often been perceived to centre on repatriation and issues of ownership (see Chapter 5), these debates have more often been about the need to fundamentally reform curatorial practice in relation to things held in museum collections (Isaac 2009; this section after Harrison in press a). Thus a major part of the Indigenous critique of museum practice has involved a critique of the categorisation, management and storage of things in ways that are not only foreign to Indigenous ontologies, but that are also potentially offensive, or even dangerous (Henry 2004; Sully 2007) from the perspective of museum pieces as object-persons. Recently, museums have begun to acknowledge Indigenous categories and curatorial practices as equal forms of expertise with those of museum curators (Chaat Smith 2008; Chavez Lamar 2008; Singer 2008). In many instances, Indigenous viewpoints about objects have been given their own space in museum catalogues and databases (see chapters in Sleeper-Smith 2009). However, while this is obviously an important step in acknowledging Indigenous knowledge-practices and forms of expertise, and emphasises the museum itself as a space for reconciliation and social reform (Kelly and Gordon 2002; Mpumlwana et al. 2002; Allen and Hamby 2011), this does not necessarily reform the system itself, as the original categories and underlying values on which they rest often remain in place. This is directly analogous to the situation with the introduction of cultural landscapes and intangible heritage as categories of World Heritage, which, while introduced as a concession to non-modern worldviews, nonetheless have simply maintained the Cartesian dualisms and underpinning philosophies of the Convention.

So, while the critique of museums and the incorporation of Indigenous categories within them have emerged as part of a project of reforming these categories, one could argue that it is necessary to go further in drawing attention to the very nature of the categories themselves and the forms of authority on which they draw, and which they subsequently reproduce. Part of this process involves an acknowledgement that classification and ordering can only ever be partially realised (cf. Law 1994), and that any attempt to categorise will always produce anomalies (Douglas 1966). By revealing the process of categorisation to be partial and incomplete, we undermine the universalising mission of the museum (Bennett 1995), and draw attention to the ways in which the categories they employ are not 'natural', but are actively formed out of particular systems of value. Such an approach contains the potential for a radical reconceptualisation of objects in museum collections and their relationships with people. For example, we might ask what would happen if we were to consider objects in museums as 'kin', as many Indigenous people do (see Hays-Gilpin and Lomatewama in press)? How would this transform curatorial practices and modes of ordering and classification within the museum, and in heritage practice more generally?

One of the key outcomes of the Advanced Seminar was a consideration of the ways in which a sense of curatorial responsibility arises from the 'weight' of things in museums (Harrison et al. in press). In making reference to the 'weight' of things, we mean not only the physical bulk of collections, which occupy vast storage facilities behind the scenes of museums around the world, but also their political and affective 'weight'. In speaking of the affective weight of things in museums, we have in mind the charismatic (Wingfield 2010) or enchanting (Gell 1998; Harrison 2006) qualities of objects, their ability to engage the senses (Edwards et al. 2006: 12), as well as their ability to act in ways that are both integral to, and generative of, human behavior, or even in ways that are person-like (either in conjunction with, or independently of, persons themselves; Jones and Cloke 2008; Olsen 2010). Things also have a political weight, in the sense in which they come to represent or stand in for various imperial and colonial processes that underlie their presence in museum collections. In addition to reminding us of varied imperial and colonial histories, things speak to the contemporary political and ethical issues of ownership of culture and its products.

The notion of 'curatorial responsibility' carries within it two concepts—'care' and 'responsibility' (see Harrison in press a). It implies certain responsibilities or obligations to things themselves, which may be separate from our obligations to those individuals and groups (Indigenous or otherwise) outside the museum who relate to these things in some way (for example, as descent communities). If we are to assume less hierarchical models of social interactions and dialogical concepts of heritage, in which objects can behave in ways that are 'person-like', should they also be treated as 'persons'? What would it mean to open a dialogue with museum objects and allow them to 'speak' for themselves?

As truth claims, which integrate radically different concepts of time and space and which demand to be taken seriously, connectivity ontologies are beginning to have a renewed impact on heritage practice in the integration of Indigenous and Western conservation practices (Sully 2007; see Hays-Gilpin and Lomatewama in press; Knowles in press). A model of heritage as emplaced, creative production, involving a number of human and non-human agents, shifts our focus to the regenerative aspects of heritage production. Heritage emerges not as a process concerned with the past and present, but a future-oriented, emergent, contingent and creative endeavour. It is not a process of meaning-making that exists only in the human mind, but one in which multiple actors, both humans and non-humans, are equally implicated in complex processes that bind them across time and space (Harrison and Rose 2010). It becomes a symmetrical process, in which curation involves not only protecting an object, place or practice for future generations of people, but also protecting people for future generations of an object, place or practice (and indeed, for past generations of both). In seeing heritage not as a discourse or process of symbolic meaning-making, but as an emergent property of the relationship between humans and non-humans, in which the creative actions of 'things' are recognised as existing in a mixed or shared relationship of symmetry with humans, the objects that form part of museum (and heritage) collections take on new forms of significance and agency in their ongoing, creative relationships with humans in the present. In part, they draw on their power as objects from the past, but similarly, they exist as part of a meshwork of relationships (both material and social) in the present. The challenge for museums, and the process of heritage management more generally, thus becomes one of finding ways of engaging creatively with these objects so as to facilitate their ongoing relationships with people and the other objects around them in the future. This means opening up a dialogue with heritage objects, places and practices as actors in their own right, rather than perceiving them merely as props that stand in for human cultures from the past, in the present.

Dialogical democracy: dialogical heritage and dialogical decision-making processes

A dialogical model of heritage also pushes us to consider more dialogical models of decision-making in the identification, listing and management of heritage. As a result of the professionalisation and bureaucratisation of heritage practice over the course of the twentieth century (see Chapter 3), 'ordinary' laypersons and communities have been increasingly locked out of involvement in decisions about what heritage to conserve and how to conserve it (Carman 2005; Smith and Waterton 2009b). Smith (2006) has described the ways in which a set of bureaucratic knowledge/power effects employed by heritage 'experts' has worked to alienate the public from an involvement in heritage, whilst simultaneously producing the expertise on which their privilege is established. However, a notion of heritage as inherently dialogical opens up the possibility of more dialogical models of heritage decision-making processes. Drawing on Michel Callon et al.'s *Acting in an Uncertain World: An Essay of Technical Democracy* (2011), which considers controversies that arise as a result of uncertainties in the science and technology arena, I refer to this as a notion of 'dialogical democracy'. I suggest these concepts of dialogical decision-making and dialogical democracy flow directly from a notion of heritage as dialogical.

Callon et al. (2011) show how 'hybrid forums', in which experts, non-experts, ordinary citizens and politicians come together, can help undermine the antagonistic bureaucratic divide between laypersons and experts. They suggest two poles along which laypersons are traditionally isolated from the production of knowledge and the decision-making processes based on that knowledge. The first pole concerns the division between specialists and laypersons, while the second concerns the separation between ordinary citizens and those who are elected to represent them (Callon et al. 2011: 35). We might think of these dualisms as another set of Cartesian coordinates, which are challenged by dialogical thinking and ontologies of connectivity. Hybrid forums, which are generally formed in the space of uncertainty that arises from the discovery of a new controversy (in the science and technology field, for example, the imminent failure of a nuclear reactor), see these asymmetries removed, as groups and individuals with a direct interest in the issue at hand are forced together with experts and politicians to come to an informed decision about how to act. Hybrid forums are defined as

> open spaces where groups can come together to discuss technical options involving the collective, hybrid because the groups involved and the spokespersons claiming to represent them are heterogeneous, including experts, politicians, technicians, and laypersons who consider themselves involved.
>
> *(Callon et al. 2011: 18)*

These might also be considered 'hybrid' forums because they simultaneously address themselves to questions and problems at a variety of scales and from a wide range of different domains, from ethics and economics to applied and theoretical technical knowledge. Importantly, mirroring issues we have considered in relation to breaking down the nature/culture divide, these forums simultaneously address themselves to technical, political, environmental and social issues, opening up a space for a consideration of the relationships between these various fields.

One of the most powerful aspects of this work on hybrid forums is the way in which controversy comes to be perceived not as a 'social' or 'political' problem to be managed, but as a mode of exploration in its own right, which has the potential to generate important new insights and forms of knowledge on issues of critical concern to the various actors involved. They are not consultative forums that are simply concerned with gaining 'consent' (see Greer et al. 2002 for a similar clarification regarding the difference between reactive or 'consent-based' research and 'community-based' research in archaeology), but are involved in the co-production of new knowledge and new ways of seeing, thinking and acting. Because such hybrid forums are generally produced spontaneously as a result of conflict and uncertainty, it is difficult to formalise them. However, Callon et al. suggest several ways in which the dialogic procedures of such forums can be characterised and hence utilised more broadly in decision-making processes. They suggest three criteria, each with two sub-criteria, which allow for an assessment of the depth of dialogue which different forms of hybrid forum facilitate—the *intensity* of dialogism (how early laypersons are involved in the exploration of possible worlds and the degree of intensity of concern for the composition of the collective); the *openness* of dialogism (the degree of diversity of groups consulted/degree of independence *vis-á-vis* established action groups and degree of control of representativeness of spokespersons of groups involved in the debate); and the *quality* of dialogism (degree of seriousness of voice and degree of openness of voice) (Callon et al. 2011: 160). In addition, they add three criteria to evaluate the implementation of procedures—the equality and conditions of access to debates, the transparency and traceability of debates and the clarity of the rules organising debates (Callon et al. 2011: 163). They use these criteria to assess a number of different forms of hybrid forum, including 'focus' or discussion groups, public inquiries, consensus conferences and citizens' panels. In assessing these varied forms of hybrid forum against their criteria, they argue that no single form is likely to produce more dialogically democratic outcomes, suggesting instead the need for constant reflection and debate on the procedures, their implementation and outcomes (Callon et al. 2011: 188).

Given the role that the question of minority representation has played within heritage and critical heritage studies more generally (see Chapters 5 and 7), it seems important to consider how the representation of minorities is addressed within such hybrid forums. The authors show how hybrid forums not only assist in the question of the representation of minorities because they work to close the gap between the represented and the concerned layperson, but also constitute arenas for the emergence of new identities. They note three particular lessons from their cases studies with regard to the representation of emergent minorities, which can be summarised as follows:

1 minorities are better represented when their spokespersons are involved in discussion from the outset and in a continuous and productive way;
2 interested groups and individuals have an important role to play in generating their own forms of knowledge which can contribute to specialist knowledge, and

this 'rebalancing' of interests in hybrid forums better serves the security of the representation of emergent minorities; and

3 general principles need to be relativized in order to deal with specific issues which are always necessarily local and singular so that the specificities of interests, concerns and competences of individual groups (including minorities) might be appropriately considered in each case.

(Callon et al. 2011: 252–3)

These general principles, and the notion of the hybrid forum, form the basis for modelling more dialogical procedures in a heritage arena, in relation to specific debates and controversies as well as more general procedures relating to the identification, listing and management of heritage in contemporary society. We might imagine circumstances in which decisions over the listing of endangered heritage sites, for example, might be made by hybrid forums that include not only experts and bureaucrats, as is often the case, but also those who would be directly affected by the conservation and/or loss of the site in question. This would allow those with an interest in the conservation of the site to speak directly with those who are involved in assessing the site, and those who make the decisions about its future. This would not simply involve community consultation or the acceptance of community submissions by expert panels, but would directly involve interested laypersons in negotiated decision-making processes. Similarly, States Parties might also form hybrid forums for the drawing up of tentative lists, and UNESCO might involve interested groups directly in their own decision-making processes regarding nominations to the World Heritage List. Decisions might be made on site in the places under discussion, so that these places might also form part of the dialogue and communicate for themselves.

The hybrid forum provides a new set of instruments for heritage decision-making, based on a model of heritage as inherently dialogical, and has important implications for the future of heritage as more open, inclusive, representative and creative. It also has the potential to overcome traditional problems in the production of static identities through heritage by providing opportunities for the continuous expression of changing and emerging identities. The various regimes and modalities of discussion outlined above have the potential to reorganise relationships between experts, politicians, bureaucrats and laypersons, which, rather than suppressing conflicts, make use of the overflows and controversies that emerge as a result of conflict and uncertainties over heritage in productive and innovative ways. Hybrid forums can structure and help foster collaborative and consultative research processes and the co-production of knowledge by experts and interested stakeholders. Dialogical heritage must be dialogically democratic, and the hybrid forum provides an important model for increasing democracy through dialogical decision-making processes.

Conclusion

While I have suggested that one of the major sources of transformation in relation to the definitions and models for the management of global heritage has developed as a result of the expansion of the categories of heritage in relation to the World Heritage Convention in the light of its claims to represent a universal set of categories of heritage, in this chapter I have explored what it might mean to take such challenges to their logical conclusion in breaking down the Cartesian dualisms and modern philosophies on which the Convention rests. Drawing on Australian and Amerindian Indigenous ontological perspectives and a broad ontology of connectivity, I have suggested that a dialogical model of heritage as relational and emergent in the connection between people, objects, places and practices not only better describes the ways in which most people think about and experience heritage as a quality of lived experience in the contemporary world, but also pushes us to consider the relationship between heritage and other social, political and environmental issues. In particular, it foregrounds issues of sustainability and the role of 'cultural' heritage conservation as part of a broader environmental agenda. Importantly, the environment becomes a 'social' issue as much as it does a 'natural' one. This opens up debates around the environment, global warming and 'natural' heritage conservation, in challenging and potentially important new ways. Thinking of heritage not as a set of tangible 'things', nor as intangible expressions and practices, but instead as relational and emergent in the dialogue between people, objects, places and practices also has implications for how we think about and manage heritage in the future. It implies notions of obligation, responsibility, care, curation and ethics, but also suggests that conservation is as much a 'social' process as it is a physical or technical one—that conservation of an object, place or practice for future generations of people also requires a symmetrical consideration of the conservation of people for a future generation of objects, places or practices of heritage. A dialogical model of heritage based on an ontology of connectivity not only flattens the hierarchies of relationships involved amongst the various heterogeneous actors, human and non-human, that bind time and place to keep the past alive in the present, but also suggests important dialogical models of heritage decision-making in hybrid forums, which break down the conventional barriers between experts, politicians, bureaucrats and interested laypersons or stakeholders. Dialogical models of heritage provide an important basis for thinking productively and actively about heritage in the future.

10

A FUTURE FOR THE PAST?

Throughout this volume, I have developed three interlinked themes—*connection, materiality* and *dialogue*—as ways of thinking about what heritage is and does in contemporary global societies. In this brief conclusion, I would like to look to the future of heritage studies and try to reinforce some of the implications of the 'toolkit of concepts' that I have developed here. In doing so, I emphasise the ways in which critical interdisciplinary approaches to heritage might have an influence on the global practice of heritage, and hence have a lasting impact on important social, political, economic and environmental issues in the future.

I have argued that heritage is a distinctly modern concern, in the sense in which the question of what is 'old' and what is 'new' belongs to a peculiarly modern sensibility. This sensibility arises from the experience of modernity and its relationship to time, ordering and uncertainty (or 'risk'). These three concepts are integrally linked—modernity must order and classify to deal with uncertainty and risk; uncertainty derives from a sense of the accelerated passage of time; linear time provides one of a series of principles of ordering and classification to manage uncertainty. Together, they are responsible for the development of our modern conception of heritage as salvage or preservation of that which is distant, old, hidden and hence authentic, as opposed to the notion of heritage as a form of creative production involving the assembly and reassembly of things on the surface and in the present, which I have emphasised throughout the book. The accelerated operation of this modern sensibility, coupled with a series of factors, including shifting economic and demographic processes of deindustrialisation and redundancy; the development of the heritage 'experience' as a marketable commodity; the growth of domestic and international leisure travel and the accompanying restructuring of the tourist gaze and its economic and social impacts; the diversification and segmentation of heritage to make it marketable to more varied audiences; and the globalisation of the World Heritage concept, have contributed to the abundance of heritage which I have suggested characterises our late-modern world. This abundance is reflected in the growth in the number and range of officially listed and conserved places, objects and practices. It is also reflected in unofficial forms in the growth of nostalgia and alternative memorial practices of individuals and groups that are not necessarily recognised by the state.

While heritage studies has tended to focus on issues relating to the politics of representation and the knowledge/power effects of the discourse of heritage, it has generally under-theorised the affective qualities of heritage—its materiality, the ways in which intangible heritage practices are mediated by and power distributed within interlinked webs of people and things, and the ways in which these people and things might be said to be in dialogue with one another and with the world. While I do not want to undermine the importance of the 'discursive turn' in critical heritage studies, I have advocated a more balanced approach, which considers both the material and the discursive simultaneously. I have drawn on actor–network theory, assemblage theory, symmetrical archaeology, and a notion of heritage as an apparatus or *dispositif* to argue the case for a material semiotic approach to heritage to bridge these two critical approaches.

Drawing on this material semiotic approach, I have explored a number of crises of definition, which I argue arose as a result of the global application of a specific set of discontinuous, modern, post-Enlightenment ideas about heritage and the past, which had developed in Euro-American contexts over the nineteenth and twentieth centuries, to countries and communities with radically different conceptions of heritage in the late twentieth and early twenty-first centuries, focusing on the implications of the 1972 World Heritage Convention. This process, coupled with the abundance and globalisation of heritage in late-modern societies (not only as a consequence of the work of UNESCO and its advisory bodies, but also of broader processes of the restructuring of global economies, the growth of international heritage tourism and the increasingly transnational flows of people, capital, ideas and images), generated a series of conceptual crises that have seen radical transformations in the way in which it is defined, managed and understood in the contemporary world. In Chapters 6–9 I explored a series of these crises, looking in detail at the World Heritage Committee's responses to various claims for representation, which it was forced to accommodate as a result of its expression as a 'universal' set of principles, representing 'universal' values. These crises saw UNESCO broaden and redefine heritage to include cultural landscapes, intangible practices, 'absent' heritage and other spectral traces, and even cultural diversity itself. More diverse and representative models of heritage were developed not only in response to these counter-claims, but also the changing place of heritage in the global economy and the requirements to appeal to broader audiences. The global practice of heritage has thus transformed dramatically over the past few decades, even while the UNESCO approach to World Heritage has become increasingly hegemonic.

I have also tried to emphasise that heritage actually has very little to do with the past, but instead emerges out of the relationship between past and present as a reflection on the future. Heritage is not a passive process, but an active assembling of a series of objects, places and practices that we choose to hold up as a mirror to the present, associated with a particular set of values that we wish to take with us into the future. As such, heritage is not inert or passive, but has the potential to engage directly with questions of contemporary global concern. Thinking of heritage as a creative engagement with the past in the present focuses our attention on our ability to take an active and informed role in the production of our own future.

The foundation of this argument is a dialogical model, in which heritage is seen as emerging from the relationship between people, objects, places and practices, and which does not distinguish between or prioritise what is 'natural' and what is 'cultural', but is instead concerned with the various ways in which humans and non-humans are linked by chains of *connectivity*, and work together to keep the past alive in the present for the future. The dialogical model of heritage as an emergent property of the relationship between people and other human and non-human actors forces us to focus on the active role of heritage, and broadens the debate from one about heritage as power, to a wider debate about the future. This also allows us to connect heritage to sustainability discourses and debates, and to broader issues related to the environment and resource management in globalised societies.

One of the implications of thinking of heritage as relational is the adoption of an ontology of connectivity, in which all things—people, objects, plants, animals—are bound together as part of a broad natural–cultural collective, in which the actions of one part of the collective have an impact on all the others, and through which each component of the collective is co-produced by the others. This connectivity ontology resonates not only with Indigenous ontological perspectivism and animist theories of life, but also with actor–network and other symmetrical approaches to the study of society. In this way, connectivity emerges as both a *method* for analysing and understanding heritage and its role in society, and an *ontology* of heritage and its emergence as part of a dialogue between people and things.

If these three linked themes of materiality, connectivity and dialogue are simultaneously tools for studying heritage and ways of making connections between heritage and other urgent contemporary social, political, economic and environmental issues in the world, then a critical interdisciplinary heritage studies can and should have a role to play in democratising heritage and in making heritage work more positively and productively. The newly emerging field of interdisciplinary heritage studies has a clear role to play in commenting critically on new developments in heritage and being more actively engaged with the production of policy and the critical discussion of its function in society. Perhaps more importantly, an interdisciplinary heritage studies has a role to play in the liberation of laypersons who have become increasingly marginalised in heritage decision-making processes. If all heritage is co-produced, then we are all simultaneously producers and consumers of heritage. In realising this we might, in the words of Jacques Rancière, become *emancipated spectators*, 'blurring the boundary between those who act and those who look, between individuals and a collective body' (2009: 19). I have argued that hybrid forums provide one model for more dialogically democratic decision-making processes that flow from a definition of heritage as dialogical.

My emphasis on dialogically democratic decision-making processes in heritage derives from the ways in which heritage has almost always tended to be used in contexts of unequal relations of power, to isolate and exclude particular individuals and social groups. These exclusionary processes have occurred at a range of different scales. At one scale, nation-states have used heritage to produce and exclude subaltern minorities and to define what constitutes citizenship, allowing them to eliminate and persecute those who do not share the histories, values or ethnicities of majorities. On another scale, bureaucrats, politicians and 'experts' have employed the knowledge/power effects of the discourse of expertise in relation to heritage to exclude laypersons from an involvement in heritage decision-making processes. Any discussion of heritage must be tested for claims that might exclude or disempower others. Within this context, the acknowledgement of diversity as a 'universal' human right has important implications for heritage. In some cases, heritage has been used to establish multiculturalism itself as part of contemporary national origin myths, but this has the potential to mask social, political and economic inequality by specifying these inequalities as a function of cultural diversity, and hence making them appear to be 'natural' and inevitable. The systemic inequalities and forms of racism that may underpin the acknowledgement of diversity complicate any account of globalisation and its impact on the management and presentation of heritage. Difference and diversity must be presented not as intrinsic, but as something to be chosen and actively promoted; not as something that is simply rooted in the past, but as an effective choice towards which societies must work in the future. Similarly, 'universal' rights must themselves also be viewed as negotiated and open to discussion and debate in response to the continually changing diversity of human cultures and their heritages. The emphasis must remain firmly on the process of constantly remaking cultures in the present, and not on an easy recourse to tradition as an excuse for the maintenance of social, economic and political inequalities, and/or for permitting the continuity of practices which are inhumane or which harm or prejudice against others. These issues raise further questions of our ethical obligations to heritage and to other parts of the natural/cultural collective to which we belong, and cautions against becoming too complacent about heritage as something that is always necessarily positive or benign. This issue will become ever more urgent in a globalised world characterised by inequality, conflict and diminishing resources.

Throughout the book, I have emphasised the role of uncertainty, threat and risk in motivating late-modern heritage practices and their dominant paradigm of salvage. In general, I have treated this late-modern sense of uncertainty and risk with suspicion. However, dialogical models of heritage and heritage decision-making also provide a way of making more productive use of this sense of uncertainty, through foregrounding controversy and crisis as the very crucibles within which the ideal collectives to make appropriate decisions about particular critical issues are formed. Hybrid forums, in which experts, non-experts, ordinary citizens and politicians come together, can help undermine the antagonistic bureaucratic divide between laypersons and experts in relation to heritage, and simultaneously address themselves to a broad range of technical, political, environmental and social issues, while opening a space for a consideration of the relationships between these various fields. These hybrid forums provide a context for the co-production of new knowledge and new ways of seeing, thinking and acting in the world. The hybrid forum provides a new set of instruments for heritage decision-making, based on a model of heritage as inherently dialogical, and has important implications for the future of heritage as more open, diverse, inclusive, representative and creative.

One of the areas in which we need to become more active in our heritage decision-making is in thinking more sustainably about heritage. This means not only making better connections between heritage and other environmental, social, economic and political issues, but also thinking sensibly and equitably about the pasts we produce in the present for the future. We live in a world in which heritage is ubiquitous, and in which we rarely reconsider the implications of past heritage decisions. To make sense of the heterogeneous piling up of traces and practices of the past in the present, we must distinguish between active and passive processes of remembering and forgetting, as well as the politics of collective memory and forgetfulness. Drawing on a broader literature on individual and collective memory, I have argued that one cannot properly form new memories and attach value to them without selecting some things to also forget. Remembering is an active process of cultivating and pruning, not one of completely archiving everything that may or may not be of value in the future. I argue that the same is true of heritage, and without closer attention to processes by which heritage might be deaccessioned or actively removed, and to the values that underpin our everyday conservation decisions, we risk being overwhelmed by memory and, in the process, making all heritage worthless. This process of actively cultivating new memories also requires us to make brave decisions to prune those forms of heritage that are inconsistent with, or hold no continuing value for, contemporary and future generations if heritage and its role in the production of social memory is to remain sustainable in the future. This does not mean returning to a canonical model of heritage, in which only the very 'best' can be conserved—that would overturn the very important work which has been done over the past few decades to make sure that heritage becomes more equal, representative and diverse. Instead, it means thinking actively about heritage and its role in contemporary society, and foregrounding the ways in which heritage is constantly produced and reproduced in the present. Actively promoting the diversity of heritage is something that I have tried to emphasise as necessary to social well being, but it is also something that is possible only through engagement with, and attention to, the process and meaning of heritage-making in the present.

I have argued that, while heritage might be said to be a *product* of late-modernity, it is also a *producer* of it. It is only through an active engagement with the pasts we produce in the present that we can generate the individual and collective memories that will bind us together in future. Understanding heritage and its production dialogically, in the connectivity of people and things, will allow not only heritage researchers and practitioners, but also informed laypersons, to exercise greater agency in the quotidian decisions that governments, NGOs, communities and other individuals make in actively forming our pasts in the present. In this way, a critical interdisciplinary heritage studies is well placed to address itself to some of the most pressing contemporary issues of social, economic, political and environmental concern.

NOTES

1 Introduction: Heritage everywhere

1 I use the term 'listing' here, but in other regional or national contexts, the terms 'designation', 'nomination' or 'inscription' may be used. In all these cases, what is meant is the identification and description of an object, place or practice to convey legal or procedural protection of some form.

3 Prehistories of World Heritage: The emergence of a concept

1 Note that separate legislation was later developed to cover the listing of historic buildings in the UK. This was not introduced until after the Second World War in the form of the Town and Country Planning Act 1944.
2 Note that the Royal Commission on the Historical Monuments of England (RCHME) was not merged with English Heritage until 1999.

4 Late-modernity and the heritage boom

1 This section draws closely on discussions of heritage and late-modernity previously published in Harrison and Schofield (2010: 128ff) and Ferguson et al. (2010).

5 Critical heritage studies and the discursive turn

1 We might think, for example, of the creation of the government department '*English Heritage*', formed in 1984 out of the far less patriotically titled 'Historic Buildings and Monuments Commission'.

6 Intangible heritage and cultural landscapes

1 This historical account draws closely on Layton (1986) and Commonwealth of Australia (2010).

8 Heritage and the 'problem' of memory

1 Meskell (2002) uses the term 'negative heritage' to describe such sites of conflict, which become 'the repository of negative memory in the collective imaginary', although I prefer to emphasise the spectral, spatial and (non)material dimensions of these 'absent presences', for the reasons developed in the preceding sections.

9 Dialogical heritage and sustainability

1 These quotations are direct transcriptions of interviews with Jaru language speakers in Kimberley Kriol, recorded by the author in 1999.

REFERENCES

Adorno, T.W. (2001) *The Culture Industry: Selected Essays on Mass Culture*, London and New York: Routledge.

Agamben, G. (2009) *What is an Apparatus? And Other Essays*, Stanford: Stanford University Press.

Agence France-Presse (2001) 'Decree from Taliban Orders Destruction of Statues', *New York Times Online* 27 February. www.nytimes.com/2001/02/27/world/27AFGH.html?ex=1202878800&en=ad6c2e9efda4456b&ei=5070

Aikawa, N. (2004) 'An Historical Overview of the Preparation of the UNESCO International Convention for the Safeguarding of the Intangible Cultural Heritage', *Museum International* 56(1–2): 137–149.

Alberti, B. and Bray, T.L. (2009) 'Introduction: Special Section, Animating Archaeology: of Subjects, Objects and Alternative Ontologies', *Cambridge Archaeological Journal* 19(3): 337–343.

Allaback, S. (2000) *Mission 66 Visitor Centers: The History of a Building Type*, Washington, DC: National Park Service, US Department of the Interior, Cultural Resources Stewardship and Partnerships Park Historic Structures and Cultural Landscapes Program.

Allen, L. and Hamby, L. (2011) 'Pathways to Knowledge: Research, Agency and Power Relations in the Context of Collaborations Between Museums and Source Communities', in S. Byrne, A. Clarke, R. Harrison and R. Torrence (eds) *Unpacking the Collection: Networks of Material and Social Agency in the Museum,* New York: Springer, pp. 209–230.

Amit-Talai, V. (1996) 'The Minority Circuit: Identity Politics and the Professionalization of Ethnic Activism', in V. Amit-Talai and C. Knowles (eds) *Re-Situating Identities: The Politics of Race, Ethnicity and Culture,* Ontario: Broadview Press, pp. 89–114.

Anderson, B. ([1983] 2006) *Imagined Communities: Reflections on the Origin and Spread of Nationalism* (revised edn), London and New York: Verso.

Ang, I. (2005) 'Multiculturalism', in T. Bennett, L. Grossberg, and M. Morris (eds) *New Keywords: A Revised Vocabulary of Culture and Society*, Malden and Oxford: Blackwell Publishing, pp. 226–229.

Appadurai, A. (1996) *Modernity at Large*, Minneapolis and New York: University of Minneapolis Press.

——([2001] 2008) 'The Globalization of Archaeology and Heritage: A Discussion with Arjun Appadurai', in G. Fairclough, R. Harrison, J.H. Jameson Jr and J. Schofield (eds) *The Heritage Reader*, Abingdon and New York: Routledge, pp. 209–218.

——(2006) *Fear of Small Numbers*, Durham and London: Duke University Press.

Appiah, K.A. (2007) *Cosmopolitanism: Ethics in a World of Strangers*, London: Penguin Books.

Ashworth, G.J. (2008) 'The Memorialization of Violence and Tragedy: Human Trauma as Heritage', in B. Graham and P. Howard (eds) *The Ashgate Companion to Heritage and Identity*, London: Ashgate, pp. 231–244.

Ashworth, G.J. and Hartmann, R. (2005) *Horror and Human Tragedy Revisited: The Management of Sites of Atrocity for Tourism*, New York: Cognizant Communication.

Ashworth, G.J., Graham, B.J. and Tunbridge, J.E. (2007) *Pluralising Pasts: Heritage, Identity and Place in Multicultural Societies*, London: Pluto Press.

Askew, M. (2010) 'The Magic List of Global Status: UNSECO, World Heritage and the Agendas of States', in S. Labadi and C. Long (eds) *Heritage and Globalisation*, Abingdon and New York: Routledge, pp. 19–44.

Augé, M. (1995) *Non-Places: Introduction to an Anthropology of Supermodernity*, London and New York: Verso.

——(2004) *Oblivion*, Minneapolis: University of Minnesota Press.

Australian Government (2005) 20th Anniversary "Handback" – a Brief Background. www.environment.gov.au/parks/publications/uluru/pubs/factsheet-handback.pdf

——(2010) *Uluru–Kata Tjuta National Park Management Plan 2010–2020*, Canberra: Director of National Parks.

Australian National Parks and Wildlife Service (1986) *Nomination of Uluru (Ayers Rock–Mount Olga) National Park for Inclusion on the World Heritage List*, Canberra: Australian National Parks and Wildlife Service.

Bandarin, F. (ed.) (2007) *World Heritage: Challenges for the Millennium*, Paris: UNESCO World Heritage Centre.

Barad, K. (2007) *Meeting the Universe Halfway: Quantum Physics and the Entanglement of Matter and Meaning*, Durham and London: Duke University Press.

Barringer, T.J. and Flynn, T. (eds) (1998) *Colonialism and the Object: Empire, Material Culture, and the Museum*, London and New York: Routledge.

Baudrillard, J. (1994) 'The System of Collecting', in J. Elsner and R. Cardinal (eds) *Cultures of Collecting*, London: Reaktion, pp. 7–24.

——(2002) *The Spirit of Terrorism*, London and New York: Verso.

Bauman, Z. (2000) *Liquid Modernity*, Cambridge and Malden: Polity Press.

——(2011) *Culture in a Liquid Modern World*, Cambridge and Malden: Polity Press.

Baumann, G. (1999) *The Multicultural Riddle: Rethinking National, Ethnic, and Religious Identities*, London and New York: Routledge.

Baxter, I. (2010) 'Global Heritage Tourism: The Value of Experiencing the Past', in G.S. Smith, P.M. Messenger and H.A. Soderland (eds) *Heritage Values in Contemporary Society*, Walnut Creek: Left Coast Press, pp. 241–254.

BBC News (2006) 'Who are the Taliban?' *BBC News Online*. http://news.bbc.co.uk/1/hi/world/south_asia/1549285.stm

Bearak, B. (2001) 'Over World Protests, Taliban are Destroying Ancient Buddhas', *New York Times Online*, 4 March. www.nytimes.com/2001/03/04/world/04AFGH.html?ex=1202878800&en=8616ae683eeed445&ei=5070

Beck, U. (1992) *Risk Society: Towards a New Modernity*, London: Sage.

Bell, D. (1973) *The Coming of Post-Industrial Society: A Venture in Social Forecasting*, London: Penguin Books.

Benavides, O.H. (2009) 'Translating Ecuadorian Modernities: Pre-Hispanic Archaeology and the Reproduction of Global Difference', in L. Meskell (ed.) *Cosmopolitan Archaeologies*, London and Durham: Duke University Press, pp. 228–248.

Bennett, J. (2010) *Vibrant Matter: A Political Ecology of Things*, Durham and London: Duke University Press.

Bennett, T. (1995) *The Birth of the Museum: History, Theory, Politics*, London and New York: Routledge.

——(2004) *Pasts Beyond Memory: Evolution, Museums, Colonialism*, London and New York: Routledge.

Bennett, T. (2005) 'Civic Laboratories: Museums, Cultural Objecthood and the Governance of the Social', *Cultural Studies* 19(5): 521–47.

——(2006) 'Exhibition, Difference and the Logic of Culture', in I. Karp, C. Krantz, L. Szwaja and T. Ybarra-Frausto (eds) *Museum Frictions: Public Cultures/Global Transformations*, Durham and London: Duke University Press, pp. 46–69.

——(2009) 'Museum, Field, Colony: Colonial Governmentality and the Circulation of Reference', *Journal of Cultural Economy* 2(1–2): 99–116.

——(2010) 'Making and Mobilising worlds: Assembling and Governing the Other', in T. Bennett and P. Joyce (eds) *Material Powers: Cultural Studies, History and the Material Turn*, London: Routledge, pp. 188–208.

——(in press a) 'The "Shuffle of Things" and the Distribution of Agency', in R. Harrison, S. Byrne and A. Clarke (eds) *Reassembling the Collection: Ethnographic Museums and Indigenous Agency*, Santa Fe: SAR Press.

Benton, T. (1999) 'From the Arengario to the Lictor's Axe: Memories of Italian Fascism', in M. Kwint, C. Breward and J. Aynsley (eds) *Material Memories: Design and Evocation*, Oxford and New York: Berg, pp. 199–218.

——(2010) 'Heritage and Changes of Regime', in T. Benton (ed.) *Understanding Heritage and Memory*, Manchester/Milton Keynes: Manchester University Press/Open University, pp. 126–163.

Benton, T. and Watson, N.J. (2010) 'Museum Practice and Heritage', in S. West (ed.) *Understanding Heritage in Practice*, Manchester/Milton Keynes: Manchester University Press/Open University, pp. 127–165.

Berman, M. (1983) *All that is Solid Melts Into Air: The Experience of Modernity*, London and New York: Verso.

Black, G. (2005) *The Engaging Museum: Developing Museums for Visitor Involvement*, London and New York: Routledge.

Boswell, D. (1999) 'Introduction to Part 2', in D. Boswell and J. Evans (eds) *Representing the Nation: A Reader*, London and New York: Routledge, pp. 111–114.

Bourdieu, P. (1984) *Distinction: A Social Critique of the Judgement of Taste*, London and New York: Routledge.

Bowker, G.C. (2005) *Memory Practices in the Sciences*, Cambridge: MIT Press.

Bowker, G.C. and Star, S.L. (2000) *Sorting Things Out: Classification and its Consequences*, Cambridge: MIT Press.

Boym, S. (2001) *The Future of Nostalgia*, New York: Basic Books.

Bradley, R. (2002) *The Past in Prehistoric Societies*, London and New York: Routledge.

Breglia, L.G. (2006) *Monumental Ambivalence: The Politics of Heritage*, Austin: University of Texas Press.

Brett, D. (1996) *The Construction of Heritage*, Cork: Cork University Press.

Briggs, M. (1952) *Goths and Vandals: A study of the Destruction, Neglect and Preservation of Historical Buildings in England*, London: Constable.

Bryant, L., Smicek, N. and Harman, G. (eds) (2011) *The Speculative Turn: Continental Materialism and Realism*, Melbourne: re.press.

Bryman, A. (2004) *The Disneyization of Society*, London, Thousand Oaks and New Delhi: Sage.

Butler, B. (2011) 'Heritage as Pharmakon and the Muses as Deconstruction: Problematising Curative Museologies and Heritage Healing', in S. Dudley, A.J. Barnes, J. Binnie, J. Petrov and J. Walklate (eds) *The Thing about Museums: Objects and Experience, Representation and Contestation, Essays in Honour of Professor Susan M. Pearce*, London and New York: Routledge; pp. 354–70.

Byrne, D. (1991) 'Western Hegemony in Archaeological Heritage Management', *History and Archaeology* 5: 269–76.

——(1995) 'Buddhist Stupa and Thai Social Practice', *World Archaeology* 27(2): 266–81.

——(1996) 'Deep Nation: Australia's Acquisition of an Indigenous Past', *Aboriginal History* 20: 82–107.

——(2003) 'The Ethos of Return: Erasure and Reinstatement of Aboriginal Visibility in the Australian Historical Landscape', *Historical Archaeology* 37(1): 73–86.

——(2007) *Surface Collection: Archaeological Travels in Southeast Asia*, Lanham: AltaMira Press.

——(2008) 'Heritage as Social Action', in G. Fairclough, R. Harrison, J.H. Jameson Jr and J. Schofield (eds) *The Heritage Reader*, Abingdon and New York: Routledge, pp. 149–73.

——(2009) 'Archaeology and the Fortress of Rationality', in L. Meskell (ed.) *Cosmopolitan Archaeologies*, Durham and London: Duke University Press, pp. 68–88.

Byrne, D. and Nugent, M. (2004) *Mapping Attachment: A Spatial Approach to Aboriginal Post-Contact Heritage*, Sydney: Department of Environment and Conservation, NSW.

Byrne, D., Brayshaw, H. and Ireland, T. (2001) *Social Significance: A Discussion Paper*, Hurstville: NSW National Parks and Wildlife Service.

Byrne, S., Clarke, A., Harrison, R. and Torrence, R. (2011) 'Networks, Agents and Objects: Frameworks for Unpacking Museum Collections', in S. Byrne, A. Clarke, R. Harrison and R. Torrence (eds) *Unpacking the Collection: Networks of Material and Social Agency in the Museum*, New York: Springer, pp. 3–26.

Callon, M. (1989) *The Laws of the Markets*, Oxford: Blackwell.

——(2003) 'The Increasing Involvement of Concerned Groups in R&D Policies: What Lessons for Public Powers?', in E. Guena, A.J. Salter and W.E. Steinmueller (eds) *Science and Innovation: Rethinking the Rationales for Funding and Governance*, Northampton, MA: Edward Elgar, pp. 30–68.

——(2005) 'Why Virtualism Paves the Way to Political Impotence: A Reply to Daniel Miller's Critique of *The Laws of the Markets*', *Economic Sociology: European Electronic Newsletter* 6(2): 3–20.

Callon, M. and Law, J. (2004) 'Introduction: Absence–Presence, Circulation, and Encountering in Complex Space', *Environment and Planning D: Society and Space* 22(1) 3–11.

Callon, M., Law, J. and Rip, A. (eds) (1986) *Mapping the Dynamics of Science and Technology: Sociology of Science in the Real World*, London: Palgrave Macmillan.

Callon, M., Lascoumes, P. and Barthe, Y. (2011) *Acting in an Uncertain World: An Essay on Technical Democracy*, Cambridge and London: MIT Press.

Calma, G. and Liddle, L. (2003) 'Uluru–Kata Tjuta National Park: Sustainable Management and Development', in UNESCO World Heritage Centre (ed.) *World Heritage Papers 7. Cultural Landscapes: The Challenges of Conservation*, Paris: UNESCO World Heritage Centre, pp. 104–119.

Cameron, F.R. (2010) 'Liquid Governmentalities, Liquid Museums and the Climate Crisis', in F.R. Cameron and L. Kelly (eds) *Hot Topics, Public Culture, Museums*, Newcastle-upon-Tyne: Cambridge Scholars, pp. 112–128.

Cameron, F. (2011a) 'From Mitigation to Creativity: The Agency of Museums and Science Centres and the Means to Govern Climate Change', *Museum and Society* 9(2): 84–89.

——(2011b) 'Guest Editorial: Climate Change as a Complex Phenomenon and the Problem of Cultural Governance', *Museum and Society* 9(2): 90–106.

Carman, J. (2002) *Archaeology and Heritage: An Introduction*, London and New York: Continuum.

——(2005) *Against Cultural Property: Archaeology, Heritage and Ownership*, London: Duckworth.

Carman, J. and Sørensen, M.L.S. (2009) 'Heritage Studies: An Outline', in M.L.S. Sørensen and J. Carman (eds) *Heritage Studies: Methods and Approaches*, Abingdon and New York: Routledge, pp. 11–28.

Casey, E.S. (1987) *Remembering: A Phenomenological Study*, Bloomington and Indianapolis: Indiana University Press.

Chaat Smith, P. (2008) 'Critical Perspectives on the Our Peoples Exhibit: A Curator's Perspective', in A. Lonetree and A.J. Cobb (eds) *The National Museum of the American Indian: Critical Conversations*, Lincoln and London: University of Nebraska Press, pp. 131–143.

Chavez Lamar, C. (2008) 'Collaborative Exhibit Development at the Smithsonian's National Museum of the American Indian', in A. Lonetree and A.J. Cobb (eds) *The National Museum of the American Indian: Critical Conversations*, Lincoln and London: University of Nebraska Press, pp. 144–164.

Chelsea Market (2011) *History*. http://chelseamarket.com/history

Choay, F. (2001) *The Invention of the Historic Monument*, Cambridge: Cambridge University Press.

Clarke, K. (2010) 'Values in Cultural Resource Management', in G.S. Smith, P.M. Messenger and H.A. Soderland (eds) *Heritage Values in Contemporary Society*, Walnut Creek: Left Coast Press, pp. 89–99.

Clavé, S.A. (2007) *The Global Theme Park Industry*, Wallingford: CABI Publishing.

Cleere, H. (2001) 'The Uneasy Bedfellows: Universality and Cultural Heritage', in R. Layton, J. Thomas and P.G. Stone (eds) *Destruction and Conservation of Cultural Property*, London and New York: Routledge, pp. 22–29.

Clifford, J. (1988) *The Predicament of Culture: Twentieth Century Ethnography, Literature and Art*, Cambridge and London: Harvard University Press.

——(1995) 'Paradise', *Visual Anthropology Review* 11(1): 92–117.

——(1997) *Routes: Travel and Translation in the Late Twentieth Century*, Cambridge and London: Harvard University Press.

Clifford, J. and Marcus, G.E. (eds) (1986) *Writing Culture: The Poetics and Politics of Ethnography*, Berkeley and London: University of California Press.

Climo, J.J. and Cattell, M.G. (eds) (2002) *Social Memory and History: Anthropological Perspectives*, Walnut Creek, Lanham and New York: AltaMira Press.

Cohen, D. (2009) *Three Lectures on Post-Industrial Society*, London and Cambridge: MIT Press.

Colwell-Chanthaphonh, C. (2003) 'Dismembering/Disremembering the Buddhas: Renderings on the Internet during the Afghan Purge of the Past', *Journal of Social Archaeology* 3(1): 75–98.

Commonwealth of Australia (2010) *Culture, History and World Heritage*. www.environment.gov.au/parks/uluru/culture-history/index.html

Connerton, P. (2008) 'Seven Types of Forgetting', *Memory Studies* 1(1): 59–71.

——(2009) *How Modernity Forgets*, Cambridge: Cambridge University Press.

Coombes, A. (1994) *Reinventing Africa: Museums, Material Culture and Popular Imagination in Late Victorian and Edwardian England*, London: Yale University Press.

——(2003) *History after Apartheid: Visual Culture and Public Memory in a Democratic South Africa*, Durham and London: Duke University Press.

Cowell, B. (2008) *The Heritage Obsession: The Battle for England's Past*, Chalford: Tempus.

Cramer, M. (2011) 'Where was the Berlin Wall?', in E.C. Schweitzer (ed.) *The Berlin Wall Today: Remnants, Ruins, and Remembrances*, New York: Berlinica Publishing, pp. 5–7.

Creigh-Tyte, S.W. and Gallimore, J. (1998) 'The Built Heritage in England: The History and Development of Government Policy', *Cultural Trends*, 8: 25–36.

Cronin, A. and Hetherington, K. (eds) (2008) Consuming the Entrepreneurial City: Image, Memory, Spectacle, New York: Routledge.

Crosette, B. (2001) 'Taliban Explains Buddha Demolition', *New York Times Online*, 19 March. www.nytimes.com/2001/03/19/world/19TALI.html?ex=1202878800&en=d4a0 8c68da5a00a3&ei=5070

Cuno, J. (2008) *Who Owns Antiquity? Museums and the Battle over our Ancient Heritage*, Princeton: Princeton University Press.

Daly, P. and Winter, T. (eds) (2011) *Routledge Handbook of Heritage in Asia*, London and New York: Routledge.

Darian-Smith, K. and Hamilton, P. (eds) (1994) *Memory and History in Twentieth-Century Australia*, Oxford, Auckland and New York: Oxford University Press.

Davison, G. ([2000] 2008) 'Heritage: From Pastiche to Patrimony' in G. Fairclough, R. Harrison, J.H. Jameson Jr and J. Schofield (eds) *The Heritage Reader*, Abingdon and New York: Routledge, pp. 31–41.

Delafons, J. (1997) *Politics and Preservation: A Policy History of the Built Heritage, 1882–1996*, London: E&Fn Spon.

Deleuze, G. and Guattari, F. ([1988] 2004) *A Thousand Plateaus: Capitalism and Schizophrenia*, London and New York: Continuum.

Deloria, V. (1969) *Custer Died for Your Sins: An Indian Manifesto*, New York: Macmillan.

Department of Planning and Community Development Victoria (2011) Intangible Heritage. www.dpcd.vic.gov.au/heritage/heritage-places-and-objects/intangible-heritage-about

Derrida, J. (1994) *Specters of Marx: The State of the Debt, the Work of Mourning, and the New International*, London and New York: Routledge.

Di Giovine, M.A. (2009) *The Heritage-scape: UNESCO, World Heritage, and Tourism*, Lanham: Lexington Books.

Dibley, B. (2011) 'Museums and a Common World: Climate Change, Cosmopolitics, Museum Practice', *Museum and Society* 9(2): 154–165.

Dicks, B. (2000) *Heritage, Place and Community*, Cardiff: University of Wales Press.

——(2003) *Culture on Display: The Production of Contemporary Visitibility*, Berkshire: Open University Press.

District Six Museum (2011) *About the Museum*. www.districtsix.co.za/frames.htm

Dolff-Bonekämper, G. (2002) 'The Berlin Wall: An Archaeological Site in Progress', in J. Schofield, W. Gray-Johnson and C.M. Beck (eds) *Matériel Culture: The Archaeology of 20th Century Conflict*, London: Routledge, pp. 236–248.

Donnachie, I. (2010) 'World Heritage', in R. Harrison (ed.) *Understanding the Politics of Heritage*, Manchester/Milton Keynes: Manchester University Press/Open University, pp. 115–153.

Douglas, M. (1966) *Purity and Danger: An Analysis of Concepts of Pollution and Taboo*, London: Routledge & Kegan Paul.

——(1992) *Risk and Blame: Essays in Cultural Theory*, London: Routledge.

Duncan, C. (1995) *Civilizing Rituals: Inside Public Art Museums*, London and New York: Routledge.

Eddy, J. and Schreuder, D. (eds) (1988) *The Rise of Colonial Nationalism. Australia, New Zealand, Canada and South Africa First Assert their Nationalities, 1800–1914*, Sydney: Allen and Unwin.

Edwards, E., Gosden, C. and Phillips, R.B. (eds) (2006) *Sensible Objects: Colonialism, Museums and Material Culture*, Abingdon and New York: Routledge.

Elias, J.L. (2007) '(Un)making Idolatry: From Mecca to Bamiyan', *Future Anterior* 4(2): 13–29.

Elsner, J. and Cardinal, R. (1994) 'Introduction', in J. Elsner and R. Cardinal (eds) *Cultures of Collecting*, London: Reaktion, pp. 1–6.

English, A. (2000) 'An Emu in the Hole: Exploring the Link between Biodiversity and Aboriginal Cultural Heritage in New South Wales, Australia', *Parks* 10(2): 13–25.

——(2001) *The Sea and the Rock Give us a Feed: Mapping and Managing Gumbaingirr Wild Resource Use Places*, Hurstville: NSW National Parks and Wildlife Service.

English, A. and Gay, L. (2005) *Living Land, Living Culture: Aboriginal Heritage and Salinity*, Sydney: Department of Environment and Conservation, NSW.

English Heritage (2010a) *Heritage Counts 2010 England*. http://hc.english-heritage.org.uk/content/pub/HC-Eng-2010

——(2010b) *Removing a Building from the List*. www.english-heritage.org.uk/content/imported-docs/a-e/guidance-delisting.doc

——(2011) *Stonehenge World Heritage Site Facts and Figures*. www.english-heritage.org.uk/daysout/properties/stonehenge/world-heritage-site/why-is-stonehenge-a-world-heritage-site/facts-and-figures

Evans, G. (2002) 'Living in a World Heritage City: Stakeholders in the Dialectic of the Universal and Particular', *International Journal of Heritage Studies* 8(2): 117–35.

Falk, J.H. and Dierking, L.D. (2000) *Learning from Museums: Visitor Experiences and the Making of Meaning*, Lanham: AltaMira Press.

Faneuil Hall Marketplace (2009) *History of Faneuil Hall*. www.faneuilhallmarketplace.com/?q=history

Ferguson, R., Harrison, R. and Weinbren, D. (2010) 'The Heritage of the Contemporary Past', in T. Benton (ed.) *Understanding Heritage and Memory*, Manchester/Milton Keynes: Manchester University Press/Open University, pp. 277–315.

Fforde, C., Hubert, J. and Turnbull, P. (eds) (2002) *The Dead and Their Possessions: Repatriation in Principle, Policy and Practice*, London and New York: Routledge.

Fixler, D.N. (2011) 'Two Architects, Two Views of Modernism: Ben Thompson and Paul Rudolph', *Architecture Boston* 14(1): 26–30.

Flood, F.B. (2002) 'Between Cult and Culture: Bamiyan, Islamic Iconoclasm, and the Museum', *The Art Bulletin* 84(4): 641–659.

Foote, K.E. (2003) *Shadowed Ground: America's Landscapes of Violence and Tragedy*, Austin: University of Texas Press.

Forty, A. (1999) 'Introduction', in A. Forty and S. Küchler (eds) *The Art of Forgetting*, Oxford and New York: Berg, pp. 1–18.

Forty, A. and Küchler, S. (eds) (1999) *The Art of Forgetting*, Oxford and New York: Berg.

Foucault, M. (2007) *Security, Territory, Population: Lectures at the College de France 1977–1978*, New York: Picador.

——(2011) *The Government of Self and Others: Lectures at the College de France, 1982–1983*, New York: Picador.

Fowler, P. (2003) *World Heritage Papers 6. World Heritage Cultural Landscapes 1992–2002*, Paris: UNESCO World Heritage Centre.

——(2004) *Landscapes for the World: Conserving a Global Heritage*, Bollington, Cheshire: Windgather Press.

Francioni, F. (ed.) (2008) *The 1972 World Heritage Convention: A Commentary*, Oxford: Oxford University Press.

Gable, E. and Handler, R. (1996) 'After Authenticity at an American Heritage Site', *American Anthropologist* 98(3): 568–78.

Gamboni, D. (2001) 'World Heritage: Shield or Target?', *Getty Conservation Institute Newsletter* 16: 5–11.

Gathercole, P. and Lowenthal, D. (eds) (1990) *The Politics of the Past*, London: Unwin Hyman.

Gell, A. (1998) *Art and Agency*, Oxford: Oxford University Press.

Giddens, A. (1990) *Consequences of Modernity*, Cambridge: Polity Press.

——(1991) *Modernity and Self-Identity: Self and Society in the Late Modern Age*, Cambridge: Polity Press.

Giddens, A. and Pierson, C. (1998) *Making Sense of Modernity: Conversations with Anthony Giddens*, Stanford: Stanford University Press.

Gilbert, J. (2006) *Indigenous Peoples' Land Rights Under International Law: From Victims to Actors*, Ardsley, NY: Transnational Publishers.

Gilmore, J.H. and Pine, B.J. (2007) *Authenticity: What Consumers Really Want*, Boston: Harvard Business School Press.

Girard, R. ([1972] 2005) *Violence and the Sacred*, London and New York: Continuum.

Golden, J. (2004) 'Targeting Heritage: The Abuse of Symbolic Sites in Modern Conflicts', in Y. Rowan and U. Baram (eds) *Marketing Heritage: Archaeology and the Consumption of the Past*, Walnut Creek: AltaMira Press, pp. 183–202.

Goodale, M. (2006) 'Toward a Critical Anthropology of Human Rights', *Current Anthropology* 47(3): 485–511.

——(2008) *Surrendering to Utopia: An Anthropology of Human Rights*, Stanford: Stanford University Press.

González-Ruibal, A. (2008) 'Time to Destroy: An Archaeology of Supermodernity', *Current Anthropology* 49(2): 247–279.

——(2009) 'Vernacular Cosmopolitanism: An Archaeological Critique of Universalistic Reason', in L. Meskell (ed.) *Cosmopolitan Archaeologies*, Durham and London: Duke University Press, pp. 113–139.

Gordon, A. (1997) *Ghostly Matters: Haunting and the Sociological Imagination*, Minneapolis: University of Minnesota Press.

Goulding, C. and Domic, D. (2008) 'Heritage, Identity and Ideological Manipulation: The Case of Croatia', *Annals of Tourism Research* 36(1): 85–102.

Goytisolo, J (2001) *Defending Threatened Cultures*. Speech delivered at the opening of the meeting of the Jury, 15 May. www.unesco.org/bpi/intangible_heritage/goytisoloe.htm

Graham, B. and P. Howard (2008) 'Heritage and Identity', in B. Graham and P. Howard (eds) *The Ashgate Companion to Heritage and Identity*, London: Ashgate, pp. 1–17.

Graham, B., Ashworth, G.J. and Tunbridge, J.E. (2000) *A Geography of Heritage: Power, Culture and Economy*, London: Arnold.

Gray, C. (2001) 'Streetscapes/"The Destruction of Penn Station"; A 1960's Protest That Tried to Save a Piece of the Past', *New York Times* May 20, p. 119. www.nytimes.com/2001/05/20/realestate/streetscapes-destruction-penn-station-1960-s-protest-that-tried-save-piece-past.html?pagewanted=1

Grayling, A.C. (2006) *Among the Dead Cities: Was the Allied Bombing of Civilians in WWII a Necessity or a Crime?*, London: Bloomsbury Publishing.

Greenberg, R., Ferguson, B.W. and Nairne, S. (eds) (1996) *Thinking about Exhibitions*, London and New York: Routledge.

Greenfield, J. ([1989] 1996) *The Return of Cultural Treasures*, Cambridge: Cambridge University Press.

Greenhalgh, P. (1988) *Ephemeral Vistas: The Expositions Universelles, Great Exhibitions and World's Fairs, 1851–1939*, Manchester: Manchester University Press.

Greer, S., Harrison, R. and McIntyre-Tamwoy, S. (2002) 'Community Based Archaeology in Australia', *World Archaeology* 34(2): 265–287.

Grillo, R.D. (2003) 'Cultural Essentialism and Cultural Anxiety', *Anthropological Theory* 3(2): 157–173.

Haber, A.F. (2009) 'Animism, Relatedness, Life: Post-Western Perspectives', *Cambridge Archaeological Journal* 19(3): 418–430.

Habermas, J. (1981) 'Modernity versus postmodernity', *New German Critique* 22: 3–14.

——(1989) *The Structural Transformation of the Public Sphere: An Inquiry into a Category of Bourgeois Society*, Massachusetts: MIT Press.

Hack, K. (2010) 'Contentious Heritage', in T. Benton (ed.) *Understanding Heritage and Memory*, Manchester/Milton Keynes: Manchester University Press/Open University, pp. 88–125.

Hage, G. (1998) *White Nation: Fantasies of White Supremacy in a Multicultural Society*, Annandale, NSW: Pluto Press.

Hall, M. (1984) 'The Burden of Tribalism: The Social Context of Southern African Iron Age Studies', *American Antiquity*: 49(3): 455–67.

——(2001) 'Cape Town's District Six and the Archaeology of Memory', in R. Layton, P. Stone and J. Thomas (eds) *The Destruction and Conservation of Cultural Property*, London and New York: Routledge, pp. 298–311.

——(2006) 'The Reappearance of the Authentic', in I. Karp, C. Krantz, L. Szwaja and T. Ybarra-Frausto (eds) *Museum Frictions: Public Cultures/Global Transformations*, Durham and London: Duke University Press, pp. 70–101.

Hall, S. (ed.) (1997) *Representation: Cultural Representations and Signifying Practices*, London, Thousand Oaks and New Delhi/Milton Keynes: Sage/Open University.

——([1999] 2008) 'Whose Heritage? Un-settling "The Heritage", Reimagining the Post-Nation' in G. Fairclough, R. Harrison, J.H. Jameson Jr and J. Schofield (eds) *The Heritage Reader*, Abingdon and New York: Routledge, pp. 219–28.

Hallam, E. and Hockey, J. (2001) *Death, Memory and Material Culture*, Oxford and New York: Berg.

Hamilakis, Y. (2007) *The Nation and its Ruins: Antiquity, Archaeology and National Imagination in Greece*, Oxford and New York: Oxford University Press.

Hamilton, P. (1994) 'The Knife Edge: Debates about Memory and History', in K. Darian-Smith and P. Hamilton (eds) *Memory and History in Twentieth-Century Australia*, Oxford, Auckland and New York: Oxford University Press, pp. 9–32.

Handler, R. and Gable, E. (1997) *The New History in an Old Museum*, Durham and London: Duke University Press.

Hardie, I. and Mackenzie, D. (2007) 'Assembling an Economic Actor: The Agencement of a Hedge Fund', *Sociological Review* 55(1): 57–80.

Harman, G. (2002) *Tool-Being: Heidegger and the Metaphysics of Objects*, Chicago: Open Court.

Harrison, D. and Hitchcock, M. (2005) *The Politics of World Heritage: Negotiating Heritage and Conservation*, Clevedon: Channel View Publications.

Harrison, R. (2002) '*Ngarranganni/Ngamungamu/Jalanijarra*: "Lost Places", Recursiveness and Hybridity at Old Lamboo Pastoral Station, Southeast Kimberley', PhD thesis, University of Western Australia.

——(2004) *Shared Landscapes: Archaeologies of Attachment to the Pastoral Industry in New South Wales*, Sydney: UNSW Press.

——(2005) 'Dreamtime, Old Time, This Time: Archaeology, Memory and the Present-Past in a Northern Australian Aboriginal Community', in T. Ireland and J. Lydon (eds) *Object Lessons: Archaeology and Heritage in Australia*, Melbourne: Australian Scholarly Publishing, pp. 243–264.

——(2006) 'An Artefact of Colonial Desire? Kimberley Points and the Technologies of Enchantment', *Current Anthropology* 47(1): 63–88.

——(2008) 'The Politics of the Past: Conflict in the Use of Heritage in the Modern World', in G. Fairclough, R. Harrison, J. Jameson and J. Schofield (eds) *The Heritage Reader*, Abingdon and New York: Routledge, pp. 177–190.

——(2010a) 'What is Heritage?', in R. Harrison (ed.) *Understanding the Politics of Heritage*, Manchester/Milton Keynes: Manchester University Press/Open University, pp. 5–42.

——(2010b) 'Stone Tools', in D. Hicks and M.C. Beaudry (eds) *The Oxford Handbook of Material Culture Studies*, Oxford and New York: Oxford University Press, pp. 521–542.

——(2010c) 'Heritage as Social Action', in S. West (ed.) *Understanding Heritage in Practice*, Manchester/Milton Keynes: Manchester University Press/Open University, pp. 240–276.

——(2011) 'Surface Assemblages: Towards an Archaeology *in* and *of* the Present', *Archaeological Dialogues* 18(2): 141–196.

——(in press a) 'Reassembling Ethnographic Museum Collections', in R. Harrison, S. Byrne and A. Clarke (eds) *Reassembling the Collection: Ethnographic Museums and Indigenous Agency*, Santa Fe: SAR Press.

——(in press b) 'Assembling and Governing Cultures "At Risk": Centers of Collection and Calculation, from the Museum to World Heritage', in R. Harrison, S. Byrne and A. Clarke (eds) *Reassembling the Collection: Ethnographic Museums and Indigenous Agency*, Santa Fe: SAR Press.

Harrison, R. and O'Donnell, D. (2010) 'Natural Heritage', in S. West (ed.) *Understanding Heritage in Practice*, Manchester/Milton Keynes: Manchester University Press/Open University, pp. 88–126.

Harrison, R. and Rose, D.B. (2010) 'Intangible Heritage', in T. Benton (ed.) *Understanding Heritage and Memory*, Manchester/Milton Keynes: Manchester University Press/Open University, pp. 238–276.

Harrison, R. and Schofield, J. (2010) *After Modernity: Archaeological Approaches to the Contemporary Past*, Oxford: Oxford University Press.

Harrison, R., Byrne, S. and Clarke, A. (eds) (in press) *Reassembling the Collection: Ethnographic Museums and Indigenous Agency*, Santa Fe: SAR Press.

Harvey, D. (1990) *The Condition of Postmodernity: An Enquiry into the Origins of Cultural Change*, Oxford: Blackwell.

Harvey, D.C. (2001) 'Heritage Pasts and Heritage Presents: Temporality, Meaning and the Scope of Heritage Studies', *International Journal of Heritage Studies* 7(4): 319–338.

——(2008) 'A History of Heritage', in B. Graham and P. Howard (eds) *The Ashgate Companion to Heritage and Identity*, London: Ashgate, pp. 19–36.

Harvey, G. (2005) *Animism: Respecting the Living World*, London: Hurst and Company.

Hassan, F.A. (2007) 'The Aswan High Dam and the International Rescue Nubia Campaign', *African Archaeological Review* 24: 73–94.

Hayden, D. (1995) *The Power of Place: Urban Landscape as Public History*, Cambridge: MIT Press.

Hays-Gilpin, K. and Lomatewama, R. (in press) 'Curating Communities at the Museum of Northern Arizona', in R. Harrison, S. Byrne and A. Clarke (eds) *Reassembling the Collection: Ethnographic Museums and Indigenous Agency*, Santa Fe: SAR Press.

Hein, G.E. (1998) *Learning in the Museum*, London and New York: Routledge.

Hellenic Ministry of Culture (2007) *The Restitution of the Parthenon Marbles*. http://odysseus.culture.gr/a/1/12/ea120.html

Henry, J.P. (2004) 'Challenges in Managing Culturally Sensitive Collections at the National Museum of the American Indian', in L.E. Sullivan and A. Edwards (eds) *Stewards of the Sacred*, Washington, DC: American Association of Museums, pp. 105–112.

Heritage Lottery Fund (2010) *Investing in Success: Heritage and the UK Tourism Economy*. www.hlf.org.uk/aboutus/howwework/Documents/HLF_Tourism_Impact_single.pdf

Herscher, A. (2010) *Violence Taking Place: The Architecture of the Kosovo Conflict*, Stanford: Stanford University Press.

Herzfeld, M. (1991) *A Place in History: Social and Monumental Time in a Cretan Town*, Princeton: Princeton University Press.

——(1997) *Cultural Intimacy: Social Poetics in the Nation-State*, New York: Routledge.

——(2004) *The Body Impolitic: Artisans and Artifice in the Global Hierarchy of Value*, Chicago and London: University of Chicago Press.

——(2005) 'Political Optics and the Occlusion of Intimate Knowledge', *American Anthropologist* 107(3): 369–376.

Hetherington, K. (1997) *The Badlands of Modernity: Heterotopia and Social Ordering*, London and New York: Routledge.

——(2002) 'Phantasmagoria/Phantasm Agora: Materiality, Spatiality and Ghosts', *Space and Culture* 11/12: 24–41.

——(2004) 'Secondhandedness: Consumption, Disposal, and Absent Presence', *Environment and Planning D: Society and Space* 22: 157–173.

——(2005) 'Memories of Capitalism: Cities, Phantasmagoria and Arcades' *International Journal of Urban and Regional Research* 29(1): 187–200.

——(2007) *Capitalism's Eye: Cultural Spaces of the Commodity*, New York: Routledge.

——(2010) 'The Ruin Revisited', in G. Pye (ed.) *Trash Culture: Objects and Obsolescence in Cultural Perspective*, Bern: Peter Lang, pp. 15–38.

Hewison, R. (1981) *In Anger: British Culture in the Cold War, 1945–60*, London: Weidenfeld and Nicolson.

——(1987) *The Heritage Industry: Britain in a Climate of Decline*, London: Methuen.

Hicks, D. (2010) 'The Material–Cultural Turn: Event and Effect', in D. Hicks and M.C. Beaudry (eds) *The Oxford Handbook of Material Culture Studies*, Oxford and New York: Oxford University Press, pp. 25–98.

Higuchi, T. and Barnes, G. (1995) 'Bamiyan: Buddhist Cave Temples in Afghanistan', *World Archaeology* 27(2): 282–302.

Hobsbawm, E. (1983a) 'Introduction: Inventing Traditions', in E. Hobsbawm and T. Ranger (eds) *The Invention of Tradition*, Cambridge: Cambridge University Press, pp. 1–14.

——(1983b) 'Mass-Producing Traditions: Europe, 1870–1914', in E. Hobsbawm and T. Ranger (eds) *The Invention of Tradition*, Cambridge: Cambridge University Press, pp. 263–307.

Hobsbawm, E. and Ranger, T. (eds) (1983) *The Invention of Tradition*, Cambridge: Cambridge University Press.

Hodder, I. (2010) 'Cultural Heritage Rights: From Ownership and Descent to Justice and Well-being', *Anthropological Quarterly* 83(4): 861–882.

Hogan, J. (ed.) (1996) *Hiroshima in History and Memory*, Cambridge, New York, Melbourne and Madrid: Cambridge University Press.

Holtorf, C. (2005) *From Stonehenge to Las Vegas: Archaeology as Popular Culture*, Walnut Creek: Altamira Press.

——(2009) 'Imagine This: Archaeology in the Experience Society', in C. Holtorf and A. Piccini (eds) *Contemporary Archaeologies: Excavating Now*, Bern: Peter Lang, pp. 47–64.

Holtorf, C. (2010a) 'Heritage Values in Contemporary Popular Culture', in G.S. Smith, P. M. Messenger and H.A. Soderland (eds) *Heritage Values in Contemporary Society*, Walnut Creek: Left Coast Press, pp. 43–54.

——(2010b) 'Meta-stories of Archaeology', *World Archaeology* 42(3): 381–393.

Hooper-Greenhill, E. (1992) *Museums and the Shaping of Knowledge*, London and New York: Routledge.

——(1994a) *Museums and their Visitors*, London and New York: Routledge.

——(ed.) (1994b) *The Educational Role of the Museum*, London and New York: Routledge.

——(1995) *Museum: Media: Message*, London and New York: Routledge.

——(1997) *Cultural Diversity: Developing Museum Audiences in Britain*, Leicester: Leicester University Press.

——(2007) *Museums and Education: Purpose, Pedagogy, Performance*, London and New York: Routledge.

Hopwood, N., Schaffer, S. and Secord, J. (eds) (2010) 'Seriality and Scientific Objects in the Nineteenth Century', *History of Science* 46(3–4): 251–502.

Horkheimer, M. and Adorno, T.W. (1972) *Dialectic of Enlightenment*, New York: Continuum Publishing.

Horne, D. (1984) *The Great Museum: The Re-Presentation of History*, London: Pluto Press.

Hosmer, C.B. (1965) *Presence of the Past: the History of the Historic Preservation Movement in the United States before Williamsburg*, New York: G.P. Putnam's Sons.

——(1981) *Preservation Comes of Age: From Williamsburg to the National Trust 1926–1949*, Charlottesville: University Press of Virginia.

Hunter, M. (1996) *Preserving the Past: The Rise of Heritage in Modern Britain*, Stroud: Sutton.

Hutchins, E. (1995) *Cognition in the Wild*, Cambridge: MIT Press.

Huyssen, A. (1995) *Twilight Memories: Marking Time in a Culture of Amnesia*, London and New York: Routledge.

——(2000) 'Present Pasts: Media, Politics, Amnesia', in A. Appadurai (ed.) *Globalization*, Durham: Duke University Press, pp. 57–77.

——(2003) *Present Pasts: Urban Palimpsests and the Politics of Memory*, Stanford: Stanford University Press.

ICOMOS (1964) *International Charter on the Conservation and Restoration of Monuments and Sites* ('Venice Charter'), Paris: International Council on Monuments and Sites.

Isaac, G. (2009) 'Responsibilities towards Knowledge: The Zuni Museum and the Reconciling of Different Knowledge Systems', in S. Sleeper-Smith (ed.) *Contesting Knowledge: Museums and Indigenous Perspectives,* London and Lincoln: University of Nebraska Press, pp. 303–321.

Jameson, F. (1984) 'Postmodernism or the Cultural Logic of Late Capitalism', *New Left Review* 146: 53–93.

——(1991) *Postmodernism, or, The Cultural Logic of Late Capitalism*, Durham: Duke University Press.

Jameson, J.H. Jr (2008) 'Presenting Archaeology to the Public: Then and Now', in G. Fairclough, R. Harrison, J.H. Jameson Jr and J. Schofield (eds) *The Heritage Reader*, London and Abingdon: Routledge, pp. 427–456.

Jensen, R. (1999) *The Dream Society: How the Coming Shift from Information to Imagination will Transform Your Business*, New York: McGraw Hill Professional.

Jokilehto, J. (2002) *A History of Architectural Conservation*, London: Butterworth-Heinemann.

Jones, O. and Cloke, P. (2008) 'Non-Human Agencies: Trees, Relationality, Time and Place', in C. Knappett and L. Malafouris (eds) *Material Agency: Towards a Non-Anthropocentric Approach*, New York: Springer, pp. 79–96.

Jones, R. and Birdsall-Jones, C. (2008) 'The Contestation of Heritage: The Colonizer and the Colonized in Australia', in B. Graham and P. Howard (eds) *The Ashgate Companion to Heritage and Identity*, London: Ashgate, pp. 365–380.

Joyce, P. and Bennett, T. (2010) 'Material Powers: Introduction', in T. Bennett and P. Joyce (eds) *Material Powers: Cultural Studies, History and the Material Turn*, Abingdon and New York: Routledge, pp. 1–21.

Kammen, M.G. (1995) 'Some Patterns and Meanings of Memory Distortion in American History', in D.L. Schacter (ed.) *Memory Distortion: How Minds, Brains and Societies Reconstruct the Past,* Cambridge: Harvard University Press, pp. 329–345.

Karp, I. and Levine, S.D. (eds) (1991) *Exhibiting Cultures: The Poetics and Politics of Museum Display,* Washington, DC and London: Smithsonian Institute Press.

Kelly, L. and Gordon, P. (2002) 'Developing a Community of Practice: Museums and Reconciliation in Australia', in R. Sandell (ed.) *Museums, Society, Inequality,* London and New York: Routledge, pp. 153–174.

Kieley, F. (1940) *A Brief History of the National Park Service,* Washington, DC: National Park Service, US Department of the Interior.

Kijas, J. (2005) *Revival, Renewal and Return: Ray Kelly and the NSW Sites of Significance Survey,* Sydney: Department of Environment and Conservation (NSW).

Kirshenblatt-Gimblett, B. (1998) *Destination Culture: Tourism, Museums, and Heritage,* Berkeley and Los Angeles: University of California Press.

——(2006) 'World Heritage and Cultural Economics', in I. Karp, C. Krantz, L. Szwaja and T. Ybarra-Frausto (eds) *Museum Frictions: Public Cultures/Global Transformations,* Durham and London: Duke University Press, pp. 161–202.

Knowles, C. (in press) 'Artefacts in Waiting: Altered Agency of Museum Objects', in R. Harrison, S. Byrne and A. Clarke (eds) *Reassembling the Collection: Ethnographic Museums and Indigenous Agency,* Santa Fe: SAR Press.

Kohl, P.L. and Fawcett, C. (eds) (1995) *Nationalism, Politics, and the Practice of Archaeology,* Cambridge: Cambridge University Press.

Kohn, R.H. (1995) 'History and the Culture Wars: The Case of the Smithsonian Institution's Enola Gay Exhibition', *Journal of American History* 82(3): 1036–1063.

Kosselleck, R. (1985) *Futures Past: On the Semantics of Historical Time,* Cambridge: MIT Press.

Kramer, J. (2006) *Switchbacks: Art, Ownership, and Nuxalk National Identity,* Vancouver: University of British Columbia Press.

Krauss, W. (2008) 'European Landscapes: Heritage, Participation and Local Communities', in B. Graham and P. Howard (eds) *The Ashgate Research Companion to Heritage and Identity,* Aldershot and Burlington: Ashgate, pp. 425–438.

Krieger, A. (2011) 'Faneuil Hall Marketplace (Quincy Market)—Boston, Massachusetts (1966–1979)', *Architecture Boston* 14(1): 20.

Küchler, S. (1999) 'The Place of Memory', in A. Forty and S. Küchler (eds) *The Art of Forgetting,* Oxford and New York: Berg, pp. 53–72.

——(2003) *Malanggan: Art, Memory, Sacrifice,* Oxford and New York: Berg.

Kurin, R. (2004) 'Safeguarding Intangible Cultural Heritage in the 2003 UNESCO Convention: A Critical Appraisal', *Museum International* 56(1–2): 66–77.

Kwint, M., Breward, C. and Aynsley, J. (eds) (1999) *Material Memories: Design and Evocation,* Oxford and New York: Berg.

Kymlicka, W. (1997) *States, Nations and Cultures,* Assen: Royal Van Gorcum.

Labadi, S. (2007) Representations of the Nation and Cultural Diversity in Discourses on World Heritage, *Journal of Social Archaeology* 7(2): 147–170.

Labadi, S. and Long, C. (eds) (2010) *Heritage and Globalisation,* Abingdon and New York: Routledge.

Ladd, B. (1997) *The Ghosts of Berlin: Confronting German History in the Urban Landscape,* Chicago: University of Chicago Press.

Laird, P.W. (1998) 'The Public's Historians', *Technology and Culture* 39(3): 474–482.

de Landa, M. (1997) *A Thousand Years of Nonlinear History,* New York: Zone Books/Swerve Editions.

——(2006a) *A New Philosophy of Society: Assemblage Theory and Social Complexity,* London and New York: Continuum.

——(2006b) *Real Virtuality: Meshworks and Hierarchies in the Digital Domain,* Rotterdam: Netherlands Architecture Institute.

Latour, B. (1987) *Science in Action: How to Follow Scientists and Engineers through Society*, Cambridge: Harvard University Press.

——(1993) *We Have Never Been Modern*, Cambridge: Harvard University Press.

——(1996) *Aramis, or The Love of Technology*, Cambridge: Harvard University Press.

——(1999) *Pandora's Hope: Essays on the Reality of Science Studies*, Cambridge: Harvard University Press.

——(2004) *Politics of Nature: How to Bring the Sciences into Democracy*, Cambridge: Harvard University Press.

——(2005) *Reassembling the Social: An Introduction to Actor–Network Theory*, Oxford: Oxford University Press.

Latour, B. and Woolgar, S. (1979) *Laboratory Life: The Social Construction of Scientific Facts*, Beverly Hills: Sage.

Law, J. (1994) *Organizing Modernity: Social Order and Social Theory*, Oxford: Blackwell.

——(2004) *After Method: Mess in Social Science Research*, London: Routledge.

Law, J. and Hassard, J. (eds) (1999) *Actor Network Theory and After*, Oxford: Blackwell.

Layton, R. (1986) *Uluru: An Aboriginal History of Ayers Rock*, Canberra: Aboriginal Studies Press.

——(ed.) (1989a) *Conflict in the Archaeology of Living Traditions*, London and New York: Routledge.

——(1989b) *Who Needs the Past? Indigenous Values and Archaeology*, London and New York: Routledge.

Layton, R. and Titchen, S. (1995) 'Uluru: An Outstanding Australian Aboriginal Cultural Landscape', in B. von Droste, H. Plachter and M. Rossler (eds) *Cultural Landscapes of Universal Value*, Stuttgart and New York: Gustav Fischer Verlag Jena with UNESCO, pp. 174–181.

Le Goff, J. (1996) *History and Memory*, New York: Columbia University Press.

Leask, A. and Fyall, A. (eds) (2006) *Managing World Heritage Sites*, Oxford: Butterworth-Heinemann.

Lennon, J.J. and Foley, M. (2000) *Dark Tourism*, New York: Continuum.

Leon, W. and Rosenzweig, R. (eds) (1989) *History Museums in the United States: A Critical Assessment*, Urbana and Chicago: University of Illinois Press.

Lidchi, H. (1997) 'The Poetics and Politics of Exhibiting Other Cultures', in S. Hall (ed.) *Representation: Cultural Representations and Signifying Practices*, London, Thousand Oaks, New Delhi/Milton Keynes: Sage/Open University, pp. 151–222.

Lilley, I. ([2000] 2008) 'Professional Attitudes to Indigenous Interests in the Native Title Era: Settler Societies Compared', in G. Fairclough, R. Harrison, J. Jameson and J. Schofield (eds) *The Heritage Reader*, Abingdon and New York: Routledge, pp. 191–208.

Linenthal, T. and Englehardt, T. (eds) (1996) *History Wars: The 'Enola Gay' and other battles for the American Past*, New York: Metropolitan Books.

Lipsitz, G. (1990) *Time Passages: Collective Memory and American Popular Culture*, Minnesota: University of Minnesota Press.

Littler, J. and Naidoo, R. (2004) 'White Past, Multicultural Present: Heritage and National Stories', in H. Brocklehurst and R. Phillips (eds) *History, Nationhood and the Question of Britain*, Basingstoke: Palgrave Macmillan, pp. 330–41.

Logan, W.S. (2002) 'Globalizing Heritage: World Heritage as a Manifestation of Modernism and Challenges from the Periphery', in D. Jones (ed.) *20th Century Heritage: Our Recent Cultural Legacy. Proceedings of the Australia ICOMOS National Conference 2001*, Adelaide and Melbourne: University of Adelaide and Australia/International Council on Monuments and Sites, pp. 51–57.

——(2007) 'Closing Pandora's Box: Human Rights Conundrums in Cultural Heritage Protection', in H. Silverman and D.F. Ruggles (eds) *Cultural Heritage and Human Rights*, New York: Springer, pp. 33–52.

——(2008) 'Cultural Diversity, Heritage and Human Rights', in B. Graham and P. Howard (eds) *The Ashgate Research Companion to Heritage and Identity*, Aldershot and Burlington: Ashgate, pp. 439–454.

Logan, W.S. and Reeves, K. (2009) 'Introduction: Remembering Places of Pain and Shame', in W.S. Logan and K. Reeves (eds) *Places of Pain and Shame: Dealing with 'Difficult Heritage'*, Abingdon and New York: Routledge, pp. 1–14.

Logan, W., Langfield, M. and Nic Craith, M. (2010) 'Intersecting Concepts and Practices', in M. Langfield, W. Logan and M. Nic Craith (eds) *Cultural Diversity, Heritage and Human Rights: Intersections in Theory and Practice*, Abingdon and New York: Routledge, pp. 3–20.

Long, C. and Labadi, S. (2010) 'Introduction', in S. Labadi and C. Long (eds) *Heritage and Globalisation*, Abingdon and New York: Routledge, pp. 1–16.

Lowenthal, D. (1985) *The Past is a Foreign Country*, Cambridge: Cambridge University Press.

——(1998) *The Heritage Crusade and the Spoils of History*, Cambridge: Cambridge University Press.

——(2004) 'The Heritage Crusade and its Contradictions', in M. Page and R. Mason (eds) *Giving Preservation a History: Histories of Historic Preservation in the United States*, London and New York: Routledge, pp. 19–44.

Lucas, G. (2004) 'Modern Disturbances: On the Ambiguities of Archaeology', *MODERNISM/modernity* 11(1): 109–20.

——(2005) *The Archaeology of Time*, London and New York: Routledge.

——(2010) 'Time and the Archaeological Archive', *Rethinking History* 14: 343–359.

Lupton, D. (1999) *Risk*, London and New York: Routledge.

Lydon, J. (2009) 'Young and Free: The Australian Past in a Global Future', in L. Meskell (ed.) *Cosmopolitan Archaeologies*, Durham and London: Duke University Press, pp. 28–47.

Lyotard, J.F. ([1979] 1984) *The Postmodern Condition: A Report on Knowledge*, Minneapolis: University of Minnesota Press.

Macdonald, S. (ed.) (1997a) *The Politics of Display: Museums, Science, Culture*, London and New York: Routledge.

——(1997b) *Reimagining Culture: Histories, Identities and the Gaelic Renaissance*, London and New York; Berg.

——(2002) *Behind the Scenes at the Science Museum*, Oxford and New York: Berg.

——(2009a) *Difficult Heritage: Negotiating the Nazi Past in Nuremberg and Beyond*, Abingdon and New York: Routledge.

——(2009b) 'Reassembling Nuremberg, Reassembling Heritage', *Journal of Cultural Economy* 2(1–2: 117–134.

Macdonald, S. and Silverstone, R. (1990) 'Rewriting the Museums: Fictions, Taxonomies, Stories and Readers', *Cultural Studies* 4(2): 176–191.

Macintyre, S. and Clark, A. (2004) *The History Wars*, Melbourne: Melbourne University Press.

Mackintosh, B. (1985) *The Historic Sites Survey and National Historic Landmarks Program: A History*, Washington, DC: History Division, National Park Service, Department of the Interior.

Mandler, P. (1997) *The Fall and Rise of the Stately Home*, New Haven and London: Yale University Press.

Manzo, K.A. (1996) *Creating Boundaries: The Politics of Race and Nation*, London and Boulder: Lynne Rienner.

Martinez Cobo, J.R. (1986) *Study of the Problem of Discrimination Against Indigenous Populations*, New York: United Nations.

Mason, R. (2002) 'Assessing Values in Conservation Planning: Methodological Issues and Choices', in M. de la Torre (ed.) *Assessing the Values of Cultural Heritage*, Los Angeles: Getty Conservation Institute, pp. 5–30.

——(2009) *The Once and Future New York: Historic Preservation and the Modern City*, Minneapolis: University of Minnesota Press

Max Hanna Sightseeing Research (1998) 'The Built Heritage in England: Properties Open to the Public, Visitors and Visitor Trends', *Cultural Trends* 8: 32–53.

Mayer-Schönberger, V. (2009) *Delete: The Virtue of Forgetting in the Digital Age*, Princeton and Oxford: Princeton University Press.

Mayr, O. (1998) 'The "Enola Gay" Fiasco: History, Politics, and the Museum', *Technology and Culture* 39(3): 462–473.

McBryde, I. (1990) '"Those Truly Outstanding Examples.": Kakadu in the Context of Australia's World Heritage Properties – A Response', in J. Domicelji and S. Domicelj (eds) *A Sense of Place: A Conversation in Three Cultures*, Canberra: Australian Heritage Commission, pp. 15–19, 46–52.

Merlan, F. (2008) 'Indigeneity: Global and Local', *Current Anthropology* 50(3): 303–333.

Merriman, N. (1991) *Beyond the Glass Case: The Past, the Heritage and the Public in Britain*, London: Leicester University Press.

——(2004) 'Introduction: Diversity and Dissonance' in N. Merriman (ed.) *Public Archaeology*, London and New York: Routledge, pp. 1–17.

Meskell, L. (2002) 'Negative Heritage and Past Mastering in Archaeology', *Anthropological Quarterly* 75(3): 57–74.

——(ed.) (2009a) *Cosmopolitan Archaeologies*, Durham and London: Duke University Press.

——(2009b) 'Cosmopolitan Heritage Ethics', in L. Meskell (ed.) *Cosmopolitan Archaeologies*, Durham and London: Duke University Press, pp. 1–27.

——(2009c) 'The Nature of Culture in Kruger National Park', in L. Meskell (ed.) *Cosmopolitan Archaeologies*, Durham and London: Duke University Press, pp. 89–112.

——(2010) 'Human Rights and Heritage Ethics', *Anthropological Quarterly* 83(4): 839–860.

Message, K. (2006) *New Museums and the Making of Culture*, Oxford and New York: Berg.

Messer, E. (1993) 'Anthropology and Human Rights', *Annual Review of Anthropology* 22: 221–249.

Mihesuah, D.A. (1995) *Repatriation Reader: Who Owns American Indian Remains?* Nebraska: University of Nebraska Press.

Miles, M. (1997) *Art, Space and the City: Public Art and Urban Futures*, London and New York: Routledge.

Mitrašinović, M. (2006) *Total Landscape, Theme Parks, Public Space*, Aldershot: Ashgate.

Moore, P. (1999) *The Destruction of Penn Station*, New York: Distributed Art Publishers.

Mpumlwana, K., Corsane, G., Pastor-Makhurane, J. and Rassool, C. (2002) 'Inclusion and the Power of Representation: South African Museums and the Cultural Politics of Social Transformation', in R. Sandell (ed.) *Museums, Society, Inequality*, London and New York: Routledge, pp. 244–261.

Murray, N., Shepherd, N. and Hall, M. (eds) (2007) *Desire Lines: Space, Memory and Identity in the Post-Apartheid City*, London and New York: Routledge.

Murtagh, K.R. (2006) *Keeping Time: The History and Theory of Preservation in America* (3rd edn), New Jersey: John Wiley and Sons.

Murzyn, MA. (2008) 'Heritage Transformation in Central and Eastern Europe', in B. Graham and P. Howard (eds) *The Ashgate Companion to Heritage and Identity*, London: Ashgate, pp. 315–346.

Museums Association (2011) *Visitors Love Museums*. www.museumsassociation.org/download?id=165106

Nagata, J. (2010) '"Elasticity" of Heritage, From Conservation to Human Rights: A Saga of Development and Resistance in Penang, Malaysia', In M. Langfield, W. Logan and M. Nic Craith (eds) *Cultural Diversity, Heritage and Human Rights: Intersections in Theory and Practice*, Abingdon and New York: Routledge, pp. 101–116.

Nakata, M. (2007) *Disciplining the Savages: Savaging the Disciplines*, Canberra: Aboriginal Studies Press.

Nash, R. (1967) *Wilderness and the American Mind*, New Haven and London: Yale University Press.

National Archives (2011) *English Heritage*. www.ndad.nationalarchives.gov.uk/AH/64/detail.html#n1

National Park Service (2011a) *National Park System Timeline* (annotated). www.nps.gov/history/history/hisnps/NPSHistory/timeline_annotated.htm

——(2011b) *National Park Service Public Use Statistics*. www.nature.nps.gov/stats

National Trust (2011) *A History of the National Trust*. www.nationaltrust.org.uk/main/w-trust/ w-thecharity/w-thecharity_our-past/w-history_trust-timeline.htm

National Trust for Historic Preservation (2011a) *Cultural Heritage Tourism 2011 Fact Sheet*. www.culturalheritagetourism.org/documents/2011CHTFactSheet6-11.pdf

——(2011b) *About the National Trust for Historic Preservation*. www.preservationnation.org/about-us

NCAM (2010) *The history of the Nubia Salvage Campaign in Sudan*, National Corporation for Antiquities and Museums in Sudan. www.numibia.net/nubia/salvage.htm

Newman, R.P. (2004) *Enola Gay and the Court of History*, New York: Peter Lang.

Nielsen, B. (2011) 'UNESCO and the "Right" Kind of Culture: Bureaucratic Production and Articulation', *Critique of Anthropology* 31(4): 273–292.

Nora, P. (ed.) (1996) *Realms of Memory: The Construction of the French Past. Volume 1: Conflicts and Divisions*, New York and Chichester: Columbia University Press.

——(1997) *Realms of Memory: The Construction of the French Past. Volume 2: Traditions*, New York and Chichester: Columbia University Press.

——(1998) *Realms of Memory: The Construction of the French Past. Volume 3: Symbols*, New York and Chichester: Columbia University Press.

O'Doherty, B. (ed.) (1972) *Museums in Crisis*, New York: G. Braziller.

O'Hanlon, M. (1993) *Paradise: Portraying the New Guinea Highlands*, London: British Museum Press.

Oelschlaeger, M. (1991) *The Idea of Wilderness: From Prehistory to the Age of Ecology*, New Haven and London: Yale University Press.

Olick, G. and Robbins, J. (1995) 'Social Memory Studies: From "Collective Memory" to the Historical Sociology of Mnemonic Practices', *Annual Review of Sociology* 24: 105–140.

Olsen, B. (2003) 'Material Culture after Text: Re-Membering Things', *Norwegian Archaeological Review* 36(2): 87–104.

——(2007) 'Keeping Things at Arm's Length: A Genealogy of Asymmetry', *World Archaeology* 39(4): 579–588.

——(2010) *In Defence of Things: Archaeology and the Ontology of Objects*, Walnut Creek and Lanham: AltaMira Press.

Olwig, K. (2001) '"Time Out of Mind"– "Mind Out of Time": Custom versus Tradition in Environmental Heritage Research and Interpretation', *International Journal of Heritage Studies* 7(4): 339–354.

Olwig, K. and Lowenthal, D. (eds) (2006) *The Nature of Cultural Heritage and the Culture of Natural Heritage: Northern Perspectives on a Contested Patrimony*, London and New York: Routledge.

Osborne, P. (1995) *The Politics of Time: Modernity and the Avante-Garde*, London: Verso.

Otero-Pailos, J. (2006) 'Creative Agents', *Future Anterior* 3(1): ii–vii.

——(2007) 'Conservation Cleaning/Cleaning Conservation', *Future Anterior* 4(1): ii–viii.

——(2008) 'Mnemonic Value and Historic Preservation', in M. Treib (ed.) *Spatial Recall: Memory in Architecture and Landscape*, London and New York: Routledge, pp. 240–59.

Padgen, E.S. (2011) 'Ben Who?', *Architecture Boston* 14(1): 3.

Page, M. and Mason, R. (2004) 'Rethinking the Roots of the Historic Preservation Movement', in M. Page and R. Mason (eds) *Giving Preservation a History: Histories of Historic Preservation in the United States*, London and New York: Routledge, pp. 1–16.

Parks Australia (2009) *Uluru–Kata Tjuta National Park Note – Please Don't Climb*. www.environment.gov.au/parks/publications/uluru/pn-please-dont-climb.html

Parry, R. (2007) *Recoding the Museum: Digital Heritage and the Technologies of Change*, Abingdon and New York: Routledge.

Pearce, S. (ed.) (1994) *Museums and the Appropriation of Culture*, London: Athlone Press.

——(1995) *On Collecting: An Investigation into Collecting in the European Tradition*, London and New York: Routledge.

Perry, M. and Burnham, B. (2001) 'A Critical Mission: The World Monuments Watch', in World Monuments Fund (ed.) *World Monuments Watch: 100 Most Endangered Sites 2002*, London: World Monuments Fund, pp. 3–4.

Pine, B.J. and Gilmore, J.H. (1999) *The Experience Economy: Work is Theater and Every Business a Stage*, Boston: Harvard Business School Press.

Poria, Y., Reichel, A. and Cohen, R. (2011) 'World Heritage Site—Is It an Effective Brand Name? A Case Study of a Religious Heritage Site', *Journal of Travel Research* 50(5): 482–495.

Pretzer, W.H. (1998) 'Reviewing Public History in Light of the "Enola Gay"', *Technology and Culture* 39(3): 457–461.

Pye, G. (ed.) (2010) *Trash Culture: Objects and Obsolescence in Cultural Perspective*, Bern: Peter Lang.

Rabinow, P. (1989) *French Modern: Norms and Forms of the Social Environment*, Cambridge: MIT Press.

——(2003) *Anthropos Today: Reflections on Modern Equipment*, Princeton: Princeton University Press.

Rancière, J. (2009) *The Emancipated Spectator*, London and New York: Verso.

Rassool, C. (2007) 'Memory and the Politics of History in the District Six Museum', in N. Murray, N. Shepherd and M. Hall (eds) *Desire Lines: Space, Memory and Identity in a Post-Apartheid City*, Abingdon and New York: Routledge, pp. 113–27.

Rassool, C. and Prosalendis, S. (eds) (2001) *Recalling Community in Cape Town: Creating and Curating the District Six Museum*, Cape Town: District Six Museum.

Rethly, A. (2008) *In the Shadow of Stalin's Boots: Visitors' Guide to Memento Park*, Budapest: Private Planet Books.

Rojek, C. (1993) *Ways of Escape: Modern Transformations in Leisure and Travel*, London, Macmillan.

Rojek, C. and Urry, J. (eds) (1997) *Touring Cultures: Transformations of Travel and Theory*, London and New York: Routledge.

Roland, A. (1998) 'Voices in the Museum', *Technology and Culture* 39(3): 483–488.

Rose, D. (1996) *Nourishing Terrains: Australian Aboriginal Views of Landscape and Wilderness*, Canberra: Australian Heritage Commission.

——(2003) *Sharing Kinship with Nature: How Reconciliation is Transforming the NSW National Parks and Wildlife Service*, Sydney: NSW National Parks and Wildlife Service.

——(2008) 'On History, Trees and Ethical Proximity', *Postcolonial Studies* 11(2): 157–67.

——(2011) *Wild Dog Dreaming: Love and Extinction*, Charlottesville and London: University of Virginia Press.

Rose, D. and Robin, R. (2004) 'The Ecological Humanities in Action: An Invitation', *Australian Humanities Review* 31–32. www.australianhumanitiesreview.org/archive/Issue-April-2004/rose.html

Rose, D., Smith, D. and Watson, C. (2003) *Indigenous Kinship with the Natural World*, Sydney: NSW National Parks and Wildlife Service.

Rosenzweig, R. and Thelen, D. (1998) *The Presence of the Past: Popular Uses of History in American Life*, New York: Columbia University Press.

Ross, M. (1996) *Planning and the Heritage: Policy and Procedures* (2nd edn), London: E&fn Spon.

Rössler, M. (1995) 'UNESCO and Cultural Landscape Protection', in B. von Droste, H. Plachter and M. Rössler (eds), *Cultural Landscapes of Universal Value*, Stuttgart and New York: Gustav Fischer Verlag Jena with UNESCO, pp. 42–49.

Rowlands, M. and Butler, B. (2007) 'Conflict and Heritage Care', *Anthropology Today* 23(1): 1–2.

Rowse, T. (2008) 'Indigenous Culture: The Politics of Vulnerability and Survival', in T. Bennett and J. Frow (eds) *The Sage Handbook of Cultural Analysis*, London: Sage, pp. 406–426.

Rowthorn, R. and Ramaswamy, R. (1997) *Deindustrialization – Its Causes and Implications*, Washington, DC: World Monetary Fund.

Ruppert, E. (2009) 'Becoming Peoples: "Counting Heads in the Northern Wilds"', *Journal of Cultural Economy* 2(1–2): 11–31.

Ruskin, J. (1849) *Seven Lamps of Architecture*, London: Smith Elder and Company.

Russell, L. (2001) *Savage Imaginings: Historical and Contemporary Constructions of Australian Aboriginalities*, Melbourne: Australian Scholarly Publishing.

Ryan, J. and Silvanto, S. (2009) 'The World Heritage List: The Making and Management of a Brand', *Place Branding and Public Diplomacy* 5: 290–300.

——(2011) 'A Brand for all the Nations: The Development of the World Heritage Brand in Emerging Markets', *Marketing Intelligence & Planning* 29(3): 305–318.

Samuel, R. (1994) *Theatres of Memory: Past and Present in Popular Culture*, London: Verso.

Said, E.W. (1978) *Orientalism*, Harmondsworth: Penguin

Säve-Söderberg, T. (1987) *Temples and Tombs of Ancient Nubia*, London: Thames and Hudson.

Scarre, C. and Scarre, G. (2006) *The Ethics of Archaeology: Philosophical Perspectives on Archaeological Practice*, Cambridge: Cambridge University Press.

Schmertz, M.F. (2011) 'A Life in Architecture: How the Boy from Minnesota became the Man who Reshaped Cities', *Architecture Boston* 14(1): 23–24.

Schlanger, N. (2010) 'Series in Progress: Antiquities of Nature, Numismatics and Stone Implements in the Emergence of Prehistoric Archaeology', *History of Science* 48(3–4): 343–369.

Schmitt, T. (2005) 'Jemaa el Fna Square in Marrakech: Changes to a Social Space and to a UNESCO Masterpiece of the Oral and Intangible Heritage of Humanity as a Result of Global Influences', *Arab World Geographer* 8(4): 173–195.

——(2008) 'The UNESCO Concept of Safeguarding Intangible Cultural Heritage: Its Background and *Marrakchi* Roots', *International Journal of Heritage Studies* 14(2): 95–111.

Scott, J.C. (1998) *Seeing Like A State: How Certain Schemes to Improve the Human Condition Have Failed*, New Haven and London: Yale University Press.

Serres, M. (1987) *Statues*, Paris: Bourin.

Serres, M. and Latour, B. (1995) *Conversation on Science, Culture and Time*, Ann Arbor: University of Michigan Press.

Shanks, M. (2007) 'Symmetrical Archaeology', *World Archaeology* 39(4): 589–596.

Shanks, M., Platt, D. and Rathje, W.L. (2004), 'The Perfume of Garbage: Modernity and the Archaeological', *MODERNISM/modernity* 11(1): 61–83.

Sharpley, R. and Stone, P.R. (eds) (2009) *The Darker Side of Travel: The Theory and Practice of Dark Tourism*, Bristol, Tonawanda and Ontario: Channel View Publications.

Shepherd, N. and Murray, N. (2007) 'Introduction: Space, Memory and Identity in the Post-Apartheid City', in N. Murray, N. Shepherd and M. Hall (eds) *Desire Lines: Space, Memory and Identity in a Post-Apartheid City*, Abingdon and New York: Routledge, pp. 1–18.

Silberman, N.A. (1989) *Between Past and Present: Archaeology, Ideology and Nationalism in the Modern Middle East*, New York: Henry Holt.

——(2010) 'Technology, Heritage Values, and Interpretation', in G.S. Smith, P.M. Messenger and H.A. Soderland (eds) *Heritage Values in Contemporary Society*, Walnut Creek, Left Coast Press, pp. 63–74.

Silverman, H. and Ruggles, D.F. (2007) 'Cultural Heritage and Human Rights', in H. Silverman and D.F. Ruggles (eds) *Cultural Heritage and Human Rights,* New York: Springer, pp. 3–22.

Simpson, M. (1996) *Making Representations: Museums in the Post-Colonial Era*, London: Routledge.

Singer, B.R. (2008) 'The Making of Who We Are: Now Showing at the National Museum of the American Indian Lelawi Theatre', in A. Lonetree and A.J. Cobb (eds) *The National Museum of the American Indian: Critical Conversations*, Lincoln and London: University of Nebraska Press, pp. 165–180.

Skounti, A. (2009) 'The Authentic Illusion: Humanity's Intangible Cultural Heritage, the Moroccan Experience', in L. Smith and N. Akagawa (eds) *Intangible Heritage*, Abingdon and New York: Routledge, pp. 74–92.

Sleeper-Smith, S. (ed.) (2009) *Contesting Knowledge: Museums and Indigenous Perspectives*, London and Lincoln: University of Nebraska Press.

Smith, L. (2004) *Archaeological Theory and the Politics of Cultural Heritage*, Abingdon and New York: Routledge.

——(2006) *Uses of Heritage*, Abingdon and New York: Routledge.

——(2007) 'Empty Gestures? Heritage and the Politics of Representation', in H. Silverman and D.F. Ruggles (eds) *Cultural Heritage and Human Rights*, New York: Springer, pp. 159–171.

Smith, L. and Waterton, E. (2009a) '"The Envy of the World"? Intangible Heritage in England', in L. Smith and N. Akagawa (eds) *Intangible Heritage*, Abingdon and New York: Routledge, pp. 289–302.

——(2009b) *Heritage, Communities and Archaeology*, London: Duckworth.

Smith, M.K. and Robinson, M. (eds) (2006) *Cultural Tourism in a Changing World: Politics, Participation and (Re)Presentation*, Clevedon and Buffalo: Channel View Publications.

Smithsonian Institution (2011) *Visitor Statistics*. http://newsdesk.si.edu/about/stats

Sorkin, M. (ed.) (1992) *Variations on a Theme Park: The New American City and the End of Public Space*, New York: Hill and Wang.

Spivak, G.C. (1996) *The Spivak Reader*, D. Landry and G. MacLean (eds), New York and London: Routledge.

Stewart, S. (1993) *On Longing: Narratives of the Miniature, the Gigantic, the Souvenir, the Collection*, Durham and London: Duke University Press.

Strathern, M. (1988) *The Gender of the Gift*, Berkeley: University of California Press.

——(2004), 'The Whole Person and its Artefacts', *Annual Review of Anthropology* 33: 1–19.

Stubbs, J.H. (2009) *Time Honored: A Global View of Architectural Conservation*, London and New York: John Wiley and Sons.

Sully, D. (ed.) (2007) *Decolonising Conservation: Caring for Maori Meeting Houses outside New Zealand*, Walnut Creek: Left Coast Press.

Sundbo, J. and Darmer, P. (2008) *Creating Experiences in the Experience Economy*, Cheltenham: Edward Elgar.

Taussig, M. (1991) *The Nervous System*, London and New York: Routledge.

——(1993) *Mimesis and Alterity: A Particular History of the Senses*, London and New York: Routledge.

Terdiman, R. (1993) *Present Past: Modernity and the Memory Crisis*, New York: Cornell University Press.

Teski, M.C. and J.J. Climo (eds) (1995) *The Labyrinth of Memory: Ethnographic Journeys*, Westport, CT: Bergin and Garvey.

Thomas, J. (2004) *Archaeology and Modernity*, London: Routledge.

——(2009) 'Sigmund Freud's Archaeological Metaphor and Archaeology's Self-Understanding', in C. Holtorf and A. Piccini (eds) *Contemporary Archaeologies: Excavating Now!*, Bern: Peter Lang, pp. 33–45.

Tilden, F. (1957) *Interpreting our Heritage*, Chapel Hill: University of North Carolina Press.

——(1977) *Interpreting Our Heritage* (3rd edn), Chapel Hill: University of North Carolina Press.

Till, K.E. (2005) *The New Berlin: Memory, Politics, Place*, Minneapolis: University of Minnesota Press.

Tilley, C., Keane, W., Küchler, S., Rowlands, M. and Spyer, P. (eds) (2006) *Handbook of Material Culture*, London: Sage.

Timothy, D.J. and Boyd, S.W. (2003) *Heritage Tourism*, Harlow: Pearson Education.

Tomlinson, J. (2007) *The Culture of Speed: The Coming of Immediacy*, London and New Delhi: Sage.

Toyne, P. and Vachon, D. (1984) *Growing Up the Country: The Pitjantjatjara Struggle for their Land*, Fitzroy: Penguin Books.

Trigger, B. (1980) 'Archaeology and the Image of the American Indian', *American Antiquity* 45(4): 662–76.

——(1984) 'Alternative Archaeologies: Nationalist, Colonialist, Imperialist', *Man* 19: 355–70.

——(1985) 'The Past as Power: Anthropology and the North American Indian', in I. McBryde (ed.) *Who Owns the Past?*, Oxford: Oxford University Press, pp. 11–40.

——([1989] 1996) *A History of Archaeological Thought*, Cambridge: Cambridge University Press.

Tsing, A.L. (2005) *Friction: An Ethnography of Global Connection*, New Jersey: Princeton University Press.

Tuhiwai Smith, L. (1999) *Decolonizing Methodologies: Research and Indigenous Peoples*, London and New York: Routledge.

Tunbridge, J.E. (2008) 'Plural and Multicultural Heritages', in B. Graham and P. Howard (eds) *The Ashgate Companion to Heritage and Identity*, London: Ashgate, pp. 299–313.

Tunbridge, J.E and Ashworth, G.J. (1996) *Dissonant Heritage: The Management of the Past as a Resource in Conflict*, Chichester: Wiley.

UNESCO (nd) *The Different Types of Cultural Heritage*. http://portal.unesco.org/culture/en/ev.php-URL_ID=1907&url_do=do_topic&url_section=201.html [no longer online].

——(1950) *Statement by Experts on Race Problems*. http://unesdoc.unesco.org/images/0012/001269/126969eb.pdf

——(1954) *Convention for the Protection of Cultural Property in the Event of Armed Conflict* ('Hague Convention'), Paris: UNESCO.

——(1966) *Declaration on the Principles of International Cultural Cooperation*, Paris: UNESCO.

——(1970) *Convention on the Means of Prohibiting and Preventing the Illicit Import, Export and Transfer of Ownership of Cultural Property*, Paris: UNESCO.

——(1972) *Convention Concerning the Protection of the World Cultural and Natural Heritage* ('World Heritage Convention'), Paris: UNESCO.

——(1987) *World Heritage Nomination: IUCN Summary 447: Uluru (Ayers Rock–Mount Olga) National Park Australia*. http://whc.unesco.org/archive/advisory_body_evaluation/447rev.pdf

——(1989) *Recommendation on the Safeguarding of Traditional Culture and Folklore*. http://portal.unesco.org/en/ev.php-URL_ID=13141&url_do=do_printpage&url_section=201.html

——(1992) WHC-92/CONF.002/10/Add Item 14 of *Provisional Agenda: Revision of the Operational Guidelines for the Implementation of the World Heritage Convention*. http://whc.unesco.org/archive/1992/whc-92-conf002-10adde.pdf

——(1994) WHC-94/CONF.003/INF.6 *Expert Meeting on the 'Global Strategy' and thematic studies for a representative World Heritage List*. http://whc.unesco.org/archive/global94.htm#debut

——(2000) *World Culture Report 2000: Cultural Diversity, Conflict and Pluralism*, Paris: UNESCO.

——(2002) *Universal Declaration on Cultural Diversity*. http://unesdoc.unesco.org/images/0012/001271/127160m.pdf

——(2003a) *Nomination File for the Cultural Landscape and Archaeological Remains of the Bamiyan Valley*. http://whc.unesco.org/en/list/208/documents

——(2003b) *Charter on the Preservation of the Digital Heritage*, Paris: UNESCO.

——(2003c) *Convention for the Safeguarding of the Intangible Cultural Heritage*, Paris: UNESCO.

——(2005) *Convention on the Protection and Promotion of the Diversity of Cultural Expressions*. http://unesdoc.unesco.org/images/0014/001429/142919e.pdf

——(2006) *World Heritage Committee Threatens to Remove Dresden Elbe Valley (Germany) from World Heritage List*. http://whc.unesco.org/en/news/265

——(2007) *Oman's Arabian Oryx Sanctuary: First Site Ever to be Deleted from UNESCO's World Heritage List*. http://whc.unesco.org/en/news/362

——(2009a) *Nomination for Inscription on the Representative List in 2009 (Reference No. 00235)*. www.unesco.org/culture/ich/doc/src/00235-Nomination_form.doc

——(2009b) *Dresden is Deleted from UNESCO's World Heritage List*. http://whc.unesco.org/en/news/522

——(2010a) *Timeline: Salvage of the Monuments of Nubia*. http://whc.unesco.org/uploads/activities/documents/activity-173-2.pdf

——(2010b) *The Rescue of Nubian Monuments and Sites*. http://whc.unesco.org/en/activities/173

——(2011a) *Melaka and George Town, Historic Cities of the Straits of Malacca*. http://whc.unesco.org/en/list/1223

——(2011b) *World Heritage Emblem*. http://whc.unesco.org/en/emblem

——(2011c) *World Heritage List Statistics*. http://whc.unesco.org/en/list/stat

——(2011d) *Statistics on States Parties*. http://whc.unesco.org/en/statesparties/stat

——(2011e) *Working Towards a Convention*. www.unesco.org/culture/ich/index.php?lg=en&pg=00004

——(2011f) *UNESCO Constitution*. http://portal.unesco.org/en/ev.php-URL_ID=15244&url_do=do_topic&url_section=201.html

United Nations (2000) *Resolution A/RES/54/185.* www.un.org/millennium/declaration/ ares552e.pdf

Urry, J. (1990) *The Tourist Gaze: Leisure and Travel in Contemporary Societies,* London: Sage.

——(1995) *Consuming Places,* London and New York: Routledge.

——(2004) 'Connections', *Environment and Planning D: Society and Space* 22(1) 27–37.

Uzzell, D. (2009) 'Where is the Discipline in Heritage Studies? A View from Environmental Psychology', in M.L.S. Sørensen and J. Carman (eds) *Heritage Studies: Methods and Approaches,* Abingdon and New York: Routledge, pp. 326–333.

Veale, S. (2001) *Remembering Country: History and Memories of Towarri National Park,* Hurstville: NSW National Parks and Wildlife Service.

Vergo, P. (1989) 'The Reticent Object' in Vergo, P. (ed.) *The New Museology,* London: Reaktion Books, pp. 41–59.

Viveiros de Castro, E.B. (2004) 'The Transformation of Objects into Subjects in Amerindian Ontologies', *Common Knowledge* 10(3): 463–485.

Virilio, P. (1986) *Speed and Politics: An Essay on Dromodology,* New York: Columbia University Press.

——(2000) *A Landscape of Events,* Cambridge: MIT Press.

——(2002) *Ground Zero,* London and New York: Verso.

Walsh, K. (1992) *The Representation of the Past: Museums and Heritage in the Post Modern World,* London and New York: Routledge.

Waterton, E., Smith, L. and Campbell, G. (2006) 'The Utility of Discourse Analysis to Heritage Studies: The Burra Charter and Social Inclusion', *International Journal of Heritage Studies* 12(4): 339–355.

Webmoor, T. (2007) 'What About "One More Turn after the Social" in Archaeological Reasoning? Taking Things Seriously', *World Archaeology* 39(4): 547–562.

——(2008) 'From Silicon Valley to the Valley of Teotihuacan: The "Yahoo!s" of New Media and Digital Heritage', *Visual Anthropology Review* 24(2): 183–200.

Webmoor, T. and Witmore, C.L. (2004) *Symmetrical Archaeology.* http://humanitieslab.stanford. edu/Symmetry/Home

——(2008) 'Things Are Us! A Commentary on Human/Things Relations under the Banner of a "Social" Archaeology', *Norwegian Archaeological Review* 41(1): 53–70.

West, S. and Ansell, J. (2010) 'A History of Heritage', in S. West (ed.) *Understanding Heritage in Practice,* Manchester/Milton Keynes: Manchester University Press/Open University, pp. 7–46.

West, S. and McKellar, E. (2010) 'Interpretation of Heritage', in S. West (ed.) *Understanding Heritage in Practice,* Manchester/Milton Keynes: Manchester University Press/Open University, pp. 166–204.

Wikan, U. (1999) 'Culture: A New Concept of Race', *Social Anthropology* 7(1): 57–64.

——(2002) *Generous Betrayal: Politics of Culture in the New Europe,* Chicago: University of Chicago Press.

Williams, P. (2007) *Memorial Museums: The Global Rush to Commemorate Atrocities,* Oxford and New York: Berg.

Williams, R. (1958) *Culture and Society 1780–1850,* London: Chatto and Windus.

Wilson, J.L. (2005) *Nostalgia: Sanctuary of Meaning,* New Jersey: Associated University Presses.

Wingfield, C. (2010) 'Touching the Buddha: Encounters with a Charismatic Object', in S. Dudley (ed.) *Museum Materialities: Objects, Engagements, Interpretations,* London and New York: Routledge, pp. 53–70.

Witmore, C.L. (2006) 'Vision, Media, Noise and the Percolation of Time: Symmetrical Approaches to the Mediation of the Material World', *Journal of Material Culture* 11(3): 267–92.

——(2007) 'Symmetrical archaeology: excerpts of a manifesto', *World Archaeology* 39(4): 546–62.

Wood, A.C. (2007) *Preserving New York: Winning the Right to Protect a City's Landmarks,* New York and Abingdon: Routledge.

Wood, P. (2004) *The Day Saddam's Statue Fell.* http://news.bbc.co.uk/1/hi/3611869.stm

Wright, P. ([1985] 2009) *On Living in an Old Country: The National Past in Contemporary Britain*, London and New York: Verso.

——(1989) 'The Quality of Visitors' Experience in Art Museums', in P. Vergo (ed.) *The New Museology*, London: Reaktion Books, pp. 119–48.

——(1991) *A Journey Through Ruins: The Last Days of London*, London: Radius.

Žižek, S. (2002) *Welcome to the Desert of the Real*, London and New York: Verso.

INDEX